Frommer's™

Thailand

with your family

From tropical adventures to sublime beaches

by Jack Barker

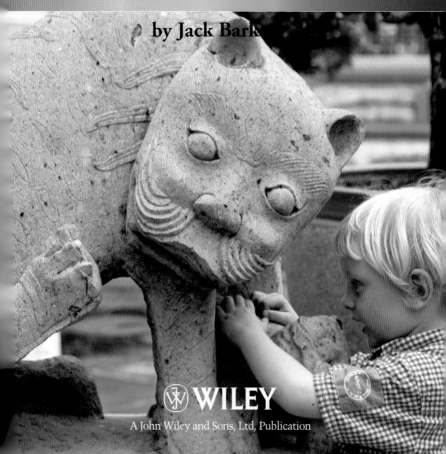

WILEY

A John Wiley and Sons, Ltd, Publication

Copyright © 2009 John Wiley & Sons Ltd, The Atrium, Southern Gate,
Chichester, West Sussex PO19 8SQ, England
Telephone (+44) 1243 779777
Email (for orders and customer service enquiries): cs-books@wiley.co.uk. Visit our Home
Page on www.wiley.com

All Rights Reserved. No part of this publication may be reproduced, stored in a retrieval system or transmitted in any form or by any means, electronic, mechanical, photocopying,
recording, scanning or otherwise, except under the terms of the Copyright, Designs and
Patents Act 1988 or under the terms of a licence issued by the Copyright Licensing Agency
Ltd, 90 Tottenham Court Road, London W1T 4LP, UK, without the permission in writing
of the Publisher. Requests to the Publisher should be addressed to the Permissions
Department, John Wiley & Sons Ltd, The Atrium, Southern Gate, Chichester, West Sussex
PO19 8SQ, England, or emailed to permreq@wiley.co.uk, or faxed to (+44) 1243 770620.

Designations used by companies to distinguish their products are often claimed as trademarks. All brand names and product names used in this book are trade names, service marks,
trademarks or registered trademarks of their respective owners. The Publisher is not associated with any product or vendor mentioned in this book.

This publication is designed to provide accurate and authoritative information in regard to
the subject matter covered. It is sold on the understanding that the Publisher is not engaged
in rendering professional services. If professional advice or other expert assistance is required,
the services of a competent professional should be sought.

UK Publisher: Sally Smith
Executive Project Editor: Daniel Mersey
Commissioning Editor: Mark Henshall
Development Editor: Kate Calvert
Project Editor: Hannah Clement
Cartographer: Jeremy Norton
Photo Research: Jill Emeny

Wiley also publishes its books in a variety of electronic formats. Some content that appears in
print may not be available in electronic books.

British Library Cataloguing in Publication Data
A catalogue record for this book is available from the British Library

ISBN: 978-0-470-51966-0

Typeset by Wiley Indianapolis Composition Services
Printed and bound in China by RR Donnelley
5 4 3 2 1

Contents

About the Author

Jack Barker is an award-winning travel writer and photographer based in the UK. In Britain he has written for the *Independent, Mail on Sunday,* the Saturday and Sunday *Telegraphs,* the *Times, Sunday Times* and *Guardian.* Abroad he has been published by the *Washington Post* and *New York Times* amongst others, and he also writes for magazines and websites worldwide. He has previously written guidebooks to Kenya, South Africa, Bali, Spain and Turkey, and updated guides to Morocco, Mauritania and Senegal.

He first visited Thailand in 1981, spending several months exploring what was then very much an emerging destination. This early exposure proved formative. Since then he's returned to Thailand and other Southeast Asian countries every year, writing about different adventures and experiences. Recently he has taken his family on several visits, introducing them to Thailand and his favourite part of the world.

Jack Barker lives in Wiltshire with his wife Nicky and children, Lucy and Wilf.

Acknowledgements

My thanks to Nicky for putting up with me during the writing of this guidebook, to Lucy for her critical help in road-testing some of Thailand's more challenging adventures, Wilf for finding unexpected pleasures in shoe-string hotels, and all three for proving that travel with young children in Thailand is fun.

An Additional Note

Please be advised that travel information is subject to change at any time and this is especially true of prices. We therefore suggest that you write or call ahead for confirmation when making your travel plans. The authors, editors and publisher cannot be held responsible for experiences of readers while travelling. Your safety is important to us however, so we encourage you to stay alert and be aware of your surroundings.

Star Ratings, Icons & Abbreviations

Hotels, restaurants and attraction listings in this guide have been ranked for quality, value, service, amenities and special features using a star-rating system. Hotels, restaurants, attractions, shopping and nightlife are rated on a scale of zero stars (recommended) to three (exceptional). In addition to the star rating system, we also use 5 feature icons that point you to the great deals, in-the-know advice and unique experiences. Throughout the book, look for:

FIND	Special finds – those places only insiders know about
MOMENT	Special moments – those experiences that memories are made of
VALUE	Great values – where to get the best deals
OVERRATED	Places or experiences not worth your time or money
GREEN	Attractions employing responsible tourism policies

The following **abbreviations** are used for credit cards:

AE	American Express
MC	Mastercard
V	Visa

A Note on Prices

In the Family-friendly Accommodation section of this book we have used a price category system.

An Invitation to the Reader

In researching this book, we discovered many wonderful places – hotels, restaurants, shops and more. We're sure you'll find others. Please tell us about them, so we can share the information with your fellow travellers in upcoming editions. If you were disappointed with a recommendation, we'd love to know that too. Please email: frommers@wiley.co.uk or write to:

Frommer's Thailand with Your Family, 1st Edition
John Wiley & Sons, Ltd
The Atrium
Southern Gate
Chichester
West Sussex, PO19 8SQ

Photo Credits

Cover Credits

Main Image: © Jack Barker
Small Images: © Shutterstock
Back Cover: © Shutterstock

Front Matter Credits

Pi: © Jack Barker; piii/piv: © Shutterstock.

Inside Images

All images: © Jack Barker with the following exceptions:
© Anantara Group: p226.
© Barry Mason/Alamy: p173.
© Chakrabongse Villas Ltd: p72.
© Canopy Adventures (Thailand) Co Ltd: p175.
© Holiday Inn Resort Phi Phi Island: p155.
© Khun Rang: p187.
© Mariohra Cruises: p74.
© May Pen Rai Bungalows: p191.
© Mom Tri's Boathouse / Four Seasons Info Media (Thailand): p158.
© Mr Chitapong Kuawong: p222.
© Neil McAllister / Alamy: p161.
© Samad Resorts Group: p111, p112.
© Sue Worden: p189.
© Tamarind Village: p221.
© The Legend: p228.
© Villa Baan-Nomella/Holidaylettings.co.uk/32266: p108.

The following images courtesy of:
Alangkarn Pattaya Show: p116.
Alila Cha-Am Hua Hin: p192.
Centara Hotels & Resorts: p114.
Chiang Dao Nest: p225.
Karma Sumai: p7, p184.
Laguna Beach Resort, Phuket: p146.
Le Meridien Phuket: p150.
Lisu Lounge: p224.
Mandarin Oriental Hotel Group, Photographed by George Apostolidis: p73.
Mandarin Oriental Hotel Group: p219.
Peace Resort, Koh Samui: p188.
Phuket Butterfly Garden: p129.
Pimalai Resort – koh Lanta: p156.
Royal Orchid Sheraton, Bangkok: p75.
Silom Convent Garden, Bagkok: p80.
Tourism Authority of Thailand: p51, p133.

1 Family Highlights of Thailand

Nowhere is the term 'developing world' as apt as in Thailand. Few countries have changed so fast and so quickly over a single generation. Children who used to play in the sand outside driftwood shacks now run deluxe air-conditioned beach resorts with swimming pools and spas: villages made of wood with dirt streets flocked with black-painted bicycles are now cities of concrete and glass, rushing headlong into the 21st century.

Despite all this, Thailand in many ways retains an almost childlike innocence; a reverence for the past alongside a fervour for the future. Anywhere in the country you can step out of the traffic into the calm oasis of a Buddhist monastery and find an open welcome from the resident monks. Travelling with children is a breeze. All Thais – and I've yet to find an exception – seem to genuinely love children, and are especially fascinated by small westerners, something they very rarely see. While adults must negotiate commercial relationships and practical matters, children are exempt. With their curious, kind and gentle personalities the Thais you meet can calm and charm the hottest, tiredest, western child.

As if this wasn't enough, Thailand is a land of exceptional natural beauty. The beaches are sublime, from the Gulf of Thailand to the long glimmering waters of the Andaman Coast. But there's nothing bland about this tropical landscape. It rears up in sheer limestone out-crops in the south and rugged mountain landscapes of the north, shel-tering minority hill tribes and riven by cave systems, tracked by rivers and – off the main roads – immediately reverting to a traditional way of life.

On an urban level, the Thai culture has blossomed with all the advantages of the modern age but has kept in touch with its tradi-tional past. Candles and sacrifices still grace spirit houses alongside each new Thai home, and temples are filled with devout Buddhists paying homage.

Thailand is nothing like Europe. Those who've visited before as backpackers will know this and long to return. In many ways it is more simple to travel here as a family than it would be in Europe. There are hotels to suit all budgets, and getting around is easy, with a huge range of transport options for every given route. In every resort city there are 'planned' attractions for children, but just as many high-lights come from the smallest encounters, the spark of new friendships with other children that transcend culture and language. And if there should ever be a problem, a missed flight, a hotel reservation gone astray, a smile and a few well-flung baht will solve most issues in a way that just wouldn't be possible in the 'developed' world. If you want to introduce your children to a new way of life, rapidly overhauling our established western model, Thailand is perfect.

BEST FAMILY EVENTS

Of all Thailand's spectacular festivals, SongKran (see p 19 and p 53) is the one that displays each Thai's inner child. The Thai New Year celebrations bring the country to a halt in frenzied waterfights that transcend cultural barriers and bond the generations. Shops set out great vats of water in the street and recruit visitors, friends and family to fight running battles with open-backed pickup trucks carrying their own barrels of water, using their height to drench pedestrians below. Coming at the height of the hot, humid build up to the rainy season everyone gets soaked – and nobody minds. The concept is that the water will wash away your sins, and occasionally spiritual insights creep in: a little old lady dabs flour on your children's cheeks for good luck, and quiet ceremonies in temples mark the start of a new year, but generally, for most children, it's the water-fights they remember. In the north the endless drenching battles go on for days; the south, more reasonably, calls a truce after one day.

BEST WATERBORNE ADVENTURE

From the canals of the capital to the tropical islands of the south, Thailand is a marine society. Fast, sleek and loud, longtailed boats spray past more genteel passenger vessels. Even mountain rivers are negotiated in rubber zodiacs and rafts made from bamboo. Of all the aquatic adventures on offer, one stands out: the sea canoe tours of Phang-nga Bay's hongs (p 133). Here you paddle through hidden, bat-filled caves to discover miraculous lagoons in the heart of sheer limestone islands, unique ecosystems concealed, over the ages, from the outside world.

BEST SNORKELLING & DIVING

Teaching children to dive is brave or possibly foolish, but snorkelling has acceptable risks – and there are few countries that can match Thailand's tropical waters for coral reefs and fish. There's superb diving in the

Elephants in Ayutthaya

Gulf of Thailand, off Pattaya and in Ang Thong National Marine Park near Koh Samui. But the ultimate snorkelling, in season, is off the Andaman Coast. Take a boat from Phuket (See p 134) and sail south to discover vivid coral reefs, bright with the colours of endless shoals of fish, with occasional glimpsed pelagics lurking in the depths.

BEST ELEPHANT EXPERIENCE

You won't see any elephants in Bangkok: they've been banned as a traffic hazard. Everywhere else in the country you will. Although some are still wild, most are domesticated, having lost their traditional role in logging and agriculture. Elephants live as long as humans, need 250kg of food each day and continue to breed: funding them is often a considerable problem. Throughout the country lone elephants roam the streets, guided by their mahout, begging shopkeepers, restaurateurs and people to buy them food. In the remote jungle interiors of the southern islands they are kept in camps, earning their living by letting westerners wash them and go for lumbering forest rides. At Phuket's Fantasea a great herd performs in unison, acting out scenes from Thai history and mythology. It's in the north, however, that they are seen at their best: around

Chiang Mai (see p 211) a selection of elephant camps put on displays where these majestic animals play football, perform musical concerts and paint works of art that would put Van Gogh to shame.

BEST BEACHES

With the huge sweep of the Gulf of Thailand and the long run of the Andaman Sea coast, Thailand has beaches to suit every mood. Not all are perfect. Photographs rarely show that the beaches of the southern Andaman, Koh Jum and Koh Lanta, and the sheltered inlets of Phang-nga Bay often slope slowly far out to sea. They're great as large ocean-sized family wading pools, but no great shakes for swimming. Others are only perfect for six months of the year: at certain times monsoon winds make many of the beaches in Samui and Phuket brooding and dangerous, as the winds bring rip-tides and waves. For year-round equanimity and perfect soft sand, I'd choose the small bays of Koh Samet: specifically the social golden sands of Haad Sai Kaew. See p 100.

BEST AQUARIUM

It's not just tourists who flock to Thailand's aquaria. Most Thais have no culture of swimming: water is seen at best as where fish come from, at worst as a drowning hazard. Children are not encouraged to swim in the sea, and certainly not to dive below its surface. A number of aquaria bring the experience to them. Startlingly sophisticated and ambitious aquaria, often built with Australian expertise, have been built in Phuket and Pattaya, and although both are excellent, the best one is where you'd least expect it: occupying an area the size of two football pitches below one of the capital's best shopping malls. Yes, the best aquarium is in Bangkok. See p 63.

BEST TIGER TREAT

Captive tigers inevitably evoke mixed feelings. That such magnificent creatures should be caged and confined seems intolerable: even worse are the 50-baht photo opportunities where tiger cubs, sucking on baby bottles of possibly tranquilised milk, are passed from tourist to tourist. Soft sentiments don't solutions make. Thailand's remote forest regions are already home to as many tigers as they can support: any captive animals released would soon be killed as they fought to establish their own territories. At Sri Racha Tiger Zoo you can see how easily they breed, where a pig acts as a surrogate mother while coachloads of Korean tourists say 'ahhh' and take photographs. I'd go for the controversial Tiger Temple (see p 70) near Kanchanaburi, where circumstances have led a pioneering Buddhist temple to

become a well-known and popular refuge for all types of animal.

BEST RIVER JOURNEYS

Roads are a recent development in Thailand. Until recently rivers were the main line of communication. In the north of the country you'll still see rafts made of bamboo crashing through shallow rapids, and you can ride on one yourself – though these days Thais will pole your boat safely down the river and you're no longer allowed to steer it yourself. From Bangkok longtail boats, named after the plume of water thrown up by the propeller dangling on the back of a truck engine, tour the backwater canals, revealing the disappearing Thailand of stilted buildings over water, where commuting is by boat and the canal waters are somehow used to wash clothes sparkling white on makeshift front-step laundries. But the first prize has to go to the inexpensive river taxis that make travelling through the capital city a pleasure, easing their way between cargo vessels, pleasure cruisers and dine'n'dance discos and also whisking you between Bangkok's greatest sights. See p 62.

BEST TEENAGE LAND CHALLENGE

There are a number of courses where aspects of Thailand's

culture are imparted to young visitors, including carving soap and fruit, Thai cookery classes and Thai boxing lessons. But the greatest – and attainable – sense of achievement can come from climbing. Climbing courses are available on Koh Phi Phi and Koh Samui as well as amongst the mountains of the north, but the greatest of all are up the sheer limestone cliffs that back Railay Beach, near Krabi. See p 142.

BEST HISTORY LESSON

Thailand's sense of tradition imbues the country, from the humblest spirit house to the grandest incense-strewn temple. Get up early on any morning and you'll see monks streaming forth to beg for the ingredients for their one daily meal. Across the border in Laos this attracts mobs of video-toting tourists, but in Thailand it's just routine. The origins of this tradition are sometimes lost in the tumultuous world of Thailand today. For a sense of the spiritual relevance of this ancient culture there are few places to beat Ayutthaya, an hour from Bangkok. Once the country's capital but now a rural hinterland, its stupas and chedis crumble in the tropical heat and an antique Buddha head, lovingly carved from stone, has been embraced by the roots of a strangler-fig tree. See p 66.

BEST ACCOMMODATION

Best Resort Hotel

In Thailand's race into the 21st century, most of the best beaches now feature at least one resort hotel. Only one has five. The Laguna Beach Resort on Phuket is the most family-friendly

View from a longtail boat in Bangkok

The ultimate private pad at Karma Sumai

member of the Laguna Resort complex, an 'integrated resort' of five leading resort hotels set on a beach and a series of inter-linked lagoons. Guests can shuttle around between all five hotels, and for a small fee make the most of their extensive facilities. This opens up 30 restaurants, 15 swimming pools and three spas. There's an 18-hole golf course, a 'Camp Laguna club' teaching teenagers abseiling, rock climbing, tennis, horse riding and more. Facilities include a waterpark, a marine centre with complimentary hobie cats, windsurfers and instruction, children's clubs for all ages, and two semi-resident elephants, Ann and baby Sara. See p 146.

Most Stylish Hotel

The Thais' natural love of beauty and harmony has, in its long recent boom, been celebrated in a number of remarkable hotels

and resorts. The Alila in Cha-am should perhaps be a member of this eclectic group, but that is, to be brutally honest, Balinese – which is not quite the same. For an icon of modern Thailand at its most urbane and sophisticated, the ultimate hotel has to be the soaring capital presence of The Banyan Tree, Bangkok. See p 74.

Best Self-Catering

For families, self-catering is often an attractive and convenient option. Freed from the choice between endless child meals and the dangers of unexpected spices in local dishes, parents can cook up comfort food for the young and make expeditions to explore at their own, unhurried pace. A number of self-catering apartments and villas are inexpensively available throughout the country, but for the ultimate private pad the Karma Samui has

Swimming pool at the Waterfront Hotel, Bophut

the edge. Four-bedroom villas look to the sea over private pools, kitchens are equipped with fridge-freezer, dishwasher, microwave and coffee machine, while laundries feature washing machines and dryers. Add huge flat-screen TVs and DVD players with a children's library of films and you have everything you could need to create your own Thai home. See p 184.

Best Beach Hotels

Thailand's tourism started with its beachfront hotels, the simple wood-and-rattan beach huts of 40 years ago spread around simple restaurants serving local food. You can still find modest establishments like these, but now you have to look further, to the outlying islands. The original pioneers have built on their success by adding sophistication: replacing bamboo with concrete, adding air-conditioning and swimming pools and, increasingly, becoming jostled by neighbours trying to cash in on

their success. A few have managed to resist the urge to expand and maintain their personal welcome, but perhaps the one that best encapsulates the small-scale charm of a great beach hotel is actually expatriate-run, the Waterfront at Bophut on Koh Samui. Family-run by a British couple, this small and idiosyncratic place has just a few rooms built right on the sand, with all the comforts of home in simply-furnished rooms set around a pool packed with floaty toys. The restaurant closes at 6.30pm each evening, so it's just as well that it is at the heart of one of Samui's most restaurant-friendly villages: there is a vast choice within easy walking distance, and babysitting is available. See p 188.

Best Guest House

The guest house culture is strong in Thailand, with simple family homes in busy city centres eking out a living by accommodating foreign visitors. Few do this with such enthusiasm as King's Home in Hua Hin (see p 194), where a small property within 200m from the Squid Piers and the beach feels rather like Dr Who's Tardis. Enter via a small entrance hall and you are led through a warren of rooms, packed with memorabilia redolent of the owner's native Holland, with huge soft beds, TVs and fridges in every room. For a cultural experience of modern Thailand central Hua Hin is hard to beat, with some of the country's best seafood served in inexpensive market restaurants and a lively, Thai-oriented beach culture.

BEST EATING OPTIONS

Best Day Out

It's rather a hack across Koh Samui from the main beach resorts, but children and their parents love the Babylon Restaurant on Bang Por Beach, and it's an excellent choice if the sea is too rough to swim. Five bouncy castles are set in a safely fenced and lightly supervised compound and although it's hardly a theme park the atmosphere is pleasant and relaxing. They were digging a swimming pool when I was there and the restaurant serves sensational Thai food at local prices on the water's edge, with distant views of the mainland. Let lunch last until late: while most of Samui's beaches get the sunrise, this one gets the sunset. See p 195.

Best Educational Dining

At almost all major resort areas there are evening dinner shows where sophisticated lighting systems and elaborate special effects showcase Thailand's history and culture. Some put on magnificent performances but miss out on the food: with others it is the other way round. For the perfect combination of fine dining and

Exotic fruit picked in Koh Samui

a genuinely spectacular display of acrobatics, stylised fights and costumed dances, the best is Bangkok's Siam Niramit. See p 83.

Best View

The expansive view over the city of Chiang Mai is just part of the pleasures of dining at the Palaad Tawanron, set above the city's fantastic zoo. There is a separate child menu, highchairs, and a clown often follows families, making balloon animals. As night falls the lights of the city sparkle in the distance, and you can also combine your meal with a twilight safari, meeting nocturnal species you might have overlooked through the day. Live music plays every night: reserve early to make sure of a table with a good view. See p 229.

Best Sunday Lunch

This quintessentially British tradition is recreated at countless British theme pubs across the country, which you'll find in almost all major resort areas. But you don't fly half-way round the world to eat roast beef and Yorkshire pudding in the tropical heat. Instead go to the BBC restaurant on Koh Samui's Great Buddha Beach, where every Sunday lunch is followed by relaxed jazz on the sands as the sun glints from the gold Buddha, out in the bay. See p 195.

Best Active Meal

They serve a seven-course lunch at the Coral Island Beach Club on a small island just off Phuket, but that's not why anyone visits. A simple day-pass opens up a world of watersports including scuba diving, power snorkelling, clear kayaks, banana boating and sea canoe expeditions. The perfect way to build up a healthy appetite in the tropical heat. See p 157.

Best Meal – Ever

I can't tie this down to one actual meal but know where it happened: on a homestay in the village of Ban Talae Nok on the Andaman Coast. A relief programme set up after the 2004 Tsunami arranges for western families to stay with local villagers, and we found a host family who might have been poor but certainly didn't starve. Fresh squid, prawns and tasty village chicken were just the protein highlights amongst a constant selection of seasonal fruits, cashew nuts and rice. Alongside a series of snacks, Thai meals are made up of several shared dishes eaten as a family, something that most visitors miss as they follow western eating patterns and buy food plate by plate. Thanks, then, to our hostess: Nooliha of Ban Talae Nok. See p 127.

2 Planning Your Trip

THAILAND

Chiang Saen
Chiang Khong
Chiang Rai
Fang
GOLDEN
TRIANGLE
Pai
NORTHERN
Mae
Hong
HILLS
Son
Chiang Mai
Nan
Lamphun
● Lampang
Phrae
Mae
Sariang
Vientiane ★
Nong Khai
Si Satchanalai
Uttaradit
Loei
Udon
Thani
Ban Chiang
Sukhothai
MAE KHONG
VALLEY
Nakhon
Phanom
Tak
Phitsanulok
Mae Sot
CENTRAL PLAINS
Chi
Khon Kaen
Kamphaeng
Phet
Phetchabun
MYANMAR
(BURMA)
ISAN
Nakhon Sawan
THAILAND
Phimai
Mun
Lopburi
Nakhon Ratchasima
(Khorat)
Ubon
Ratchathani
WESTERN
THAILAND
Surin
Nam Tok
Kanchanaburi
Ayutthaya
Sam Rong
Nakhon
Pathom
Bangkok ★
Chon Buri
CAMBODIA
Phetchaburi
Bangsaen
Cha-Am
Hua Hin
Pattaya
Andaman
Sea
Prachuap
Khiri Khan
Rayong
Chanthaburi
CHANTHABURI
PROVINCE
Koh Samet
SOUTHEASTERN
COAST
Chumphon
Koh Tao
Koh Chang
Trat
Ranong
Koh Phangan
Koh Mak
Koh Kut
Phnom Penh ★
Koh Surin
(Surin National
Marine Park)
Koh Samui
Khao
Lak
Surat
Thani
Khanom
Phang Nga
Nakhon
Si Thammarat
Gulf of Thailand
(Gulf of Siam)
SOUTHERN
PENINSULA
● Phuket
Koh
Phi Phi
Koh
Jum
Krabi
Koh
Lanta
Andaman
Sea
Songkhla
Hat Yai
Pattani
Koh Tarutao
(Tarutao National Park)
Narathiwat
Sungai Kolok
MALAYSIA

LAOS
VIETNAM
Yom
Wong
Khwae Noi
Ping
Wang
Chao Phraya

VIETNAM

★ Capital City
● Town / City
Main Route
Rail

0   100 mi
0   100 km

You may have spent a few months of your youth lazing around on Thai beaches, backpacking your way around without a care in the world. With children the experience is different. In many ways it's better – all Thais seem to love children and go out of their way to help – but in one key respect it is worse. What you had then was time (if not money). Unless you've taken your children out of school, when travelling as a family your time will almost certainly be limited. Thailand is the size of France, with a population larger than the UK's – 64 million and rising – so you can't hope to see it all. What you can do is focus clearly on just a few areas, planning to make the most of each precious day.

Thais travelling in their own country use their own networks of family and friends. The tourist industry has therefore been shaped by visiting foreigners. Older, well-heeled travellers are well catered for, as are penny-pinching backpackers. Beyond a few international resorts, however, travelling families are a novelty. This book seeks out those hotels and attractions suitable for all ages, whatever their travel tastes. From visceral adventures to serene cultural highlights Thailand has plenty to offer young and old alike. Enjoy.

THE REGIONS IN BRIEF

Bangkok is Thailand's gateway city – a crowded, dynamic Asian capital. Get it wrong and the city is an ordeal: plan it right and there are some great adventures to be had.

This is where Thailand's cultural attractions are centred, and where life is lived at its fastest. It isn't essential to spend any time at all in the city: Bangkok is easily sidestepped with internal flights or even chartered taxis to other parts of the country. But brave the madness and you can have a lot of fun here. Pick a hotel with pool, stick to river transport and the BTS overground rail network, and you'll discover a vibrant metropolis that makes London look tired.

Timeless rural Thailand starts immediately outside the city and easy rail and bus links make it easy to explore.

East of the capital – and barely an hour's drive from the international airport – you hit Thailand's first beach resort, Pattaya. The central entertainment here is sin, but there are some quiet family resorts too and top-quality family entertainments. An hour further to the east is the gem-like island of Koh Samet, with small lodges stacked over small, inviting coves and backed by a National Park hinterland.

South, down the country's elephant-trunk isthmus and the Andaman Coast, tourism is focused on Phuket. With good air connections to Bangkok and other parts of the Far East, this is resort central, an expensive place but with plenty to do and see. Explore the sheer limestone mountains of Phang-nga Bay, or pack up your bags and go further, to Koh Phi Phi, Krabi or Koh Jum, to escape from the fly and flop brigade.

The Andaman Coast is great during the UK winter, but summer is a different matter, with the southwest monsoon sweeping in, bringing rain and whipping up the sea. Flip across to the eastern side of the narrow isthmus. At this time of year the Gulf of Thailand is more sheltered and comes into its own. The island of Koh Samui has, with its own busy airport, developed fastest, while a short boat-ride reaches quieter, more laid-back Koh Phangan.

While the southern islands soak up international package travellers, domestic tourists and expatriates holidaying from work in the capital tend to focus on the mainland beaches around Hua Hin. These are easy to reach from Bangkok by road and rail and offer authentic experiences of Thailand at leisure.

Northern Thailand is another world: a mountainous region a key few degrees cooler, where even the capital, Chiang Mai, sets off at a slower pace. This is the place for cultural immersion: cooking courses, elephant adventures, hill-tribe treks and river journeys on bamboo rafts.

VISITOR INFORMATION

The first place for information about Thailand is the state-run Tourist Authority of Thailand (TAT). It publishes a range of glossy brochures but generally focuses on marketing-department themes: until recently the emphasis has been on 'chic' – not so relevant to families. In the UK TAT is at 49 Albemarle Street, London W1X 3FE, *0870 900 2007, www.tourismthailand. co.uk*. Log on to the Internet for its regular *Travel Thailand* e-newsletter.

For warnings and advice contact the Foreign Office on *0845 850 2829* or *www.fco.gov.uk/travel.*

Any number of private Thai websites have been established, generally to steer you to hotel booking engines or associated tour operations. Although some have been updated, much of the information dates back to the early years of the Internet boom and is at least 10 years out of date. In addition, hotel descriptions are biased if not simply supplied by the establishment. They do often offer good rates, however, so can be useful when booking a hotel you have already chosen or as leverage in trying to arrange for a discount directly.

Good sites to browse include *www.gothailand.com*, *www.1stop bangkok.com*, *www.bangkok.com*, *www.thailand.com*, *www.asiatravel tips.com*: all these will link to further sites focusing on specific islands and towns.

For customer feedback on hotels, tour operators and activities the big beast of the Internet is still *www.tripadvisor.com*, with *www.igougo.com*, *www.trivago.com* and *http://travel.yahoo.com* fast catching up. Be aware these can be and occasionally are manipulated by devious but convincing e-marketing specialists. For discussion boards of all issues Thai, the newsgroup at *www.thaizer.com* is comprehensive and up to date.

So far most child travel websites have little content on Thailand, but the situation can only improve. There are some wry observations on *www.alltravellingkidsfamilyvacations.com*, although the site overall is overwhelmingly geared to travel in the US. *www.familytravelthailand.com* claims to have a selection of the best family hotels in Thailand but I don't think all their properties are ideal for children. There's some information on *www.takethefamily.com* but more on *www.babygoes2.com*.

Entry Requirements & Customs

Passports & Visas

Passports must be valid for at least six months from the date of entry. Tourist Visas (technically Tourist Visa Exemptions) issued at the border are free and last for a maximum of 30 days. Before expiry you'll have to hop across the nearest border to return with another stamp in your passport. Alternatively it is possible to extend your visa at an immigration office, found in most towns, although current regulations only allow an extra 14 days and the fee is 1200B per passport: for families that gets expensive. It's no longer legal for travel agents to extend your visa on your behalf.

60-day tourist visas cost 1000B at the border (although an outrageous £25 in the UK), require two passport photos and must be obtained within three months of your proposed date of travel. The Thai Embassy is at 29–30 Queens Gate, London SW7 5JB, ☎ *020 7589 2944*, and forms can be downloaded from *www.thaiembassyuk.org.uk*. Allow several days for processing. These visas can be extended for a further 30 days from any regional immigration office.

Overstaying your visa is not advisable. If you make it to the airport or border with an expired visa you'll be charged 500B for each day – and each passport – even if you're just over the limit. Serious overstays can result in much higher fines and sometimes prison, deportation and blacklisting from the country for life. Visa regulations can change without warning so check with the embassy before you leave.

Customs

UK duty-free costs are higher than those in Thailand so there doesn't seem much point importing duty free unless you want a particular brand.

Money

The currency of Thailand is the baht, which can be written ฿, B, Bt or Bht. Technically it is divided into 100 satang, with tiny copper coins representing 25 and 50 satang, but few tourists will come across these. Silver coins are 1B (which come in three very similar varieties, all legal), the little-seen 2B, and the slightly larger 5B coins with a copper rim. 10B coins are larger and silver with a copper inset. Bank notes are in denominations of 20B (green), 50B (blue), 100B (red), 500B (purple) and 1000B (brown).

There are no restrictions on the import of foreign currencies or travellers' cheques, but the limit on foreign currency that can be exported is 50,000B (approximately £1000).

There is no black market in foreign currencies in Thailand, so be very suspicious of anyone offering to change money 'unofficially'.

Exchange bureaux are plentiful and competitive, and there are thousands of ATMs in the country, readily dispensing cash for Visa, MasterCard, Cirrus (*www.mastercard.com*) and PLUS (*www.visa.com*) networks stretch across the country, but bear in mind that UK banks charge a fee, usually £1.75–£2.50, every time you use your card in an ATM machine, and this is on top of any fee that will be charged in Thailand.

It is therefore best to make substantial withdrawals but, whatever your personal withdrawal limit, you will usually only be able to draw a maximum of 20,000B (£400) per day.

MasterCard can be used to withdraw cash at Siam Commercial and Bangkok banks; Visa at the Thai Farmers' and Bangkok banks; American Express at the Bangkok Bank and JCB at the Siam Commercial Bank.

Be careful where you leave your card: there have been countless incidences of ghost transactions appearing on accounts when travellers have left their cards behind while going off trekking or rafting.

When paying by credit card many hotels, resorts and restaurants will add 3–5% to the final bill to cover costs: this means it is usually better to pay in cash.

Exchange rates can vary considerably as both currencies are volatile members of different economic systems, but at time of writing £1=50B.

TIP ❯❯ **Get Your Card Approved for Roaming** ❮❮

Call your credit or debit card issuer before you go to Thailand and tell them when and where you are going. It's seen as a centre for credit card fraud and many companies block unexpected access. It can be a long and expensive telephone call home to get your card cleared from abroad.

What Things Cost

Seasoned travellers complain that Thailand is not as cheap as it was and it's true that prices – like standards – have gone up across the board. However, although many Thais are very wealthy, wages average around £3 a day, and in rural areas a lot of people earn even less.

So, unlike in the UK, a family can still travel very inexpensively. A family of four who travel by bus or train, eat at roadside stalls or local restaurants, stay in fan-cooled hostel rooms and steer clear of cities and any island with an airport, can live for as little as £20 per day. You will find that generally in Thailand every extra baht you spend is rewarded with considerable extra comfort, but at a certain level taxes kick in. Only the most modest hotels and restaurants avoid paying tax as increasingly they are being drawn into the official economy. This will add 17–18% to your hotel bill, so when you're getting a price for a room, check whether the rate includes tax.

Rates at mid- and upper-range hotels are highly seasonal: over Christmas and New Year rooms are likely to be twice the summer rate. Even on Koh Samui, for example, a family can expect to find a well-equipped air-conditioned beachfront suite sleeping four for £40 per night, but over Christmas you'll be paying £100 for the same room, and will need to book ahead. Meals will add a lot to this if you eat in the resort or hotel restaurant. Small shacks nearby will charge a fraction of the price and won't add tax and service to the total. See also 'Saving On Your Hotel Room' p 32.

Most sights and attractions operate dual prices, with foreigners paying up to four times as much as Thais. Getting a family into Phuket's Fantasea or the aquarium in Bangkok will set you back £30 or so. However, few monasteries charge at all, and when they do prices are low (and usually controversial). Always interesting and atmospheric, on a tight budget the religious sites can become compelling.

Most sites have reductions for children, usually based on height, most with a measure by the turnstile to work out who is entitled to a discount. You can tell a lot about a place by the cut-off point they choose, which varies from 0.9m and 1.5m. Children under four are rarely charged for any attraction – they're more likely to be given a lolly and a pat on the head.

Despite huge Tesco Lotus supermarkets now operating in most Thai cities, it is generally a mini market culture. You don't need to walk far before you come across a shop packed with all the essentials you're likely to need on a daily basis.

Prices will seem low to British eyes but Thais and long-term travellers will notice they do vary from shop to shop, with hotel boutiques particularly expensive.

When to Go

The best time to visit Thailand is from November to February, when the weather is at its coolest and driest. From March to April it is increasingly hot, and from May to October increasingly wet.

There are significant regional differences, which mean that at any time of year there's a beach at its best.

The southwest monsoon strikes the Andaman coast first and hardest: from May to November the sea is often too rough to swim in and it's no fun being on exposed western beaches, even if it's not raining. Krabi, Koh Phi Phi and Koh Lanta are also affected, and many southern resorts and hotels close altogether.

Sheltered by the mainland in the Gulf of Thailand, Koh Samui is much less affected by the southwest monsoon. Instead it gets the northeast monsoon that brings the heaviest rain in October and November. Pattaya and Koh Samet, confused by mixed influences from both monsoons, have a burst of rain in March and soak through September and October, but continue to pack in the crowds whether it's raining or not.

The rainfall varies from year to year but often by September mud roads are washed out all over the country and much of Bangkok is flooded.

Northern Thailand sees more extremes of temperature: it's cool from November to February, and may even see a very occasional frost at higher altitudes, increasingly hot from March to May, and wet thereafter, with most rain falling in August and September.

Festivals & Holidays

There are a number of official holidays that follow the western calendar. These aren't usually associated with any particular celebrations and usually just mean that banks and some museums are inexplicably shut. Others follow the lunar calendar and are variable: usually these are accompanied by all the bells and whistles you'd expect from an intrinsically devout society. Around Loi Krathong and Songran, particularly, it's difficult to find seats on flights, buses and trains as everyone rushes home to celebrate.

Thai holidays are shown below:

January

New Year's Day
Public holiday.
1st Jan.

February

Chinese New Year
Thailand has a huge Chinese population and they celebrate their New Year with gusto. Many Chinese-run shops and businesses will close for two weeks so they can give offerings and pray.

There are some spectacular processions, especially in Bangkok.

Lunar, late Jan/early Feb.

Flower Festival

Celebrating northern Thailand's blooming season, Chiang Mai comes alive with parades, floats and beauty contests.

First weekend of Jan.

Magha Puja

Buddhist celebration of the occasion when his disciples gathered to hear a sermon. In temples throughout the country there are candle-lit processions.

Lunar, full moon, public holiday.

March

King's Cup Annual Elephant Polo

Major seven-day polo tournament in Chiang Rai where international polo teams play from the backs of elephants. Entry free, proceeds in aid of Thailand's main elephant charities.

Last week of March.

April

Chakri Day

Celebrates the founding of the incumbent Chakri Dynasty.

6th Apr.

Songkran

This Buddhist New Year national festival doesn't make much of an impact in the Muslim areas of the south, but most of Thailand is turned into a wholesale water-fight. Parades, dancing and processions are enlivened by water being tipped over everyone, western or Thai. In Chiang Mai and the north this continues for days and even children get tired of it. In other places the madness lasts just a day.

Lunar, public holiday, usually 13–16th Apr.

May/June

Labour Day

Public holiday.

1st May.

Coronation Day

Public holiday.

5th May.

Visakha Puja

Celebrating Buddha's birth, enlightenment and death. Candlelit processions at monasteries.

Lunar, full moon, public holiday.

Ploughing Ceremony

Sacred bulls decorated with flowers pull a ceremonial plough to mark the beginning of the rice-planting season.

Lunar, public holiday.

Koh Samui Regatta

Competitive yacht races off Koh Samui.

First week in June.

July

Asalha Puja/Khao Phansa

Commemorates Buddha's first sermon and marks the beginning of Buddhist Lent.

Lunar, full moon, public holiday.

August

Pattaya Festival
Parades, fireworks and a food festival.

First week in Aug.

Queen's Birthday
Public holiday.

12th Aug.

October

Vegetarian Festival
In Phuket a spectacular but bizarre nine-day fasting ritual that ends with devotees piercing their bodies while in a religious trance. Not for the faint-hearted and might give children unwise ideas.

Lunar, second week in Oct.

In memory of King Chulangkom
Public holiday.

23rd Oct.

OK Phansa
End of Buddhist Lent and the beginning of Krathin. Two days of fairs and processions, and presents given to monks.

Lunar, three months after Asalha Puja.

November

Loi Krathong
Marks the end of the rainy season, with boats containing candles pushed out on to lakes, rivers and seas. Used to be made out of leaves, now often polystyrene: the morning after is not a pretty sight.

Lunar, full moon.

Elephant Roundup
Elephant parades and cultural performances in Surin.

Third weekend of Nov.

December

Constitution Day
Public holiday.

10th Dec.

King's Birthday
Public holiday.

15th Dec.

New Year's Eve
Public holiday.

31st Dec.

Check with the Tourist Authority of Thailand (UK ☏ *0870 900 2007*, *www.tourismthailand.co.uk*) for more information.

What to Pack

If you're spending all your time in one hotel or resort then you need little more than the clothes you stand up in, and maybe some tampons and swimming nappies, both of which are hard to find in Thailand. Almost everything else is readily available, usually rather cheaper than back home.

If you're planning to travel around more it's still important not to take too much, as the heat makes carting a lot of luggage something of a sweaty nightmare. The items that cause the most anguish are listed here.

Baby Milk This is available in Thailand but is generally sweeter than UK versions. Use bottled water and try your best to sterilise equipment.

Child Car Seat Bring one if you are planning on renting a car as they're not supplied by Thai car rental companies. Given the damage which may be inflicted by baggage handling, make it a polystyrene one, not hard plastic which can sustain invisible cracks which make the seat useless in a crash.

Highchairs Major resorts might have highchairs: smaller establishments might not. Consider a fabric harness that clips on to normal chairs, or a backpack baby carrier that folds out to form a small child support.

Pram/Travel Buggy These can be useful to restrain toddlers and stop them racing off into traffic, as emergency daytime sleeping stations, and child seats at restaurants without highchairs (most of the cheap ones). However, they are little use on the broken pavements of most Thai cities, bog down quickly in sandy beaches (although the three-wheelers are better) and take a lot of space. Usually it's easier to carry children than manhandle a pram about the place, and if you decide you do need a pram you can always buy one, perhaps from Tesco Lotus: prices are lower than in the UK.

Slings and Baby Carriers For parents happy to use them, slings, available at The Carrying Kind (*www.thecarryingkind.com*), offer many of the benefits of buggies and are not reliant on smooth pavements. Baby carriers work well for parents accustomed to using backpacks, with the best brands available at outdoor specialist shops. Locals strap their babies on with saris which you could buy on the spot, although keeping them secure is something that takes practice.

Sunscreen Brand-name suncreams and lotions are available in most resort areas.

Sweaters/Warm Clothes You'll only need these if you're travelling to the north, and even then only in the evenings.

Travel Cots Mid-range and expensive hotels and resorts will have some child cots and usually supply them free. Cheaper hotels will often charge for travel cots and may only have one – if any. Make sure you specify that you need a cot in advance. If not on offer it's generally preferable to risk being woken early rather than lug a travel cot around everywhere you go.

Waterproof Clothes In Thailand's tropical heat even lightweight plastic waterproofs soon leave you soaking with condensation and perspiration: an umbrella is better. Rain is often heavy and dramatic and most Thais simply take shelter until the rain has passed: so should you.

Insurance & Health

Healthcare in Thailand is generally good and inexpensive. Travel insurance is recommended, if for no other reason than the traffic. If you are involved in a road accident bills can escalate quickly past any amount you could raise on a mortgage.

Make sure the policy covers you and all your family for scuba diving and any other adventure sports you might attempt, and provides emergency airlifts if required. It is cheaper and often better to buy your travel insurance from a specialist agency rather than tour operators as they simply regard travel insurance as a profit zone.

Thai chemists can supply most drugs without prescription, but possibly under different trade names. If you require specific medicines it is best to bring those you need.

Immunisations

Thailand is a tropical country with a fair range of tropical diseases. Before you leave confirm your family has had the primary courses and boosters given as routine by the NHS.

Immunisation is usually advised for diphtheria, tetanus, poliomyelitis and hepatitis A. Sometimes typhoid, tuberculosis, rabies, Japanese B encephalitis and hepatitis B are also recommended. Travellers over nine months old coming from an area where yellow fever is endemic will need a certificate against yellow fever.

Travelling Safely with Children in Thailand

Without exception Thais seem to love children. Often you'll have people coming up to touch young blonde babies because they think it brings luck. In hotels you'll often find waiting staff taking your children away and playing with them for ages.

This doesn't mean that travelling in Thailand with children is without its hazards. Foremost among them is the traffic. Even adults struggle to cope with the buzzing flood in the cities, and road accidents are much more common in Thailand than the UK.

TIP ⟩⟩ Avoiding Insect Bites ⟨

Malaria and dengue fever are mosquito-borne diseases and even disregarding such life-threatening issues, no one likes being bitten. Minimise bites in the evening by lighting mosquito coils and placing them upwind. Apply repellent frequently (although not DEET for infants) as most brands don't seem to stay effective for long. Finally, sleep under mosquito nets, fans or in air-conditioned rooms; the critters don't like moving air or the cold. When sitting outside at nightfall look after your ankles: mosquitoes are lazy and although it's the ones on your arms you see, most are low to the ground, feasting on your ankles. Better to wear thick socks and look like frumpy than end up bitten to pieces below the table.

Hang on to children in crowded areas: it's easy for them to get swept away and lost.

Keep an eye on children around water. On some beaches there are vicious undertows and lifeguards are rare. A few will put up red flags when conditions are dangerous but these are in the minority. Most rural Thais would no more go swimming – for fun – than fly to the moon: most can't even swim. Take local advice, preferably from a local dive shop, be vigilant, and test the waters carefully. If you feel the slightest risk of an undertow stick to the nearest hotel pool.

Mobile Phones

Dialling home prefix the country code (44 for the UK) with 001.

GSM 900Hz and 1800Hz phones work in Thailand, but it's advisable to call your service provider to enable roaming, checking the coverage and how much it will cost.

It may well be cheaper to get a rechargeable Thai SIM card (available at any 7/11) so you can make calls within Thailand for 5B for the first minute, 2B per minute thereafter.

If you buy a SIM card issued by the Communications Authority of Thailand (CAT) you can make international calls through Voice-Over-Internet-Protocol (VOIP), prefixing the country code by 009 instead of 001. This is much cheaper.

Mobile phone numbers have recently been restructured from nine to 10 digits, with 8 being added between the initial 0 and the number. If you find nine-digit mobile numbers on old brochures or advertisements you can sometimes get through by adding this 8.

Landline Phones

There are still some coin-operated phone boxes in Thailand, taking the smallest, most modern type of 1B coin. This can work well for local calls but not for long distance, which often costs 15B per minute. Domestic phone cards cost 100B and can be used in steel phone boxes.

Internet cafés and even people renting out their mobile phones from trestle-tables offices on the street offer cheap long-distance and international rates. Hotel phones attract a hefty surcharge for all calls.

The Internet

The web has taken Thailand by storm. Even tiny establishments usually have their own websites and Internet access, and Internet cafés are everywhere and usually cheap. Almost all guest houses have their own computers, charging 20–40B per hour. Expensive hotels are a different matter: business centres charge way over the odds and many of the top hotels that boast wireless access charge exorbitant amounts for access.

Calling Thailand from Abroad

The country code for Thailand is 66, after which leave out the initial 0 of the telephone number.

Getting There

Bangkok is a major world transport hub served by countless airlines.

Non-stop flights are provided by:

British Airways *www.british airways.com*, 0844 493 0787

Qantas *www.quantas.com*, 020 8846 0466

Thai Airways *www.thaiairways. co.uk*, 0870 606 0911

Eva Air *www.evaair.com*, 020 7380 8300

Numerous airlines fly to Thailand via the Middle East, including Etihad, Emirates, Gulf Air (which offers nannies on some flights) and you can also fly via the Far East using Singapore Airlines, Cathay Pacific or Sri Lankan Airways. These are often cheaper, but bear in mind the extra disruption of changing planes with small children.

Don't just look at the price: check there are seat-back video screens and what else is on offer. Currently Taiwanese operator Eva provides the best standards of service in economy on this route.

Other airlines currently operating between the UK and Bangkok are: Aeroflot, Jet Airways, Air Astana, Kenya Airways, Air China, Korean Air, Air France, Kuwait Airways, Air India, Lufthansa, Alitalia, Mahan Air, ANA, Oman Air, Asiana Airlines, Pakistan International Airways, Austrian Airlines, Biman, Qatar Airways, Royal Brunei, Royal Jordanian, SAS, Egypt Air, EL AL, South African Airways, SWISS, Finnair, Transaero Airlines, Gulf Air, Turkish Airlines, Japan Airlines, Uzbekistan Airways. Take your pick.

Flying with Children

Long-haul flights with children need not be too much of a trial.

Make sure the airline you use has seat-back screens with films on demand and a children's channel.

Arrange to sit near the front, which is quieter, or at the back where you're more likely to get spare rows or extra seats.

You need extra seats. Ask the stewardess to allocate you any spare seats well before the flight doors have closed. If there seem to be any spare rows or seats, make your move as early as you dare.

Try to fly with a Far Eastern airline. They are much more tolerant. If you manage to get your children to sleep on the floor under your feet Far Eastern stewardesses usually don't bat an eye, while European stewardesses seem to insist they are woken up and returned to their seat.

Try to sit near other families with children the same age. They might make friends and other parents are likely to be more tolerant – or at least less surprised by – any noise the children might make.

Don't rely on the airline supplying colouring sets and toys – although many do – bring your own. Let them gain ownership of their games by helping them pack – and making them carry – their own daypacks.

Give the children window seats. There are fuelling trucks for them to look at while you're on the ground, views in daytime, and it's harder for them to escape to run up and down the aisle. Once they've discovered how much fun this can be it's hard to get them to stop.

Take plenty of wipes and, if required, nappies.

Tour Operators

It used to be that tour operators got the best fares on routes to Thailand, which they packaged together with discounted hotels to offer a complete travel service at unbeatable prices. Some still do: if you're after a conventional holiday experience look at Kuoni (☏ 01306 747002, *www.kuoni.co. uk*), West East Travel (☏ 0870 220 1001, *www.westeasttravel.co.uk*), Destinology (☏ 01204 474400, *www.destinology.co.uk*), Dreamticket (☏ 0845 880 0244, *www. dreamticket.com*), Carrier (☏ 0161 491 7630, *www.carrier.co.uk*) and Aspire Holidays (☏ 0845 458 9455, *www.aspireholidays.co.uk*). All cater specifically for families but will tend to focus on a few set itineraries that follow similar, if popular, formats. Accommodation is likely to be of a higher standard than you need: that's where the money is.

Prebooked Itineraries

Travelling on a pre-planned route around the country with a driver and guide can be a good way for families to experience Thailand. Known as Fully Itinerised Travel (FIT), this can take all the stress out of the travel arrangements. You know in advance that each hotel has been booked and how many beds are provided, and that the transport will be new, well driven and big enough to fit your family. In addition your family can strike up a relationship with the guide who will get to know your tastes and interests, and often suggest sights and experiences beyond your normal plans, help with children, and offer countless insights into what you can see and do. Usually they'll show you round the country for a few days and then leave you to finish your holiday on a beach. Often it's sad to part as they have become good family friends. Good operators for this include Audley Travel (☏ 01993 838000, *www.audleytravel.com*), Kuoni (☏ 01306 747002, *www. kuoni.co.uk*), Key 2 Thailand (☏ 020 7963 6676, *www.key2 thailand-holidays.co.uk*) and West East Travel (☏ 0870 220 1001, *www. westeasttravel.co.uk*), which is linked to Thai Airways and knows the destination better than anyone. Costs are slightly higher with a car and driver, but not by as much as you'd expect.

Group Travel

Depending on your family, travelling in a group with other families might be a good way to go. Your children will have immediate friends (or enemies) their own age, and you too might get on with the other travellers. Often this sort of travel has a whole range of activities packed into a programme, which can be a good thing. What you miss are the chance encounters with the locals: generally you'll have a guide and inevitably spend more time relating to the other people in your group than the Thais. Costs, on the other hand, are likely to be lower than you could ever hope to arrange travelling independently. Good operators include Explore (☏ *0845 013 1537*, *www.explore.co.uk*), Exodus (☏ *0845 863 9600*, *www.exodus. com*) and the Australian company Intrepid (☏ *0207 354 6169*, *www.intrepid.com*). All have special group programmes for families and will also arrange FIT tours.

Whichever tour operator you choose, make sure they're fully bonded. Travelling with an ATOL registered tour operator does have one big advantage: it means your funds are safe if any of the people providing the main elements of your holiday – the airlines, hotels or tour operator themselves – go bust.

Fly for Less

The Internet has revolutionised buying cheap air tickets, but you don't need to be online to score a deal: most of the major operators also have telesales desks which offer much the same rates. Good places to try include Ebookers (☏ *087 223 5000*, *www. flightbookers.co.uk*) and Opodo (☏ *0871 277 0090*, *www.opodo.co. uk*). Online price comparison sites can save significant amounts of money and time. Good examples include *www.kayak.co.uk*, *www.travelsupermarket.co.uk*, *www.traveljungle.co.uk* and *www. skyscanner.net*. However, for all their bells and whistles – and the endless minutes where the computer claims to be checking every possible operator and combination of flights – *www.cheap flights.co.uk* still seems to come up with better rates, despite its more traditional format.

Paying by credit card often attracts a surcharge when buying cut-price tickets, but is advisable for the protection it gives should the airline go bust.

Remember it's not all about price. You can check out the facilities offered on many international flight routes, right down to the legroom available for each particular seat, on *www. seatguru.com*.

Getting Around Thailand

By Air Thailand's domestic air network is accessible, efficient and not expensive. If connecting with internal flights it is best to use the glitzy new Suvarnabhumi Airport (code BKK), from where Thai Airways flights scoot off in all directions round the country. Connecting is a breeze, even if you've just got off a long intercontinental flight, making it possible to sidestep Bangkok altogether on the way in.

Bangkok's newly reopened Don Muang Airport (code DMK) is now the country's largest domestic hub: flights from here tend to be slightly cheaper.

Since 2007 airport tax has been included in the price of all international and domestic air tickets.

By Car Renting a car is easy in Thailand but driving is not. Bangkok is particularly hard to navigate, with constant traffic jams, misleading signs and many one-way streets. In rural areas the situation eases, but Thai drivers are unashamedly reckless. Each year there are 250 road fatalities on Phuket alone, and thousands of injuries: no one seems to care. You'll need to be confident and fluid in your driving, and quick to react to the unexpected. Driving is (usually) on the left.

Among the many car-rental agencies, both Avis (☎ 02255 5300) and Budget (☎ 02566 5067) have convenient offices around the country, and you can hire a car with or without a driver. All drivers should have an international driver's license and the rental companies will want to see a credit card. Self-drive rates start around 1500B a day for a family-sized car, more for luxury vehicles or SUVs.

Local tour operators will rent cars for considerably less but may not include insurance: this can be a serious problem as it's an offence to drive uninsured, as will become all-too apparent if you are in an accident. Do not leave your passport as collateral for vehicle rentals, no matter how often you're asked. If the renter has your passport and you have an accident or damage the vehicle you'll be in a very poor bargaining position. Leave a credit card deposit instead.

Petrol stations are easily found, from proper serviced outlets to small stalls selling petrol in bottles who can be useful should you run dry.

By Scooter Thai families often squeeze on to a small scooter and in rural areas, and if you're competent, careful and sober, it can be quite an adventure for your family. Rental rates are between 150B– 250B per day and you don't usually need a driving licence. Don't leave your passport as a deposit: a credit-card runout is perfectly adequate.

Be aware that there are fatalities every day on Thailand's roads. By law only the driver needs to wear a crash helmet (this is enforced on tourist islands such as Phuket and Koh

Samui and in road-block blitzes in other cities) but the rental brain buckets supplied are unpadded and almost useless: you are better off using cycle helmets brought from home or purchased locally.

All passengers should wear proper shoes as even a minor skid on gravel can do a lot of damage to flip-flopped feet. Hanging on to the bars is tremendously exciting for young children but only for very short journeys. Otherwise the hot wind and the constant blinking against dust and flies soon get tiring. On the plus side it's easy to hop on and off, and scooters are very convenient to park.

By Train Thailand's railway system radiates from Bangkok's Hualamphong Railway Station (📞 02223 7010), with a separate line heading out to Kanchanaburi from a second station, Bangkok Noi. Regular services to Chiang Mai in the north, and south to Surat Thani are the most useful to families, as sleeper seats can be reserved in advance for 12-hour overnight journeys.

First-class sleepers have air-conditioned compartments with washbasin, while second-class sleepers have bunks with curtains and either ceiling fans or air-conditioning, depending on the ticket price. On night journeys look after your possessions as theft is quite common. First-class travel is charged at about 1B per kilometre.

By Bus Thailand has a very efficient and inexpensive bus system, with air-conditioned buses that, like the trains, seem to charge about 1B per kilometre. Non-air-conditioned buses are even cheaper.

Stick to government buses operating from each city's proper bus terminal. These are a good way for short or intermediate journeys. Long-distance buses tend to travel overnight and woe betide those whose children can't sleep.

Long-Distance Taxi It might seem extravagant, but inter-city taxi travel is convenient, comfortable and – after you've multiplied bus or air tickets by four – cost-effective for families. Taxis will seat three in comfort, four if one is small, and usually have working air-conditioning. Try your hotel travel desk first for a quote, and they can make the arrangements. Allow about 800B per hour of travel. Larger families will need to rent a minibus but this only costs about 20% more and gives plenty of room to play on the way.

INSIDER TIP ▶

Few drivers speak or read English. Try to have the address of where you want to go in Thai script, or marked on a map that is also written in Thai. Even if you really like the guy, don't set off in a taxi before you're sure he knows where you're trying to go. Try another driver or see if there's anyone in the vicinity to translate.

When waving down a taxi, turn your palm down and wave them in with your fingers.

If you take the expressway you pay the fee. Give the driver the money as you queue, rather than holding things up at the kiosk.

By Taxi, Tuk-Tuk & Songthaew

In Bangkok and many provincial areas by law taxis are meant to charge by the meter. Many don't, parking up near expensive hotels and quoting outrageous fares.

Just occasionally, if your children are tired and you need to get them home, it might be worth bargaining the price down a fraction and taking the hit: in principle you should get out and find a more amenable driver but in several places, including Phuket and Koh Samui, it may prove impossible to find one.

Taxis are cheap compared to the UK, partly because many run on LPG. Fares start at 35B which will get you one kilometre. Then it creeps up slowly. Even a 20km ride, long by Bangkok standards, would cost 134B, just over £2. For typical city-centre trips most fares should come in at around 50B, although there is a timer to allow for when traffic is bad.

Foreigners will be lucky to hire a *tuk-tuk* even for a short journey for less than 50B. Don't let them take you to any shops as they'll get a commission.

In most provincial areas pickup trucks with racked seats in the back, *songthaews*, cruise the main streets offering a communal taxi service at cheap, set fees, but if they're empty they often behave like an unmetered taxi. As with *tuk-tuks*, always agree the fare in advance. Few taxi, *tuk-tuk* or *songthaew* drivers speak even basic English, so have a copy of your hotel's name, street address and district written in Thai with you at all times.

Tipping is always expected and can't always be avoided because drivers rarely admit to having any change. Go prepared with plenty of small-denomination notes.

Accommodation

The most developed parts of Thailand have the greatest range of accommodation. Visit Bangkok, Phuket, Chiang Mai, Pattaya or Koh Samui and you'll be able to choose from international chains such as the Mandarin Oriental group, The Peninsula, Hilton, Accor, Sheraton and Marriott: many chains have their flagship properties here. In addition home-grown chains such as Dusit and Amari have resort and city properties that can compete with the best. Thailand has its own star rating system that counts facilities but favours larger properties and tends to miss the big picture.

These days the trend is to smaller, independent boutique hotels. They won't be able to match the big properties for facilities but win on personalised service – and you're less likely to get lost in them.

By providing designer toiletries, branded robes, in-room DVD or CD players and Jacuzzis among countless other

TIP ⟩ **Save on Extra Beds** ⟨

Experienced travellers save on accommodation by carrying a bedroll for their children. Bulky, but not heavy, these can hugely reduce your hotel bill because most hotels don't charge for one child in their parents' room if they don't require extra bedding, and many allow two under 12.

little luxuries, five-star properties feel happy charging as much as 28,000B a night for a double room (see the 'Very Expensive' category in each destination chapter). At this point service tends to be icily professional as well: not many families will be able to completely relax with young children in so perfected an environment.

Most hotels in the 'Expensive' category have almost as many deluxe amenities but rooms are generally less palatial in size. You can still expect perks like silk bathrobes, CD and DVD players, facilities are usually high quality, and service intimidatingly smooth. Expect to pay around 15,000B per night.

'Moderate' hotels and resorts can be an excellent choice, as at this level character has not been ironed out by professionalism. Family rooms start at about 8000B in season and all the ones listed here provide good value for money. They will have swimming pools, good restaurants, toiletries, satellite television, in-room safes and international direct dialling from your room. In smaller cities and towns, this category is about the best you can do. Some of these moderately priced options also have good family room configurations. At all budgets you

run the risk of mattresses with very little give, and you'll definitely find them in this category as they tend to get harder the less you spend, unless you've found a resort run by a westerner.

Most hotels in this price bracket raise rates as they modernise rooms, so you can stay more cheaply in the yet-to-be-revamped ones, while still sharing the same facilities.

The published rate might be intimidating, but these are the places with the flexibility to discount significantly and in low season you might pick up a good family room for as little as 1800B, and a bad one for even less.

Moderate, Expensive and Very Expensive hotels will charge 17–18% service and VAT. This accentuates the gap in cost with the least expensive properties which have not yet been caught in the taxation net.

Accommodation on a Budget

The number of inexpensive hotels has been shrinking over recent years, as even the most modest establishments dig swimming pools and add spas to justify higher prices. And because tourism has generally been built up by couples and single travellers, the usual choice in this category is one big bed or two small. 'Family Rooms', when they have them, tend to be one big bed and one small. The Thais don't see any problem with fitting even large families on two such beds. However, this book has selected hotels that have a range of different rooms to suit various family sizes.

As a general rule proximity to airports means higher prices. If you're travelling on a budget it's worth taking a boat to another island, or a bus to another town to get more comfort for your baht.

The least expensive places provide very few facilities. There might be a shower but it will either be cold or heated by an instant electric heater with lethal wiring. There may be air-conditioning but you will have to pay extra to get it unlocked. They won't have a cot, and the beds will have a hard. They will have a restaurant, however, and this will often be excellent value, and these places are actually the most accommodating to children, welcoming them in to the general chaos. Some, just a few, are a delight: dirt-cheap outposts of comfort on far-flung beaches, or friendly havens in the heart of busy towns.

Reassuringly for the family traveller, Thailand has a huge number of hotels. With the possible exception of Koh Samet on a holiday weekend you will always find somewhere, however modest, to lay your children for the night.

INSIDER TIP

If you're staying in a very cheap hotel or in a private home you may well come across *Mandi* bathrooms. These have large reservoirs of water and a ladle to shower. Don't under any circumstances get soap in the main water reservoir: soap yourself down and stand well clear when you rinse yourself off.

Laundry in Thailand

One of the beauties of travel in Thailand is that you'll rarely have to do your own washing. Same-day laundry and dry cleaning are offered by most smart hotels – at a price that closely reflects their room rate so often very expensive. Budget travellers will find plenty of service laundries clustered around their lodges charging as little as 20B per kg, which includes incredibly neat ironing and folding. Culturally Thais would not normally wash socks or underwear except for close family. These days they make an exception for foreigners, but you should bear this in mind if staying with local families. In the unlikely event you've done your own laundry, don't hang your socks or underwear high: it's thought very rude. Look for somewhere low and discreet.

Surfing for Hotels

The Internet has revolutionised hotel booking in Thailand. A number of consolidators offer good rates for properties in resort areas and you should at least check their prices before calling or emailing the property direct. Make sure to print out the exact terms of your booking as there are innumerable cases of included breakfasts not being provided, room classes changed and cots strangely unavailable: a printed piece of paper can make a huge difference to your negotiating position at the front desk. Good places to try include *www. asiarooms.com*, *www.sawadee. com*, *www.gothailand.com*, *www. agoda.com* and *www.1stop bangkok.com*. There are also independent sites for the various resort areas.

For many families renting a villa is an ideal way to explore at your own pace. Rates are low. The money that would struggle to get you a dated and draughty shed in Europe will in Thailand get you a luxury pad with pool, DVD player, washing machine and possibly even a cook. A good place to look is *www. holidaylettings.co.uk*.

Saving on Your Hotel Room

Rates given in this book are the rack rate, the maximum charged. Except in high season or holidays you should be able to negotiate a discount.

● Ask about special rates or other discounts. Say how long you might be staying, even if this is just two nights. Take advantage of any discounts for family members such as being a student or a pensioner.

● Dial direct. Don't book a chain hotel through head office. You're likely to get a better price from the individual hotel's front desk.

● Book online. Internet-only prices are lower. Check with the consolidators listed above.

● Remember the law of supply and demand. A hotel with empty rooms needs your business: you're the best chance they have of filling the restaurant. Be ready to appear to walk away.

● Avoid excess charges and hidden costs. Make sure you know what is included in the room rate and what is extra. Ordering an extra bed can trigger a charge while a child under 12 sharing existing bedding usually goes free. Don't take drinks or let children pilfer sweets from the minibar: there's almost bound to be a minimarket within a few hundred yards, selling exactly the same products for much less. Don't use the room phone – surcharges can be exorbitant – and if wifi is offered, make sure it's free.

● Ask whether local taxes and service charges are included in your room rate. Check prices in the restaurant, bearing in mind tax and service charges, and consider walking a few paces to the nearest tax-free alternative.

● Look for self-catering. Many family guestrooms in Thai hotels have a kitchenette – something always mentioned under 'Amenities' in this book's hotel listings. This means you can knock up a comfort meal of minimart pasta without running up the expense of yet another child's menu meal.

Private Villas & Timeshare

Koh Samui and Phuket are Timeshare Central, and properties are impressively specified. I've stayed in several villas I'd be more than happy to swap for my UK home and your children may well support the idea of an immediate life change.

Don't leap into purchase though. There are strict restrictions on foreign ownership of land, speculators have been known to build developments on land they don't own, and many foreigners have lost their life savings in real estate scams. You should talk to a lawyer – and not the one suggested by the vendor. Even if the deal is genuine service charges can be significant. Also bear in mind it's a long way away, flights are expensive, and although Thailand is lovely, so are many other countries. Think it over.

Dining

Thai cuisine must be one of the finest in the world (see Appendix for further details). The seafood is superb and appeals to every taste, while even the most modest hand-cart street-vendor chef cooks with flair. Fried rice and noodles – specify *Mai Ao Prik* or

'not spicy' – appeal to most children, and you can always order a banana pancake or an omelette if required.

Where most parents go wrong is to try to recreate their home diet. Bread is not a part of Thai culture, and outside major resorts the local bread is not like bread at home and your children are likely to be disappointed. McDonald's restaurants are everywhere, but the burgers are not the same and the cheesy chips look as though a vulture with a stomach disorder has recently flown overhead. You're better off introducing them to fried squid sold from street-vendors and embrace Thai culture rather than trying to recreate home.

In rural areas Thai food might be the only option, but in any resort area the full gamut of world cuisines is on offer – often cooked by a native-born chef. Italians, French, Swedes and Germans have all set up new lives in Thailand, and many have opened restaurants. Should Thai food pall there's likely to be an Australian steak house within a few paces and certainly no more than a short taxi ride away.

In all events, you're never far from food of some sort as the Thais seem to have a horror of spending too long between snacks, eating lightly, healthily and very often. Any attraction without its own restaurant will quickly attract a food vendor or two.

When it comes to fine food, many of the best restaurants are in the major resorts and hotels. This is where you'll find the most formal environments and delicious cuisines. The major resorts are also where you're most likely to find highchairs. Elsewhere you might have to resort to stacking two plastic chairs together to give your child the height to reach the table.

Table Manners

Thais are as practical about table manners as your children. If something is best eaten with the hands, then that is what they'll do. Seeds or bones can be spat out – though probably into a napkin. Noodle soups are sucked up from close range, helped by chopsticks and a Chinese spoon. You'll only see knives in more expensive restaurants. Rice dishes are eaten with a spoon and fork, with the fork being used to load the spoon, held in the right, used for eating. Follow local customs or eat as you like: though Thailand is even more class-conscious than the UK table manners are not a major indicator.

Tipping

In cheaper Thai restaurants tipping is not expected. In smarter, more expensive places it most certainly is – at up to 20% on top of the 10% 'service charge' that is often automatically added.

Cultural Matters

In Thailand the head is the most important part of the body. It is very rude to pat anyone on the head – even a child. Correspondingly the feet are the lowest part and regarded with some horror. Don't point your feet at people, step over food, or – horror of horrors – poke people with your foot. When seated don't point your feet outwards: curl your legs under your body, even if this isn't comfortable. Even very young Thai children know this.

Dress

Thais dress conservatively. Going bare-chested is not acceptable for women or generally men – Thais react with distrust. To enter a monastery you'll need to cover your shoulders and legs, and remove shoes. Those with most visitors have kiosks that rent acceptable clothes to westerners.

Wai

You won't get far in Thailand before you meet your first *wai*, the respectful, prayer-like greeting. The higher the hands, the greater the respect. Don't be shy: even if you feel deeply ridiculous – embarrassment will keep your hands low which is disrespectful. It's only polite and always appreciated – although you shouldn't '*wai*' children or monks.

Long Live the King

Don't be rude about the Thai royal family, past or present. This won't win you any friends and may lead to jail. In cinemas you have to stand for the national anthem, and if you hear it played in the streets you, like everyone else, are required to stop whatever you're doing and stand still, respectfully.

Keep Cool

Above all else Thais value cool, calm behaviour and a 'cool heart'. Foreigners are all considered to have 'hot hearts' but in any situation losing your temper is seen as a serious loss of face. Stay calm and collected in all situations: a smile is your best weapon in any negotiations.

Farangs

You'll often hear yourself referred to as 'farang'. This is a corruption of the word 'French' and dates back to Thailand's first encounters with the western world. It's not intended to be rude: just accept that in Thailand you are an outsider and always, to a great extent, will remain one.

Shopping

Shopping in Thailand is part of the national psyche, a complex dance of cultures with trade at its heart. Bangkok often seems to be one huge market, and countless stalls and shops line every road.

Apart from department stores, resort boutiques and mini markets prices are generally negotiable: though even asking prices often seem low, bargaining is key. Prices are rarely shown and the magic question 'How much' launches a battle of wits that becomes serious as soon as you make your counter-offer. Once uttered, an offer can't be withdrawn – it can only be adjusted upwards. If the vendor drops to any price you have suggested the deal will be assumed to be done.

Many of the goods on sale are unashamedly counterfeit. Brand-name clothes, near-Croc shoes and fake designer bags are everywhere. Most tempting perhaps are the endless pirate CDs and DVDs, of variable quality but minimal cost. Bringing these back to the UK is an offence and such items, if discovered, will be confiscated.

Don't Get Stoned

Don't buy gems in Thailand unless you know what you're doing. Selling pebbles and bits of coloured glass is a bit of a sport here and foreigners are favourite targets. If anyone tells you a particular stone can be sold for more money in the UK they are lying. They would export it themselves. Assume any gems, even from reputable shops and accompanied by (worthless) certificates are valueless, and 99% of the time you'll be right.

The Active Family

Thailand presents some unique opportunities to push yourself – and your family. Head out to the rural areas for unforgettable adventures. Here routes have opened up Thailand's natural wild side, with safe soft-adventure options that are well planned and suitable for all ages. For planning specifics see the regional chapters, but here is an overview.

Diving & Snorkelling

If your plans are centred on the beach, the most obvious activity is snorkelling or perhaps scuba diving. Coral reefs grace the waters of the Andaman Sea, off Thailand's southwest coast, and the Gulf of Thailand. More than 80 species of coral have been discovered in the Gulf that can be dived year round, while the deeper and more saline Andaman has more than 210 species, but a shorter diving season. Marine life also includes hundreds of species of fish, plus numerous varieties of crustaceans and sea turtles.

Snorkelling is something most children over the age of five can master, although it helps if they can swim. They have to be confident in the water and able to clear their snorkel when swamped. They also have to understand that shallow breaths, through a snorkel, just change old used air. This results in oxygen deprivation, to which the clinical reaction is panic. Parents should be aware of this, but snorkelling is a magical experience and well worth experiencing as a family: just be careful and alert.

Diving is a different matter. Thai dive schools will accept children as young as eight on diving courses, but many experienced divers wouldn't dream of letting their children dive so young. The problem is that scuba diving doesn't feel dangerous but it is. Unless you are confident that you can explain to your children that they have to breathe out as they ascend – and rely on them to remember this in an emergency – then you should emphatically not send them down with breathing gear. If they take a full breath three metres down and hold their breath until they reach the surface they'll probably die – and there's nothing the decompression facilities in Pattaya or Phuket will be able to do about it.

Children have a natural aptitude for diving and enjoy it hugely, but be aware of the risks. Best stick to the snorkelling expeditions from Koh Lanta, Koh Phi Phi, Krabi, Koh Samui and Pattaya.

Trekking & Rafting

Thailand's mountainous northern jungles have become a haven for trekkers. At the same time, human rights organisations have pointed out the damage caused to remote hill-tribe villages, reducing communities to human zoos. Choose your operator carefully and look out for NGO-led projects where the local people benefit from your visit.

Most treks are little more than three or four hours on a jungle path, along with a ride on an elephant and a drift down the river on a bamboo raft. For a more authentic experience take your family on a proper trek lasting three nights or more.

River rafting in rubber dinghies, bamboo rafts and kayaks are increasingly popular in Thailand, with operators mounting expeditions from Chiang Mai and Pai. Winding through dense jungles, past rock formations and local villages, these trips include camping and sometimes trekking. Rapids are rarely extreme but are big enough to be loads of fun, and safety measures are taken seriously.

Properly organised, climbing can be fun and safe for some children as young as six. Thailand is home to one of the world's top 10 climbing walls, with countless sheer limestone cliffs. Rock climbing at Railay Beach in Krabi (see p 142) is world famous. Views are superb and safety procedures closely observed. A few small outfits accept children for training or will organize climbs for more expert families, providing all the necessary equipment and a personal climbing guide.

Getting Prepared

● Read the news. Thailand's two English-language dailies are the *Bangkok Post* (**www.bangkokpost.com**) and *The Nation* (**www.nationmultimedia.com**)

● There are a few blogs and info sites in Thailand although they can be well out of date. Check out **www.bangkokrecorder.com** and **www.angloinfo.com**. New Zealand writer Stickman (**www.stickmanbangkok.com**) has a cautionary 'warts and all' guide to Thailand and the Thailand Guru (**www.thailandguru.com**) has some good advice for expats.

● For planning your trip **www.weather2travel.com** is an excellent source of seasonal information. Just before you fly Intellicast (**www.intellicast.com**) and Weather.com (**www.weather.com**) give up-to-date forecasts.

● Check current exchange rates at the Universal Currency Converter (**www.xe.com**).

Getting the Children Interested in Thailand

● Show them a map and point out Thailand, then log on to Google Earth and zoom in close. They're sure to get excited when they see one of the islands and the beaches.

● Elephants are usually a hit and are found everywhere in Thailand so are a safe expectation to arouse alongside the charitable work done in refuges for them. Turtles are more elusive, but still of interest to children even if you're not likely to be near the turtle nesting beaches of Phuket.

● *The King and I* might be fun advance viewing, and *The Man with the Golden Gun* is good if you're likely to visit Phang-nga Bay.

● Encourage children to keep a scrapbook, starting before you leave and introducing photographs from brochures and magazines featuring Thailand.

● While on holiday collect everything; entrance tickets (which often have photographs), brochures and maps, and encourage them to keep a diary of their visit. Postcards can be stuck in as you go along but remember to leave space for family photographs to be added later.

FAST FACTS

Alcohol The official drinking age in Thailand is 18. You can readily buy and drink alcohol, even in supermarkets, but licensing laws apply and legally drinks can only be served after 5pm. On some public holidays and election days, no liquor can be sold at all. Most restaurants, bars and nightclubs sell drink, and you can pick up bottles of imported and local liquor from convenience stores. Night spots must now close at 1am (and the rule is being policed vigorously). In cheaper restaurants it is usual to bring your own local Thai spirits, bought from mini markets, and the restaurant will provide ice and sell you mixers.

Baby Equipment Large international resorts and hotels will have highchairs. Small beach-front hotels probably will not. Plastic chairs can be stacked if you need to raise your child up, and tables can be pushed down into the sand to adjust the level. All hotels except the very cheapest will have child cots, although they may have only one – and it might be already taken. Cots can be bought, relatively cheaply, from Tesco Lotus.

Breastfeeding In Thailand breastfeeding in public is not acceptable.

Business Hours Government offices (including branch post offices) are open Monday to Friday 8.30am–4.30pm, closing for lunch midday–1pm. Businesses are generally open 8am–5pm. Shops often stay open 8am–7pm or later, seven days a week. Department stores are generally open 10am–8pm. All TAT visitor centres are open daily 8.30am–4.30pm.

Chemists Throughout the country chemists stock brand-name medications and toiletries as well as less expensive local equivalents. Pharmacists usually speak some English, and a number of drugs that require a prescription elsewhere can be bought over the counter.

Distances Thailand is firmly metric and distances are in kilometres. On long journeys you'll find highways marked with little white-painted concrete blocks marking the kilometre distance to the next major town.

Electricity All outlets – except in some luxury hotels – are 220 volts AC (50 cycles). Most outlets have two round-pronged, European-style holes, although there are also some flat-pronged sockets available: you will need an adapter for UK plugs.

Embassies & Consulates

Most countries have consular representation in Bangkok, and the USA, Australia, Canada and the UK also have consulates in Chiang Mai.

Emergencies Throughout the country, the emergency number you should use is ☎ *1699* or ☎ *1155* for the Tourist Police (see Police below). Ambulances must be summoned from hospitals rather than through a central service (see hospital listings in each city). You can also contact your embassy or consulate.

Lost Credit Cards Notify your credit card company the minute you discover a card has been lost or stolen, and file a report at the nearest police station as the credit card company or insurer will require a police report or formal record of the loss. Most card companies have an emergency toll-free number to call if your card is lost or stolen. Make a note of it before you travel. Some may wire a cash advance or deliver an emergency credit card in a day or two.

If you need emergency cash over the weekend when all banks are closed Western Union

(*www.westernunion.com*) can arrange for funds to be wired.

Mail You can pick up mail while you travel by using a *poste restante*, which is a counter at a post office where your mail is kept, normally for a maximum of two months. Mail is addressed to you, care of Poste Restante, GPO, Name of City. You'll need proof of ID, must sign a receipt and pay 1B per letter. Hours of operation are the same as the post office. (See individual chapters for local post offices and their hours.)

Newspapers & Magazines

The English-language dailies are the *Bangkok Post* and *The Nation*, distributed in the morning in the capital and later in the day around the country. They cover the domestic political scene, as well as international news from Associated Press and Reuters wire services. Each costs 25B. UK papers are widely available in major resorts, downloaded online and reprinted on computer paper.

Police Thailand's Tourist Police (☎ *1699* or ☎ *1155*), have offices in every city (see specific chapters), speak English (and other foreign languages) and are open 24 hours each day. These language skills make them your first recourse rather than the regular police, who will simply be baffled.

Safety Anonymous violent crime in Thailand is rare, though it does exist. However, petty crime such as purse snatching or pick pocketing is common.

Overland travellers should take care on overnight buses and trains for small-time thieves. Beware also of credit card scams. Carry a minimum of cards, don't allow them out of your sight and keep all receipts. Don't carry unnecessary valuables either, and keep those you do have in your hotel's safe. Pay particular attention to your things, especially purses and wallets, on public transport.

Be wary of strangers who offer to guide you (particularly in Bangkok), take you shopping (especially to jewellery shops) or buy you food or drink, especially near tourist sights. These are well-known scams and usually lead to some sort of swindle. Walk away and maybe call the Tourist Police (see above).

Shipping By air is quite costly, but most major international delivery services have offices in Bangkok and the provinces including DHL Thailand, Grand Amarin Tower Building, Phetchaburi Road (℡ 02207 0600); Federal Express, at Rama IV Road (℡ 1782) and UPS Parcel Delivery Service, 16/1 Sukhumvit Soi 44/1 (℡ 02712 3300). Many businesses will also package and mail merchandise for a reasonable price.

Smoking More than five years ago Thailand banned smoking in public places such as restaurants and airports. Some bars that don't serve food can get away with smokers, or have created smoker-friendly outdoor spaces, including upmarket private cigar

bars. If in doubt, ask about non-smoking sections. A few years ago, the former Prime Minister Thaksin prohibited the display of cigarettes anywhere. Recently it has been outlawed in all air-conditioned public spaces, including hotel bedrooms. There's a 2000B fine for discarding cigarette butts on the street, and anti-smoking regulations are increasingly being enforced.

Taxes and Service Charges

Hotels charge a 7% government value-added tax (VAT) and typically add a 10% service charge. Hotel restaurants add 8.25% government tax. Smaller hotels (almost always) either ignore these taxes or quote inclusive prices. Costs quoted here include service charges and taxes.

Theft Report any loss of valuables to the Thai police station nearest to the district where the loss took place. If you think it took place in a taxi, find a friendly Thai speaker who can place an alert with the local taxi radio stations. If you've lost your passport call your embassy for an emergency one. This will allow you to board a plane but you will need to get a replacement entry visa too. To be safe, always carry a copy of your passport (and visa) when you travel, and if you lose the originals make copies of the Thai police report, which you will need to obtain replacements.

Time Zone Thailand is seven hours ahead of GMT (Greenwich Mean Time). During winter months, this means that Bangkok is seven hours ahead of London, in the summer eight hours ahead.

Tipping If no service charge is added in an expensive restaurant, a 10–15% tip is appropriate, even if a 20% tip is hoped for. In local shops, tipping is not common but airport and hotel porters expect tips; 50B is acceptable. Feel free to reward good service wherever you find it but bear in mind the minimum wage, even in Bangkok, is 165B per day. Tipping taxi drivers is appreciated but never tip those who refuse to switch on their meter, insisting on a rate for the trip. Carry small bills for tips, especially when travelling around as few taxi or *tuk-tuk* drivers will admit to having any change, hoping to round the price up. Watch their faces when you suggest rounding it down.

Toilets Public toilets are rare and never free. If you do find one the attendant will expect 1B for a quick visit, more if a child has been changed. The country's better restaurants and hotels will have western toilets. Shops and budget hotels will have an Asian squat toilet – a ceramic platform mounted over a hole in the ground. Near the toilet is a water bucket or sink with a small ladle. The water is for flushing the toilet. Toilet paper is not provided, but some have tissue dispensers (5B). Dispose of it in the wastebasket provided as it will clog up the narrow drains.

Water Don't drink the tap water here, even in the major hotels. Most hotels provide bottled water and you should use it for brushing your teeth as well as drinking. Most restaurants serve bottled or boiled water and ice made from boiled water, but do ask to be sure. Because you don't know what water it has been made from, ice is always best avoided.

What You Can Bring into Thailand It is prohibited by law to bring narcotics, pornography, firearms and ammunition, blood, live animals and agricultural products without a licence.

Tourists are allowed to enter the country with 1 litre of alcohol and 200 cigarettes (or 250g of cigars or smoking tobacco) per adult, duty free, and there is no official limit on perfume. Customs no longer restrict photographic film, PCs or cameras, as long as they are taken out of the country on departure.

What You Can Take Home from Thailand Pay more attention to what you can import to your home country. UK citizens can check details with HM Customs & Excise at ☎ *0845 010 9000* (from outside the UK, ☎ *+44 20 8929 0152*), or go to **www.hmce. gov.uk**.

Thai export customs are generally lax. The exception is cultural treasures. It is forbidden to take antique or authentic Buddha images or Bodhisattva images or fragments out of the kingdom, and special permission is needed to remove antique artefacts. You will be required to submit the object along with two 5×7-inch photographs showing a frontal view of the object, your passport and a photocopy of your passport notarised by your home embassy. The authorisation process takes eight days. For further details, contact the Department of Fine Arts, Na Phra That Road, next to Thammasat University (☏ *02221 7811* or ☏ *02225 2652*), open weekdays 9am–4pm. This is only an issue if the object in question is an antique, especially one that has been removed from a temple or palace, or a piece that has particular historic value to the kingdom. If you purchase a small Buddha image or reproduction, whether an amulet or a statue, you can ship it home or pack it in your bag. Most antiques you buy won't be remotely old, and any antique dealer will be able to notify you about which objects require special permission.

3 Bangkok

BANGKOK

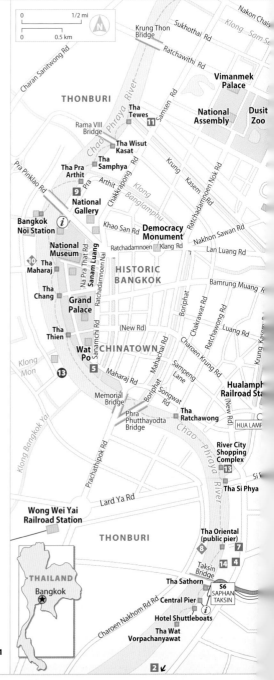

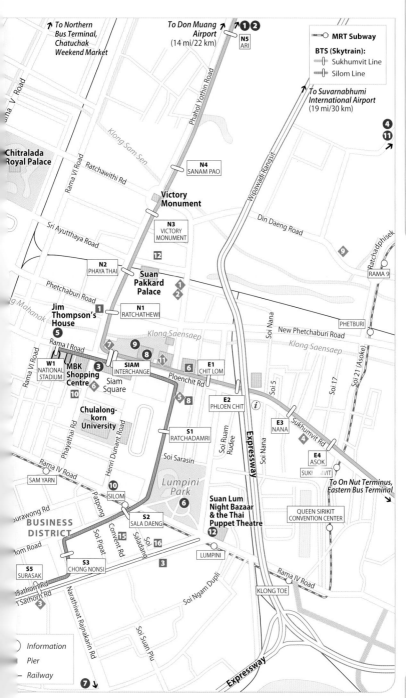

To Northern
Bus Terminal,
Chatuchak
Weekend Market

To Don Muang
Airport
(14 mi/22 km)

1 **2**

N5
ARI

MRT Subway

BTS (Skytrain):
Sukhumvit Line
Silom Line

To Suvarnabhumi
International Airport
(19 mi/30 km)

4
11

Chitralada
Royal Palace

Rama V Road

Ratchawithi Rd

Klong Sam Sen

Phahol Yothin Road

N4
SANAM PAO

Wipawadi-Rangsit

Din Daeng Road

Ratchadphisek

Rama VI Road

**Victory
Monument**

N3
VICTORY
MONUMENT

12

RAMA 9

9

Sri Ayutthaya Road

N2
PHAYA THAI

Phetchaburi Road

**Suan
Pakkard
Palace**

1
2

Soi Nana

New Phetchaburi Road

PHETBURI

g Mahanak

**Jim
Thompson's
House**

1
5

N1
RATCHATHEWI

Klong Saensaep

Klong Saensaep

Rama I Road

7

9

Soi 5

Soi 17

Soi 21 (Asoke)

W1
NATIONAL
STADIUM

**MBK
Shopping
Centre**

3

6

8

11

SIAM
INTERCHANGE

Ploenchit Rd

6

E1
CHIT LOM

Rama VI Road

10

Siam
Square

5

8

E2
PHLOEN CHIT

i

E3
NANA

Sukhumvit Rd

Phayathai Rd

**Chulalong-
korn
University**

S1
RATCHADAMRI

Soi Ruam
Rudee

Soi Nana

4

E4
ASOK

SUKHUMVIT

Henri Dunant Road

Soi Sarasin

To On Nut Terminus,
Eastern Bus Terminal

Rama IV Road

SAM YARN

10

SILOM

*Lumpini
Park*

6

**Suan Lum
Night Bazaar
& the Thai
Puppet Theatre**

12

QUEEN SIRIKIT
CONVENTION CENTER

urawong Rd

**BUSINESS
DISTRICT**

Patpong

S2
SALA DAENG

15

Convent Rd

Saladang

Soi

16

lom Road

S5
SURASAK

S3
CHONG NONSI

3

LUMPINI

Rama IV Road

KLONG TOE

Sathorn Rd

T Sathorn Rd

3

Narathiwat Rajnakarin Rd

Soi Ngam Dupli

Soi Suan Plu

Expressway

Information

Pier

Railway

7

Expressway

45

Crowded and chaotic, Thailand's capital city, Bangkok presents something of a challenge to families with children. Many make the perfectly rational decision to sidestep the capital altogether, choosing a connecting internal flight or a quick and easy taxi transfer from the cool and well-organised international airport to whisk them straight to a beach. And if you do want to experience Thai culture it is often easier to do so in a part of the country that is less pressured. The 'City of Angels', however, combines several must-see attractions for grown-ups, as well as plenty of entertaining opportunities for children.

Getting about can be difficult but, with the river running through the centre of the city, the everyday challenge of getting from A to B can become part of a captivating adventure. And for little rural ingénues like mine even the cool and slick Skytrain and subway can prove a hit. Meanwhile every *soi* (small street) contains something of interest – a tiny little shrine, a handcart selling colourful Thai sweets, or a rickety little shophouse where mounds of trade goods are used as improvised furniture by other children the same age.

While the famous Thai smile might have become a little strained at the sight of yet another adult western tourist, the people of Bangkok love to see western children wandering around the city. Mine were constantly being touched – for luck – by strangers. They were also taken off for little chats in restaurants and shops, and made a fuss of. My daughter could hardly pass a cosmetic shop without getting a nail or two painted by friendly beauticians, and my hot-looking son kept being given fans.

A little planning will mean all ages can get a lot from their time here. At first sight Bangkok is a taste of urban Asia at its most dynamic, but on an individual level it is endlessly friendly, helpful and warm.

ESSENTIALS

Getting There

Most travellers first arrive in Bangkok at the new Suvarnabhumi (pronounced 'Su-wan-na-poom') Airport, a glittering and spacious introduction to a city where claustrophobia and crowds generally rule.

The airport is 30km east of central Bangkok and there are various ways of getting into town. Ignore the touts that often cluster around as you emerge from the arrivals gate offering limousine services.

There are official taxis licensed to serve the airport, with vehicles less than five years old. These are booked at the taxi desk where you say where you are going and are given a bit of paper with the number of your taxi and the fare: keep this for later reference. On top of the taxi fare, about 300B to most destinations, you will also have to pay the 50B airport fee and

Thai Tongue-Twister

The locals know their capital as 'Krung Thep', the 'City of Angels', but this is an abbreviation. Its official title, Krungthepmahanakhon Amonrattana-kosin Mahintharayutthaya Mahadilokphop Noppharatratchathaniburirom Udomratchaniwetmahasathan Amonphimanawatansthit Sakkathattiya-witsanukamprasit, is the longest placename in the world.

65B toll fees for the expressway into town. If you've been given large notes by an ATM it's worth asking at one of the exchange bureaux for some small denominations, *torn satang* in Thai. The journey can take as little as 30 minutes, depending where you are going, but can take 90 minutes or more in rush hour or rain.

The strict licensing regulations means that larger families might not fit in one vehicle in which case you could consider the larger limousines, official ones available with set fares at the Limousine Service Desk near arrivals on level two.

A free shuttle bus links the airport with the transport centre where you find car hire and the bus station. But airport express buses charge 150B per person so families will find taxis cheaper as well as more convenient.

By the time this book goes to press the high-speed rail link should be operational, running along an elevated track to Makkasan station for the MRT subway. Red trains will offer a stopping commuter service and pink trains a fast non-stop service.

Moving on from Bangkok

By Air International flights, most of Thai Airways domestic flights and several other domestic airlines fly from Suvarnabhumi International Airport (02132 1888, *www. bangkokairportonline.com*). By the time of publication this should be linked into the Skytrain subway network, any Bangkok taxi will be prepared to negotiate a rate to get you there, and a number of Khao San Road minibuses offer regular services. Allow plenty of time for the journey – up to two hours in rush hour.

Some domestic operators, including Thai Airways, Nok Air and One Two Three Go, still leave from Don Muang Airport (*www.donmuangairportonline. com*). In rush hour this can be reached cheaply and reliably by rail from Hualamphong station. Most trains heading north stop at Don Muang, albeit briefly, with the last at 10.45pm. After that you'll need to use a taxi.

By Bus Countless minibus operators sell convenient tickets, often including ferries if needed, to the popular tourist destinations. The advantage is that they'll often pick you up from your hotel. The drawback is that you don't know how old or crowded the vehicle will be.

For long-distance travel in air-conditioned buses there are three main stations. The Eastern Bus Terminal serves Pattaya, Ban Phe (for Koh Samet) and Trat (for Koh Chang). The Northern Bus Terminal serves Pattaya, Ayutthaya, Kanchanaburi, as well as Chiang Mai, Chiang Rai and Isaan. The Southern Bus Terminal serves Kanchanaburi as well as Cha-am, Hua Hin, Koh Samui, Krabi and Phuket. Reservations are advised around major Thai holidays such as Songkran or the Chinese New Year.

By Rail Although some trains leave from the smaller terminal of Bangkok Noi, most trains, including useful services to Ayutthaya, Chiang Mai and Hua Hin, go from Hualamphong station, to the south of Yaowarat (Chinatown) and the Silom district.

VISITOR INFORMATION

Bangkok has its own city-wide tourist authority, the Bangkok Tourism Division, with offices at 17/1 Thanon Phra Athit, under the Pinklao Bridge in Banglamphu, ℂ 02225 7612-4 **www.bangkoktourist.com**, open 9am–7pm, with 27 information booths scattered around the city's most popular tourist sights, open 9am–5pm.

Information about Thailand beyond the capital is dealt with by the Tourist Authority of Thailand (TAT). There are TAT desks at Terminals 1 (ℂ 02523 8972-3) and Terminal 2 (ℂ 02535 2669): both are open from 8am until midnight. The main office in town (ℂ 02281 0422) is on Ratchadamnoen Nok Avenue, open daily from 8.30am–4.30pm. Many tour operators and travel agents around the capital have stickers saying 'TAT Tourist Information' but this does not demonstrate impartiality and in fact the Tourist Authority never uses this wording in its stationery or publicity.

Publications

Two magazines – *Metro* and *Untamed Travel* – are on sale at hotel shops and 7/11s: *Metro* has events listings while *Untamed Travel* is aimed more at backpackers. The best city map/colourfully annotated guide is *Nancy Chandler's Map of Bangkok* (100B: make sure you're being sold the latest version, 23rd edition or later). *BK Magazine* is a free publication you can pick up from many of the city's restaurants and hotels and all branches of Starbucks.

Thaiways has maps, tips and facts covering Pattaya, Chiang Mai and Phuket. *Bangkok Dining & Entertainment* concentrates on restaurant reviews and nightlife. The two English-language papers, the *Bangkok Post* and *The Nation* both have lifestyle sections with information on the city's ephemeral highlights.

Orientation

Bangkok's core is a densely populated kernel called Rattanakosin, the so-called 'Royal Island', which fills a gentle meander of the Chao Phraya River cut off by a small canal. At its heart are the Royal Palaces and a number of temples. To the north of the Royal Island is Banglamphu and the Khao San Road, while to the south it diffuses into the maze of streets and alleys that make up Yaowarat, Chinatown. South again and you'll find the Silom/Sathon area, where the BTS Skytrain meets the river taxi service at the river's edge.

The main modern city centre spreads to the west of the Royal Island along Rama I, coalescing into a battleground of megamalls around Siam Square. Here Rama I turns into Sukhumvit Road and heads off to Pattaya, but you only need to follow it as far as the BTS Skytrain terminal at On Nut. From here taxi travel is the way to reach outlying suburbs.

Getting Around

Bangkok is not easy for families on foot. Pavements are narrow, broken and often colonised by restaurants or stalls, and traffic moves as fast as it can. Even when the cars are gridlocked, motorcycles still thread through – often in unpredictable directions.

By Taxi The best way to get around is by metered taxi. When they stick to the meter these are very cheap, invariably air-conditioned, and drivers reasonably knowledgeable. Unfortunately it can be very hard to find a taxi prepared to use the meter. The

Tuk-tuk painted with Ayutthaya's temples

Boarding a Express River Taxi

rate starts at 35B and that should cover you for the first kilometre but it goes up too slowly for a young, ambitious urban Thai and the drivers that seek out westerners tend to be the least accommodating, using the traffic to justify sky-high rates for any journey. Drivers may refuse to take you at all, if it's getting near their shift change between 3pm–4pm, the traffic or weather is bad, or if they don't want to go where you do.

Tuk-tuks, the two-stroke three-wheelers, are even worse. Most families will take a *tuk-tuk* at some time – many children insist on it – but it's best to use them only for short journeys. *Tuk-tuk* drivers rarely speak English, never admit to having change, often overcharge, and your journey, through the choking exhaust of near-stationary cars, will neither be particularly fast nor safe: weighed down with a western family *tuk-tuks* have been known to flip. *Tuk-tuk* charges also start at 35B but as a foreigner who doesn't speak Thai you'll rarely persuade them to take you anywhere for that.

By River Bangkok improves dramatically when you take to the water. Express River Taxi Boats run up the Chao Phraya River, stopping at a number of marked piers to let passengers on and off. Every child I've met loves this way of travel as this is a busy river, with cargo barges constantly plying its length, and ferries shuttling to and fro. It is inexpensive into the bargain, with adult fares from 6B–15B and young children often waved through. These boats can drop you close to many of the most important sights, temples and attractions, and the riverfront is lined with stilted restaurants, smart hotels and glossy, air-conditioned shopping centres. Slower, open-sided ferries run across the river from most landings, charging 3B per adult, should you find yourselves stranded on the wrong bank.

By Mass Transit Away from the river, getting around Bangkok has been transformed by the newly built Skytrain (BTS), which is very useful and air-conditioned, and the less glitzy but efficient subway (MRT) line.

The BTS is open 6am–midnight. The Silom Line runs from the river at Saphan Taksin through Siam Square to the National Stadium. The Sukhumvit Line drops down from Mo Chit (Chatuchak Market) in the north to interchange at Siam and heads off down the Sukhumvit Road as far as On Nut for all points east.

Tickets are sold at vending machines and cost 15B–40B, depending on distance. Children are half price or, if they're small enough to carry, free. Travelling as a family means you will need a lot of 10B coins to feed the ticket machines and it's more convenient to buy one-day passes (120B), or more flexibly, 'Stored Value Cards'. These cost 30B but can be topped up with 100B or more: sweep them over sensors on the turnstile and they're automatically debited. Latest maps and ticket info is online at ***www.bts.co.th/en/bt strain.asp***.

The MRT is open 5am–midnight, it goes west from Hualamphong station and loops through Bangkok's urban heartland, finishing at Bang Sue in the north. Interchanges with the BTS are rarely completely straightforward and usually involve a bit of a walk.

Interchange combinations are Silom (MRT) with Sala Daeng (BTS), Sukhumvit (MRT) with Asok (BTS), and, most easily, at Mo Chit.

Ticket prices are similar to those of the BTS, but are not interchangeable. There are plastic disc tickets and 120B one-day passes – more information on ***www.bangkok-city.com/mrta. htm***. Note: you can call the BTS a Skytrain but only other

The Skytrain

westerners will have a clue what you're talking about. With taxi drivers, particularly, the term will only confuse.

Planning Your Outings

In this hectic city expeditions can become something of an ordeal if your hotel is badly sited. Some are marooned in a permanent gridlock of traffic, far from subway, Skytrain and river transport routes. The hotels recommended below are well located to help spend minimum time on the road.

Bangkok's often oppressive heat saps child energy. It's sensible to start early in the day and link a few – and not too many – attractions into logical itineraries, with a clear idea in advance of how you will get from one to another.

Given the difficulties of getting about, it can pay to hire a taxi for the day (about 1800B) so you are sure of transport as and when you need it.

If I had one day in Bangkok I would spend it on the river, reaching the water by taking the Skytrain to Saphan Taksin. From here I would take a high-speed tour of the *klongs,* or simply – and economically – use the Express River Taxis like the residents do, to effortlessly and atmospherically flit between attractions. These include Pak Klong Talaat vegetable market, Wat Arun, the Royal Palaces, and the major temples: Wat Pho, Wat Phra Kaew and Wat Maharat.

A cluster of the main attractions are marooned far from the river, but around Siam station, a major interchange between Skytrain and subway.

Here a raised walkway runs above the main roads, linking into the Siam Paragon with its Aquarium and IMAX. Drop down to street level and it's only a few metres to the Erawan Shrine, and Jim Thomson's house is within walking distance, though it's better to arrive fresh by flagging down a *tuk-tuk.*

Lumpini Park is not that far from here, where you can relax by renting a pedalo on the lake, people-watch on the lawns, catch a show at the Snake Farm, or move on to Suan Lum Night Bazaar and the Puppet Theatre.

Out-of-centre attractions take more planning because of travelling times. Try to avoid rush hours which, in Bangkok, last almost all day.

Family-Friendly Events

January/February

Chinese New Year

Chinese New Year is celebrated throughout Thailand, but is at its most exuberant in Bangkok. Lion and dragon dances thread through the streets, firecrackers go off on every side, there are firework displays and quiet, incense-shrouded ceremonies that involve lots of toy money being given and burned. The exact date will vary according to the Lunar Calendar but is always in late January or February, when celebrations last for three days. In 2010 it starts on 14th February, in 2011 on 3rd February and 2012 on 23rd January.

It's debateable whether this is a good time to be travelling with your family. The celebrations are lavish, but so are the crowds. Much of the capital is shut down and transport is booked out, as are hotels. However, if you are in Bangkok at this time head down to Yaowarat Road and Charon Krung Roads in the heart of the city's Chinatown district for the best of the displays, and graze your way along innumerable fast-food stalls selling traditional Thai delicacies.

March

International Kite Festival, Sanam Luang Parade Ground

Just by the Royal Palace – and almost by Royal Decree – this contest draws in teams from Japan, New Zealand, Korea and beyond. Fast, manoeuvrable 'female' kites do battle with slow but powerful 'male' kites in the skies above the Thai capital, lifted by the hot, seasonal *Tapao* wind. A fun festival for all ages, this is more than a spectator sport as there are also plenty of colourful kites on sale which you can fly in Bangkok's many public parks.

April

The Phra Chedi Klang Nam Fair – Samut Prakarn

If you haven't experienced a temple fair, this could be your moment. Whole communities come together in huge crowds, with a plethora of entertainments, food stalls and shows. The Phra Chedi Klang Nam Fair is one of the country's largest temple fairs. Head for the Wat on the river's edge at Prapadaeng, about 15km south of Bangkok, on the Thonburi side of the river.

Songkran

Although Bangkok, like everywhere in Thailand, drenches all and sundry through the Songkran celebrations, to get a true sense of the celebration head up to Ayutthaya. Without the distractions of modern urban life Phra Nakhon Si Ayutthaya is a good place to see the important ceremonies in action: fish and birds are released for good luck, and Buddhas are bathed. This doesn't mean the celebrations are in any way muted. Elephants are brought in as mobile water-cannons, everyone gets drenched, and a floral float contest ends with a 'Miss Songkran' competition.

July

Asalaha Puja

Asalaha Puja, on the night of the full moon in July, is the third most important Buddhist holiday and commemorates the moment when Buddha preached to his first five disciples. Local farmers approached Buddha and asked him to stop the monks going on their morning rounds: they were, apparently, trampling on the rice shoots. They suggested the idea of giving food direct to the monks, a practice that has continued ever since. Evening candlelit processions are staged in all temples.

October

Chinatown Vegetarian Food Festival

Thousands of shop-houses line the streets offering household goods, presents, toys and clothes, all at supposedly wholesale prices. Along the busy trading streets of Yawaraj stalls are also set up selling traditional dishes, glutinous rices, double-boiled clear soups, *rad na* noodles and *kui teow lod*, steamed rice-noodle rolls with various fillings.

November

Golden Mount Fair

Held in the first week of November at Bangkok's Golden Mount, this is a noisy and exuberant temple fair. Carnival rides, food stalls and a general trading frenzy mark the start of the cool, dry season.

Loi Krathong

Although a nationwide celebration, Bangkok, with its 10 million people, is one of the most spectacular places to experience the night of the November Full Moon. Along the city's canals and the Chao Phraya River countless candle-laden boats set sail on the smooth waters, praying for blessings in a mesmerising display of dots of light on the shimmering waters.

December

Ayutthaya World Heritage Fair

A week of celebrations is based round spectacular light shows at Phra Nakhon Si Ayutthaya, one of the greatest temples of Thailand's old capital.

FAST FACTS

ATMs In cash-driven Bangkok you're probably closer to an ATM than you are to the nearest rat – you'll find one outside most 7/11s. There are also plenty of exchange bureaux and banks.

Car Hire It would be a brave parent who planned to self-drive Bangkok. The traffic is idiosyncratic at best, signposting positively bewildering, and parking next to impossible. Someone must do it as Avis (*02251 1131-2*, *www.avisthailand.com*) and Budget (*02134 4006-7*, *www.budget.co.th*) have offices at the airport. Prices are from 2500B per day.

Chemists Generally open from 7am until midnight and usually good English is spoken.

Embassies The British Embassy is at 14 Wireless Road, Lumpini, Pathumwan, Bangkok 10330, *02305 8333*, *http://ukin thailand.fco.gov.uk*. Office hours are 8am–midday and 12.45am–4.30pm Monday to Thursday, 8am–1pm Friday. The American Embassy is at 120–22 Wireless Rd, *02205 4000*; Canada on the

15th floor, Abdulrahim Place, 990 Rama IV Road, ☏ 02636 0540; Australia at 37 South Sathorn Road, ☏ 02344 6300; and New Zealand at 93 Wireless Road, ☏ 02254 2530.

Dentists Dentistry is a huge business in Bangkok and even if you don't have an emergency it can be well worth getting your family's teeth sorted out while you're there. The experience is quite unlike anything you'll come across in the UK, with minimalist décor and technology to the fore. The Siam Family Dental Clinic has superb waiting areas, with toys and TVs for children, and presentations on tablet PCs. Their easiest branch to find is by Siam BTS station at Siam Square Soi 4, ☏ 02255 6645, *www.dentists-bangkok.com*. Alternatively, if a 32 square metre Kiddies Sliding Area is important to you in a dentist's waiting room – and of course it should be – the Home Dental Centre at 15/63 Moo 1 Soi Supapong Srinakarin Road, Nongborn Pravet 10260, ☏ 02748 3180-1, *www.homedental center.com*, is open Monday to Saturday 9am–8pm.

Hospitals Bangkok has the most sophisticated medical facilities in the country and given the traffic that's probably just as well. Bangkok General Hospital (☏ 02310 3000, *www.bangkok hospital.com*) is the flagship of one of the leading national medicare chains with a special department for foreigners and multilingual translators. Another good, modern hospital is the Samitivej Hospital (133 Soi 49, Sukhumvit Road, ☏ 02392 0011-9, *www.samitivej.co.th*): English is spoken. You may need your passport and travel insurance documents: these hospitals take major credit cards but it might not take that long to reach your credit limit.

Internet Almost all the hotels and guest houses in Bangkok offer Internet access: the more expensive the hotel the more expensive the access. Internet café or guest house charges start at about 20B an hour.

TIP ▶ **Snagging a Meter Taxi** ◀

A hot, harassed family has almost no chance of flagging down a Bangkok taxi on the street *and* persuading the driver to use the meter.

Walk away! Drag your bedraggled tribe into the closest smart hotel – not just near it as that's where the most rapacious drivers lurk – and see if your western status can win some charity from the bellboys. If there are no meter taxis in line, ask if you can call a taxi: ☏ 1681 (yes, four-digit number) or ☏ 02319 9911 while your family chills in the air-conditioned lobby. The extra cost is 20B (to be added to the metered fare): a small price to pay.

Post Office The central post office is near the river on Thanon Charoen Krung between Thanon Surawong and Thanon Si Phraya). The Overseas Call Office is open 24 hours but the post office itself is open from Monday to Friday 8am–8pm, Saturday and Sunday 8am–midday. Helpfully, they also sell packaging materials should you wish to mail purchases home: the rates are lower for packages loosely secured with string, allowing customs officials to peer in.

Safety There is little violent crime in Bangkok but there are plenty of scams. Most common – so common you almost believe they are doing it for fun – are the gemstone cons. A standard ploy is to divert tourists from well-known attractions – usually by saying they are closed – and go instead to a jewellery shop where your guide will get paid 'Tea Money' for any overpriced tat you're persuaded to buy.

But as ever the greatest risk is the traffic: look both ways before getting off the pavement.

Travel Agents Given the logistical problems of packing in a serious day's sightseeing in this frenetic capital there's a lot to be said for handing the planning over to a travel agent or tour operator. Freed from map reading, working unfamiliar transport systems and unusual opening hours, the whole family can relax and enjoy the ride. See p 25.

WHAT TO SEE & DO

Children's Top 10 Attractions

❶ **Tour** the canals on a long-tailed speedboat. See p 61.

❷ **Release** a bird and make a wish. See p 57.

❸ **Swat** 3D fish in an IMAX adventure. See p 63.

❹ **Cuddle** a tiger cub. See p 71.

❺ **Buy** blooms at the flower market.

❻ **Fly** a kite with the locals. See p 60.

❼ **Follow** Jack's beanstalk to the house of a giant. See p 60.

❽ **Take** the River Bus. See p 62.

❾ **Climb** a broken-crockery Stupa to look down on the city. See p 57.

❿ **Pedal** round the paddies. See p 58.

Bangkok Children's Discovery Museum ★★ FIND VALUE

Chatuchak Park, Chatuchak MRT, ☎ *02272 4575.*

You could easily spend a day at this fantastic and interactive museum. In three buildings displays clearly explain such important matters as how we get electricity, how babies are made and how cars work.

There are cooking classes (Thai food) in My Little Kitchen, the chance to record your own radio or TV show, and a fascinating Robot Zoo that explains animal functions. For example Velcro shoes simulate walking like a bee, and children get to see how echolocation works. At every stage there are buttons to press and levers to move, little ones can touch everything, and there are signs in English. When and if you need time out there's an outdoor playground with some scientific-themed climbing frames and a number of food stalls.

Open Tues–Fri 9am–5pm, Sat and Sun 10am–6pm. Mon closed except on public holidays. **Admission** 140B adults, 120B children. **Amenities** café.

Bangkok's Holiest Spirit House ☆☆☆ ALL AGES

Most Thai houses have Spirit Houses built in their grounds, rather like British bird-houses but much more exotic; little *salas* (pavilions) to house the possibly spiteful *nats* (spirits) displaced by the building works. Although sometimes these are neglected, far more often they're actively tended with soft-drink and fruit sacrifices made daily, incense burned and prayers said.

None, to my family, have ever managed to compete with the **Erawan Shrine** which we stumbled across by the Central World Plaza Shopping Centre, on a busy road junction where the traffic was at a standstill under the soaring concrete arches of Bangkok's BTS Skytrain.

This was once a simple Spirit House erected by the builders of the Erawan Hotel, but the construction was plagued with problems. Spiritual consultants suggested they rebuilt the Spirit House with a statue of Brahma, *Pha Prom* in Thai, in the middle. This did the trick, and the Erawan Hotel has now grown into the hugely plush Grand Hyatt Erawan. Erawan Shrine, as it is now called, has grown in importance in its wake.

It is always thronged, and at 9pm it was packed. Privately hired dancing groups performed classical routines to impress a central, four-headed, four-armed statue, surrounded by hand-carved elephants. Worshippers shuffled slowly around in a clockwise direction, eyes closed or half-closed, intent. On every side candles were being lit, wreathes of jasmine laid, and lotus stems elegantly positioned.

After a magical experience our children bought small birds in little cages from a good-luck seller by the gate. Released with a wish, the tiny creatures fluttered free into the night.

Admission free.

Bangkok's Temples ☆☆ VALUE
ALL AGES

Unsurprisingly Thailand's capital houses the most impressive and important temples in the country, the largest golden Buddhas, most extravagant buildings, and the most intense crowds of devotees, where pilgrims converge from all across the country.

The big city temples didn't really work for my family. They

Climbing the temple steps at Wat Arun

were just too big, pressured by tour groups, and the city offered too many other, more exciting things to do. The most important temple of Wat Phra Kaeo that houses the tiny Emerald Buddha, attached to the Grand Palace (Open daily 8.30am–3.30pm, admission 200B), became part of an excursion that included Wat Pho with its gold reclining Buddha 46 metres long. It was all too hot, especially with the rigorous enforcement of dress regulations (no short skirts, shorts, bare shoulders, or flip-flops, though once you get in you have to take off any newly rented shoes). The less-touristy temple of Wat Traimit, with its glimmering vast, seated gold Buddha, is much more atmospheric, but this might have been because we stumbled across it by accident, in Chinatown.

Likewise the unexceptional architecture of Wat Chana Songkhram, a tranquil oasis of spiritual peace next to the crazed backpacker life of the Khao San Road, was affecting.

The children's favourite, however, was Wat Arun, the Temple of the Dawn, reached by an open-sided two-baht cross-river ferry. They could freely climb terrifyingly steep steps up a Stupa mosaiced with broken crockery salvaged from a river shipwreck. Watch out with young children: steps are steep without ropes and unprotected drops abound. From dizzying heights views are over the sweeping meanders of the Chao Phraya, busy with barges and the ceaseless traffic of trade.

Bike Tours ★★ ALL AGES

Absolute Explorers, 99/1 Udomsuk 43–45, Sukhumvit Soi 103, Bangjak, Prakanong, 10260, 📞 *087077 9696,* **www.absoluteexplorer.com**.

If Bangkok's traffic is getting you down it is surprisingly quick and easy to reach the countryside for a relaxing cycle ride among rice paddies and small villages. Several tours visit Koh Kret but some operators also take you out on a two-day tour, including an unforgettable night staying in a village. Among various operators one of the best – and most child-friendly – is Absolute Explorers, which offers a range of experiences using trains to reach the countryside. They are careful to make sure children have bikes to suit their abilities (or if under four, a seat behind dad or an exciting ride in a Wallace & Gromit motorbike sidecar). They also provide good guides who will make sure you have enough food and water and interpret for the villagers you'll meet. Their most popular one-day tour starts with one hour on a local train – an adventure in itself – before cycling gently round a few villages, stopping often for chats with the locals, lunch and photos. The meeting point is at 9.50am daily in the lobby of the Bangkok Palace Hotel, Petchaburi Road Soi 35, by Makkasan station: expect to be home by 6pm.

Prices per day in groups of up to six from 1300B adults, 900B under 12, under fours free. Negotiate for a private family tour.

Cool off on Ice ★ ★ FIND
AGE FIVE AND UP

Sub Zero Ice Skate Club on the Esplanade, Ratchada Road, MRT Thailand Cultural Centre, ☎ 02354 2134.

Imperial World Ice Skating, 999 Sukhumvit Road, Samrong Nua: take the BTS to On Nut station and then a taxi, ☎ 02756 8217-9.

Take a break from the heat at one of Bangkok's two ice rinks. Newest is the Sub Zero Ice Skate Club by the MRT Thailand Cultural Centre station. Drinks and snacks are served on 'ice bars' and there are plenty of Thais who just hang out here. In the day it's very child-friendly but at night disco lights come on, live DJs play, 'Angel Dancers' glide around, and it gets seriously clubby. More serious skating is on offer at Bangkok's one and only Olympic-size rink,

Imperial World Ice Skating, a taxi ride from On Nut BTS station.

Sub Zero Ice Skate Club: two sessions, from 11am–5pm (200B adults, 100B children) and a night session, from 5.30pm–1am (250B adults, 150B children: at weekends entry costs 300B for adults).

Imperial World Ice Skating, sessions from 10am–2.45pm and 3.10pm–8pm. There's a pro shop and lessons are available, from 300B–3000B per hour, depending on level. Admission is 150B including skate rental, though dads might struggle to find skates big enough: non-skaters are charged 30B.

Dream World ★ ★ ALL AGES

62 Moo 1, Rangsit-Nakornnayok Road, Km.7 Thanyaburi, Patumthani, ☎ 02533 1152, ☎ 02533 1447, www.dreamworld-th.com.

An hour from central Bangkok outside rush hour: Book a meter taxi from your hotel and expect to pay 1200B, or take bus 188 from the northern bus terminal.

Bangkok's closest thing to a theme park might try to be Disney but is refreshingly other. There's only one big roller-coaster and it won't impress children trained on Alton Towers, but you can spend a long time here without anyone getting bored, enjoying several mini-trains and mini-cars rattling along rails, Cinderella's Pumpkin Castle and Sleeping Beauty's Castle. Though it can get busy at weekends there are rarely queues at the rides designed for younger children. The park is proudest of its snow field that allows tropical

Thais to build snowmen and slip on ice, but my favourite was the Giant's House at the end of the Beanstalk, where children can clamber on outsize furniture in a home that would suit a being 15 metres tall.

Best of all are the Thai children: polite but playful, making the experience unusually gentle, tolerant, smiling and fun.

Don't be tempted by older guidebooks and a plethora of websites to visit Bangkok's original theme park, Magic Land: it has been closed for years.

Open daily 10am–5pm,until 7pm on weekends and holidays. **Admission** children under 0.9m free, others 450B.

Fly a Kite ★ ★ VALUE ALL AGES

Lumpini Park is a fascinating green lung in the heart of the city, a few paces from Silom station on the MRT subway system. You can rent a boat to pedal around the water, but more to the point you can watch the people. Tai chi, traditional dances and even sword fights are just some of the activities to enjoy. From February to May you are also very likely to see kites being flown, and you can always buy and fly one of your own.

In the 13th century Sukothai era kites were used by priests to make resonant noises to scare off evil spirits, and packed with explosives to form early aerial bombs. Even now they are used by farmers to keep birds off crops, and in urban Thailand they have become almost an art form. Designs are many and varied, with birds and mythical animals, kites with bells, and others bearing lamps, often seen flying over ceremonial occasions. February to April are the main kiting months, peaking at the Thailand International Kite Competition in March, when the hot *Tapao* wind is at its strongest, held at the Sanam Luang Royal Parade Ground, just to the north of Bangkok's Royal Palace.

Jim Thompson's House
AGE SIX AND UP

Soi Kasemsan 2 Song, opposite the National Stadium on Rama I Road, 2216 7368, www.jimthompson house.com.

This peaceful oasis in the heart of the city provides a welcome opportunity to see traditional 200-year-old Thai buildings and browse an idiosyncratic collection of priceless Thai artworks in the atmosphere of a private house and garden. Jim Thompson was an American adventurer who did much to rescue Thailand's silk industry when the Thais themselves were more interested in emulating the west. Until he disappeared in 1967 – mysteriously going for a stroll in Malaysia and never coming back – he was a leading textile magnate and socialite known throughout the Far East.

The property has been little changed since he left. Even the place settings remain the same. It comprises six traditional Thai timber buildings that Thompson brought from the provinces, rebuilt in his garden grounds and furnished with antiques, fabrics and Thai works of art. Guided tours gently draw your attention to the various areas of interest and there are visiting exhibitions, generally relating to textile production in other parts of Asia. It's not dry or dusty, and children too young to maintain concentration find the traffic-free garden with its pond full of koi carp enough of an attraction in itself. The restaurant is cheaper than it looks and serves both Thai and western food.

Open 9am–5pm. **Admission** 100B adult, 50B children (anyone under 25). Guided tours compulsory: last tour 4.30pm. **Amenities** restaurant.

Longtail Klong Tours ☆ ☆ ☆
ALL AGES

Thrilling and fascinating, a long-tail tour of Bangkok's backwater canals sets out along the narrow *klongs* (canals) that thread through suburban Thonburi on the western side of the river in a fast boat powered by a poorly silenced truck engine cantilevered over a long propshaft. Once your boatman has let off steam powering through the river traffic, slow down to catch revealing glimpses of a vanishing way of life, where houses are stilted over water and transport is by boat. Small trading boats (ignore the ones who paddle across to offer you over-priced handicrafts) circulate selling snacks, people wash their clothes on front steps, and funeral parlours tier racks of new coffins over the water.

Most tours will make stops to see rural temples, devout and restful havens where the bustle of Bangkok's traffic seems an age away. My children's favourite stop was to see a snake show at the Thonburi Snake Farm (100B adults, 50B children) on Klong Wat Sai: a wild-west adventure where piratical snake-handlers throw venomous snakes around to a barely comprehensible commentary in amplified Thaiglish. A rather miserable zoo cast something of a pall but then a vendor – selling framed, mounted scorpions, butterflies and bats – draped a ten-foot python around my daughter's shoulders and she was thrilled again.

Most tours sold by tour operators will pack you in with 20 tourists, but it's relatively easy to charter a whole boat yourself. If you simply turn up, as a family, at the official longtailed boat booking office at Saphan Taksin station at the end of the BTS Skytrain. You will pay the same per person prices but are far more likely to end up with a boat – and guide – to yourself.

You can guarantee a boat of your own if you charter a vessel from the Boat Tour Centre (✆ 02235 3108) at Tha Si Phraya pier or the Mitchaopaya Travel Service (✆ 02623 6169) – and other freelance operators – who operate from pier Tha Chang, Tha Tien and Tha Maharat. Costs for half-day group tours generally range from 1000B per person, with children 75% of the adult price.

River Taxi Travel ★ ★ VALUE

ALL AGES

The Express River Taxis that run like floating buses along the Chao Phraya River perfectly combine fun and functionality. You can travel amongst the Thais on standard vessels while the same company also runs a Tourist Boat Service that can save you time and money. It runs every half hour from 9.30am to 4pm, and covers a slightly shorter route than the standard commuter Express Boats. The Tourist Boats run between the Central Pier by Saphan Taksin Skytrain station in the south, to Phra Arthit in the north. Day passes, costing 100B, come with a map/guide worth 50B, and can also be used on the River Express boats.

You can buy day passes at Saphan Taksin, Sathron, Maharaj, Phra Arthit and at Tourist Information Centres at Siam, and Nana BTS stations, or simply pay at the desk on the pier (if there is one) or on board a standard Express Boat.

The Tourist Boat stops at the major tourist destinations. From Saphan Taksin it heads north to:

Pier 1 (Oriental): The famous luxury Oriental Hotel – dress right and you might be able to use their pool.

Pier 3 (Si Phraya): A block from the river, Charoen Krung Road (New Road) is the oldest street in Bangkok, dating back to 1861.

Pier 5 (Ratchavongse): Chinatown. Pass a short belt of wholesale traders and reach narrow, broken alleys packed with atmosphere and more plastic toys and gadgets you either want or can name.

Tourist Pier (no number): 'Princess Mother Memorial Park'. The usual commuter buses don't stop here and nor should you. It's a small park developed in memory of the mother of the present monarch.

Pier 8 (Tha Tien): The best thing for me about this pier is the small restaurant to the right, looking from the wooden walkway that wobbles across the river shallows. Though the restaurant teeters on stilts, with the owners' family home in the dining area, they are great with children. Wat Arun is just across the water, reached by a two baht open-sided ferry. Others value it because it is close to Bangkok's leading tourist highlights of Wat Pho (Reclining Buddha), the National Thai Massage School and Ayutthaya-style temple. From these don't come back to the river if you're going on to see the Grand Palace and the Emerald Buddha as it's closer to walk direct.

Tourist Pier 'Maharaj' (no number): for the National Museum, Wat Mahathat, Grand Palace and Temple of the Emerald Buddha, the old city and Rattanakosin.

Pier 10 (Tha Wang Lang): Crosses to the western bank near the Siriraj Hospital, where a medical museum includes forensic specimens and skeletal Siamese twins. Might raise a frisson in morbid young minds.

Pier 13 (Phra Arthit): From here you can take the two-baht ferry crossing to (with a short walk) the Royal Barge Museum on the western bank, but most people use the stop for Banglamphu and backpacker central, the Khao San Road.

Samut Prakan Crocodile Farm `OVERRATED` ALL AGES

555 Moo 7 Taiban Road, 10270 Thailand, 02703 4891, 32km from the centre.

Children usually love the Samut Prakan Crocodile Farm, though adults are rarely so enthusiastic. Among more than 60,000 crocodiles is the largest currently in captivity, a monster six metres long. Perhaps the most memorable experience is taking a wobbly bridge over a seething mass of crocs who are visibly hungry and would love you to fall in.

There's a Dinosaur Museum and various shows run through the day, including disco-dancing elephants, crocodile-wrestling displays, and a monkey show where the animals wear clothes and even make-up. Visitors are constantly encouraged to buy food to feed the animals – mine loved feeding hippo, elephant and especially the crocs – but it was rather worrying how hungry they seemed to be.

Open daily 7am–6pm. Admission 300B, Amenities café, shop selling croc-skin products.

Siam Ocean World and the Krungsri IMAX Cinema ★ ★ ★
ALL AGES

Siam Ocean World, ☎ 02687 2000, www.siamoceanworld.co.th.

Krungsri IMAX Cinema, ☎ 02129 4631, www.imaxthai.com. Siam Paragon Mall: take the walkway from Siam BTS station.

You could spend a full family day at the Siam Paragon Shopping Mall – without buying a thing.

On the ground floor and spreading across the lowest two floors of the Mall is Siam Ocean World, an impressive aquarium covering an area the size of two football pitches and divided into several different departments. There are sections for open ocean pelagics, rocky foreshore with seal and penguin, a collection of the weirdest-looking underwater species imaginable, and even a patch of tropical rainforest – all under Bangkok's city streets – as well as a touch pool and children's play area. Perhaps most impressive is the beautifully lit section devoted to sea jellies, bringing a strange and exotic beauty to this underwater world. For an extra payment children can walk on an artificial ocean floor or learn how to snorkel.

Above the aquarium are floors and floors of shopping: designer shops, computer outlets and restaurants. On the 6th floor is a huge Cineplex – think armchair cinema, with champagne – and the Krungsri IMAX Cinema. Movies filmed this way – such as *Batman* and *Harry Potter* – are released here well before even the USA, dialogue is invariably in English, and the wraparound scheme means the experience is visceral. The IMAX cinema also shows stunning 3d films. My children were frantically batting away shoals of fish that seemed to be swimming through their hair, and large sharks looming close made them shriek with delight.

Watch out when stepping straight into any of these cinemas from the hot streets though, the air-conditioning is fixed at a polar level.

Siam Ocean World: **Open** *daily 9am–10pm.* **Admission** *850B adults, 650B children (0.8m–1.2m).*

Krungsri IMAX: **Open** *daily, 10am–10pm.* **Admission***: 200B, under 1.2m free.*

Siam Water Park and Safari World ★ ★ ALL AGES

Miniburi suburb, east of town: best take a taxi for 700B maximum and buy entrance locally as most tours are overpriced. Siam Water Park, ☏ *02919 7200, www.siamparkcity. com. Safari World,* ☏ *02914 4100-19, www.safariworld.com.*

It would be hard to argue a case for Safari World on its own but on a hot day – in Bangkok that's all of them – the Siam Water Park is paradise for families. The combination of the two attractions, conveniently close to each other in the Miniburi suburb east of Bangkok, makes for a compelling day out.

Siam Water Park, *Suan Siam*, is centred round a giant pool complete with artificial surf, whirlpools, fountains and waterfalls. Watch out for the huge waterslides as some sensitive western bottoms find them just too abrasive and after 400 metres of excitement have regretted the experience for days. There are also a few amusement park rides such as a basic roller-coaster as

Fancy a Splash?

With temperatures often in the high 30s, it's quite likely your children might suddenly demand a wet adventure in Bangkok. Two suburban shopping malls offer the waterpark experience without paying tourist prices. Go to Ban Kapee suburb and the Fantasia Lagoon on top of The Mall Department Store offers huge water slides and whirlpools with Fantasia Island – next door – providing theme park rides. Open 8am–8.45pm, admission 80B adults, 50B children, ☏ 02173 1000. More wet thrills are available at Leoland Water Park, 11am–6pm weekdays, 10am–7pm weekends; 250B adults, 150B children, on the roof of Central City Bangna Mall. It's nowhere near the city centre – from London it might be Croydon – but there's a free shuttle bus to it from On Nut, the eastern terminal of the MRT subway. It is hoped that while your children play you'll blow your wad in seven floors of retail heaven.

Time Out from Toddlers

In Bangkok with small children and need a break? Try children out aged from one to four at KiDO (*www.kidothailand.com*), a childcare franchise aimed at working Thais and expats that also takes in children by the half-day or day. Open 8am–5pm, the atmosphere is efficient, educational, caring – and fun. There are two branches. One is at Q-House Lumpini (Floor 1, by Lumpini MRT station, ☎ *02677 7511*), and at Central World Plaza (6th floor, Zone C, ☎ *02613 1713*). Day rates from 750B. Nervous parents can log on to the Internet and see how their little darlings are getting on by webcam. Fullakids is an American-run chain of four nursery and daycare centres, three of which are near Asoke, Chidlom and Victory Monument BTS stations. They operate from 7.30am–7.30pm and charge 600B per day. Call ☎ *081 612 3214* or go to *http://fullakid.com*.

well as a small zoo where children can pet the goats.

Although western visitors are most impressed by the sight of Bengal tigers, Safari World concentrates on those animals rarely seen by Thais. The park is split into several sections. The safari park, toured in an enclosed vehicle along an 8km route, gets close to giraffe, ostrich, zebra and lion. But this is of course Thailand and the experience soon gets theatrical: sea lions perform in their own spectacular show, dolphins perform memorable tricks, and imported white tigers from Russia do a lumbering dance. And the world's most endangered primates, orang-utans, facing extinction within the next generation, are here kitted out with shorts and boxing gloves to engage in show-fights. Parents cringe but most children roar with approval.

*Siam Water Park: **Open** daily 10am–6pm. **Admission** 400B adults, 300B children, under 1m free.*

*Safari World: **Open** daily 9am–4.30pm. **Admission** 400B adults, 300B children.*

Snake Farm VALUE ALL AGES

Corner of Henry Dunant and Rama IV Roads, Sala Daeng BTS station, ☎ 02252 0161.

This is the place to see poisonous snakes with a clear conscience. Established by the Pasteur Institute and run by the Thai Red Cross, it was set up to produce anti-venom serum for snake-bite victims nationwide. Cobras, Malayan pit vipers, king cobras, banded kraits and Russell vipers are amongst the species 'milked'. The process involves goading the snakes into fury before they bite into clingfilm and dribble their poison into a jar. About half an hour before each show there's a sideshow explaining the history of the place. There are plenty of chances to touch snakes and a huge carpet python for photo opportunities. My children preferred the less PC, less crowded and less slick display at the *klong*-side Snake Farm in Thonburi (see p 61).

Open *weekdays 8.30am–4.30pm, shows 11am and 3.30pm. Weekends and holidays 8.30am–midday, show 11am.* **Admission:** *70B.*

Thai Puppet Theatre ★ ★ FIND
AGE SIX AND UP

Joe Louis Theatre, 1875 Suan Lum Night Bazaar, Thanon Rama IV, 📞 *02252 9683-4, www.thaipuppet. com.*

This extraordinary show requires patience in children but is quite unlike anything they will have seen before. Operated at shoulder level by three puppeteers who are leading classical dancers, child-sized jointed puppets perform stories from the Ramayana (holy revered text of Hindus). Dancers and music are of a far higher standard than other touted dinner shows and the theatre itself is magical: a vivid insight into classical Thai music and culture. If you suspect this might be a bit slow and ceremonial for your children, take them instead to Siam Niramit, listed under restaurants (meal is included), see p 83.

Performances *daily, 7pm–9.15pm.* **Admission** *900B adults, 300B children, under fours free (no seat).* **Credit:** *MC, V.*

EXCURSIONS FROM BANGKOK

There are a number of very rewarding day-trips that can be made from Bangkok, but long travel times mean it's always a better idea to spend a night or two outside the capital: out-of-town hotels are cheaper, small towns calmer and you'll have more time to explore.

Tours sold by travel agents throughout Bangkok include travelling by road or river to Ayutthaya, Thailand's previous capital, packed with ruined temples and historic sites, and the provincial town of Kanchanaburi, with its Tiger Temple and the Bridge on the River Kwai.

Ayutthaya ★ ★ ★

The northern city of Sukothai is regarded as the birthplace of

Temple, Ayutthaya

Buddha's head tangled in the roots at Wat Phra Mahathat

Thai culture, but Ayutthaya, 80km north of Bangkok, is seen as its crowning glory. This was the national capital from the mid-14th century until the late 18th century. Then, at about the time colonial America started tossing tea into Boston Harbour, the Burmese attacked, sacking the city.

Ruined temples might not seem an obvious family attraction but they can be.

Scattered around a relatively peaceful provincial town, the gradually crumbling temples and stupas offer atmospheric glimpses into an ancient culture that rival Pagan in Burma and echo Angkor Wat in Cambodia. Unlike its more famous equivalents you can explore freely at your own pace, by bicycle or, more easily, in a chartered *tuk-tuk*.

Of the many temples perhaps the best is Wat Mahathat. This is best known for its iconic Buddha head entwined by the roots of a strangler fig tree, but of equal interest to most children are the stalls selling religious paraphernalia outside the temple gates. The plastic buckets packed with toys are intended for sacrifice but also make a good party pack.

Less popular temples are also worth visiting as you are likely to have them to yourself and children can run free.

If you can spare the time it is well worth spending a night here but most people visit on day-trips out of Bangkok.

Getting There

The least expensive one-day tours are little more than mini-van runs and allow only three to four hours to rush around a few highlight temples. Packages that zip out early in the morning by road, see the ruins and come back by boat along the Chao Phraya River, with a buffet lunch along the way provide a better experience. Lotus Tours (☎ 02476 5207-8, *www.thailand highlight.com*) uses a sleek, fast riverboat with glazed windows;

Bridge on the River Kwai

Grand Pearl Cruises (*02861 0255*) makes daytime use of a huge floating dinner/dance club, and *The Ayutthaya Princess* is a stately two-storey royal-looking barge. Most charge 1800B per adult, 1350B per child.

Lotus picks you up from your hotel at 6.30am, the Grand Pearl pick up is at River City Pier at 7.30am, and *The Ayutthaya Princess* leaves the Sheraton Pier at 8am.

Alternatively – and more cheaply – it's an easy trip to make yourself, using the trains that leave Bangkok's Hualamphong railway station (*02223 7010*) daily every hour from 6.40am–10pm or A/C buses from the Northern Bus Terminal (*05378 0556*) that leave every 15 minutes. It should cost 300B to hire a *samlor*, a scaled-up *tuk-tuk*, to tour the ruins for half a day, 400B with a guide.

Kanchanaburi ★★★

Many Bangkok tour operators sell one-day tours to Kanchanaburi focused on its headline attractions – the Bridge on the River Kwai, the so-called 'Tiger Temple', or the nearest chance to drift downriver on bamboo rafts and ride through the jungle on an elephant. Unfortunately you can't do any of these experiences justice on a day-trip. Kanchanaburi is 130km from Bangkok and it takes too long to get there. So save on your Bangkok hotel costs and take one or more nights to explore this relaxed and delightful provincial Thai town.

The Second World War might be another world for today's children but they can always relate to old trains and bridges. Out of town, they will love the Tiger Temple, riding elephants and rafting, river cruises and cave temples.

If you stay overnight an unexpected highlight – for the children if not the grownups – is that inexpensive floating hotels, moored in the river, are something of a Kanchanaburi speciality.

Getting There

Tours to Kanchanaburi booked through agents are usually much the same price. A two-day, one-night trip will cost 3500B, including a visit to the Tiger Temple (see p 70), the Bridge over the River Kwai (see p 70), a night on a floating hotel, and a day in the jungle, including a waterfall, an elephant ride and a rafting expedition. Operators include Lotus Tours (☎ 02476 5207-8, www.thailandhighlight. com) and World Travel Services (☎ 02233 5900, www.wts-thailand. com).

Avoid tours that include Damnoen Saduak floating market. It is not far off your route but by the time you reach there, it will be well swamped by tourists and most people find it disappointing.

It's easy to get to Kanchanaburi independently. The train journey is scenic and, despite wooden seats, a pleasure if your children are up to 2½ non-air-conditioned hours as they can wander up and down making friends.

Frequent third-class departures leave from Bangkok Noi station (☎ 02411 3102) to Kanchanaburi station (☎ 03456 1052) and tickets cost just 100B. There are also frequent A/C buses that take two hours from the Southern Bus Terminal (☎ 02434 5557).

Fast Facts

Tourist Information Kanchanaburi's TAT office (open daily 8.30am–4.30pm, ☎ 03451 1200) is on Saengchuto Road. There are several ATMs and for medical care the Thanakan Hospital (☎ 03462 2366-75) is at 20/20 Thanon Saeng Chuto, south of town.

There are countless tour operators for rafting, trekking, elephant rides, waterfalls and cave temples (which are particularly hard to find unaided). Established operators include Toi's Tours (☎ 03451 4209, www. toistours.com); Good Times Travel (☎ 03462 4441, www.good-times-travel.com); and BT Travel Centre (☎ 03462 5198, www.b-t-travel.com), though your first stop should, if you have a hotel, be the in-house travel desk.

Hotels include the immense Felix River Kwai Resort (9/1 Moo 3 Tambon, Kanchanaburi, ☎ 03451 5061, www.felixhotels. com), with rooms at around 3500B, although most children will prefer to try the often rather basic floating raft hotels. One is the Sugar Cane 1 (22 Soi Pakistan, Maenam Kwai Road, Kanchanaburi 71000, ☎ 03462 4520, www.sugarcaneguesthouse. com) which charges about 550B for a double room – primitive but fun. On overnight tours from Bangkok your hotel will be included and arranged.

Member of the Kanchanaburi Monkey Theatre

Attractions

Kanchanaburi Monkey School FIND ALL AGES

106 Moo 3, Khao Poon Road, Nongya, Muang, Kanchanaburi, ☎ 06914 8013.

Kanchanaburi also has rather a sweet little Monkey Theatre. Trained monkeys pick coconuts, ride bicycles, do mathematical tricks, pot baseballs and swim – rather miserably – in a small, greenish pond. If this is your only chance to see a monkey theatre you should. Quite fun and very Thai.

Open *9am–5pm. Shows whenever four or more visitors appear.*
Admission *120B adults, 60B children, infants free.* **Amenities** *drinks stall.*

The Bridge over the River Kwai ALL AGES

Made famous by a film your children have probably never seen, the Bridge over the River Kwai that your family will see isn't even original: it's a concrete look-alike, crossed by a tourist train that goes nowhere. Hopping on this slow-moving locomotive is likely to be your children's highlight, although a train from the period is edged by souvenir stalls in a hangar nearby and all ages can clamber on board and get their picture taken.

The best museum is the Death Railway Museum (80B adults, 40B children), across the road from a huge war cemetery, but your children will need an interest in the Second World War to enjoy the exhibits.

The railway line built through the jungle by starving prisoners of war remains in use, but to see the timber supports and swinging corners you'll need another day to board the train that heads out through a jungled tribal region towards **Burma**: the train now stops at a memorial at Hellfire Pass.

Tiger Temple ✩ ✩ ✩ ALL AGES

Wat Pa Luang Ta Bua Yannasampanno, Saiyok District, Kanchanaburi Province, 71150,

☏ 03453 1557, www.tigertemple.org. 40km from Kanchanaburi on highway 323, signposted from km 21.

Traditionally monasteries have acted as a refuge for animals in distress: Wat Pa Luang Ta Bua acquired its reputation in 1994 when it treated an injured boar and released it, only for it to return with a family of 10.

The first tiger arrived in 1999, a cub that was due to be stuffed and had already been injected with formaldehyde before the taxidermist lost his nerve. That one died but soon two more cubs arrived. In this region on the Burmese border a poacher can get US$5800 for an adult tiger and within a year eight cubs, often as young as a week old, were handed in. The monks had to learn to look after them.

Unfortunately Buddhist monks don't believe in contraception, and as new cubs arrived they joined a resident population that was already breeding. Now there are 40 resident tigers, living (generally caged) alongside countless chickens, deer and other animal refugees.

At every stage the head monk has shown sharp business sense and used the tigers to pay their way. Coachloads of tourists are charged to have their photographs taken with tigers, and the revenue used to build a huge tiger compound, with plans to establish a separate Tiger Island.

Western and Thai views on the treatment of animals can differ hugely and parents will have to use their own judgement at animal attractions in Thailand, but critics of this wildlife refuge can never suggest an alternative home for such displaced tigers.

Open *daily 1pm–4pm. Until 1.30pm visitors can pet cubs, then help lead the adult tigers to a canyon where you give your camera to a guide to take pictures of yourself with a tiger. Avoid red clothes because it irritates the tigers, and don't wear shorts or show shoulders because that's not acceptable to the monks. The best moment is at the end, at around 3.45pm when the coaches have gone, and food is handed out to the considerable menagerie.*

FAMILY-FRIENDLY ACCOMMODATION

The sheer variety of accommodation in Bangkok is almost unbelievable, a result of being the major travel hub for Southeast Asia, and a leading tourist destination for the last 50 years. Options range from ultra-cheap rooms, packed between paper walls around the Khao San Road, to some of the best hotels in the world. Even the finest hotels are eminently affordable by UK standards, and every baht spent is amply rewarded, with mid-range hotels offering especially good value.

The only problem for families is that the tendency in smarter hotels is to chic minimalism and a certain formality that sits uneasily with youthful exuberance. However, this is moderated by the fact that all Thais seem to love children and at every level hotel staff go out of their way to make their youngest guests feel welcome and appreciated.

VERY EXPENSIVE

Chakrabongse Villas ★ ★ FIND

396 Maharaj Road, Tatier, Bangkok 10200, ☏ 02224 6686, www.thai villas.com.

This collection of just four independent villas is set in the luxuriant grounds of Chakrabongse House, a royal-owned estate on the banks of the Chao Phraya River. Despite being within easy walking distance of the Royal Palaces their parkland setting feels almost rural: birds are everywhere and there's the occasion plosh of a fish in the river. The best villa for families is the two-bedroom Chinese House, a symphony of polished dark wood, carved furniture and oriental screens, while the Thai House is a traditional building

Chakrabongse Villas

from Ayutthaya, dismantled and reassembled with modern facilities. Facilities are those of a five-star hotel but they are so unobtrusive and considerate you scarcely notice them: it's all about privacy in this very Thai setting.

Breakfast is served in the Riverside Dining *Sala*. Dinner has to be ordered by 2pm so the chef can ensure fresh ingredients for a truly Thai feast. The villa staff will help with expeditions, and there is a private, royal *tuktuk* to travel to the Royal Palaces. Travel along the river by taking the launch from your private pier, or stroll through the grounds to the Express River Taxi pier nearby.

Rooms three units. **Rates** *Garden Suite 8000B–10,000B, River House 13,000B–16,000B, Chinese House 23,000B–25,000B.* **Credit** *MC, V.* **Amenities** *swimming pool.* **In room** *A/C.*

Mandarin Oriental ★ ★ ★

48 Oriental Avenue, 10500, ☏ 02659 9000, www.mandarinoriental.com.

An ice-cream cone and the chance to swim every day might be enough to keep any child happy but the Mandarin Oriental, the grand old lady of Thailand's top hotels, has a far more ambitious programme to help them get the most from the city. They are welcomed as Very Important People. The hotel has a fully functional Day Care Centre that operates 3pm–11pm with fun, supervised activities

Somerset Suite, Mandarin Oriental

for children of all ages (including video games, plush toys, crayons and computers) and a qualified nurse on hand at all times.

The hotel has two swimming pools with wading pool, all restaurants have child-friendly menu options, and gifts for children staying in suites include stuffed animals and books. Cots are free of charge and tennis coaches can be hired at the hotel's own tennis courts. Also, rather usefully, the hotel also operates daily river tours to the ancient capital of Ayutthaya (see p 166), two hours upstream.

Rooms 393 rooms and suites. *Rates Superior River Wing (standard) 14,000B–20,000B, Deluxe Suite 41,000B–47,000B. Amenities nine restaurants, spa, country club across the river with free scheduled shuttle. In room butler service, Internet, A/C, Bose CD player with library, TV with in-house movies, fridge, daily fruit and flowers.*

EXPENSIVE

Bangkok Marriott Resort & Spa ☆ ☆ ☆ FIND

257/1–3 Charoen Nakhon Road, Bangkok 10600, ☏ 02476 0022, www.marriotthotels.com.

This is a an excellent place for families to stay in Bangkok, well away from the craziness of the centre and making the most of the climate in what could almost be a beach resort even though it's many miles from the sea. It is located on the western bank of the Chao Phraya a few kilometres south of the centre. Access to the city centre at Central Pier and Saphan Taksin BTS station is a 20-minute journey by shuttle boat or taxi. The hotel is built in three wings round landscaped gardens with lily ponds, fountains and a large pool, all decorated for some reason with more than a hundred elephant sculptures in ceramic, stone, wood and brass. Send your children

Cruise boat, Bangkok Marriott Resort & Spa

out to count them and they'll be gone for hours.

Rooms are beautifully decorated in a muted Thai style, and each has a private balcony or terrace. There's a children's club to let parents make the most of the Mandara Spa, but there's also plenty for families to do together, including floodlit tennis courts, dinner cruises on the river, and a nightly buffet and cultural show at the Terrace Restaurant.

Rooms *413.* **Rates** *deluxe 5800B– 6800B, junior suite 9360B–9800B, deluxe suite 12,300B–12,800B.* **Credit** *AE, DC, MC, V.* **Amenities** *five restaurants, fitness centre, salon, children's club and programmes, airport transfers, shopping arcade, babysitting, laundry/dry cleaning.* **In room** *A/C, satellite TV, dataport, fridge.*

The Banyan Tree ★ ★ ★

21/100 South Sathorn Road, Sathorn, Pathumwan, 10120, ☎ *02679 1200,* *www.banyantree.com.*

Challenge your children with some of the most stunning and

contemporary restaurants in Thailand – or indeed the world – at the Banyan Tree. This immense all-suite skyscraper has some of the city's most exceptional panoramas, not least from the rooftop restaurant Vertigo, where split-level dining is framed by a stunning city light show. Trendy, chic spaces might seem just too adult, but Asian families break the ice, introducing their own children and setting a light, informal atmosphere in the rarefied elegance.

To get you out and about the hotel also offers the *Apsara I*, a restored rice barge that takes diners out on the river for cocktails and sunset cruises.

The hotel is reasonably close to Lumpini MRT station and on the far side of family walking distance to Sala Daeng BTS station, but if you're staying here the cost of a taxi is likely to be the least of your concerns.

Rooms *216 units. From 11,500B for a Standard Suite to 70,000B for a Presidential Suite.* **Credit** *AE, MC, V.* **Amenities** *six restaurants, two bars,*

pool, fitness centre and spa, laundry.
In room DVD players on request,
WiFi, A/C, satellite TV, fridge.

Royal Orchid Sheraton ★ ★

*2 Charoen Krung Road, Soi 30
(Captain Bush Lane), Siphya,
Bangrak, 10500,* 📞 *02266 0123,
www.starwoodhotels.com.*

In one of the best riverside locations, the Royal Orchid
Sheraton Hotel & Towers has
panoramic views of the Chao
Phraya River.

The site is next door to the
River City Shopping Mall, one
of the city's original retail mega-
outlets, with its own Express
River Taxi stop and long-tailed
boat booking offices.

All rooms interconnect but
also feature complimentary cribs
and rollaway beds. Firmly placed
on the Condé Nast Traveler's
2008 Gold List, it is consistently
voted among the top 50 Asian
hotels.

Rooms 734 rooms and suites. *Rates*
*double 8500B–15,000B, suites good
value. Junior Suites good value at
8000B-1400B.* **Credit** *AE, DC, MC, V.*

Amenities *two pools including a
family-friendly garden pool with café,
four restaurants, tennis courts, spa.*
In room A/C, flat-screen cable TVs
with movie channels, cribs, rollaway
beds, hypoallergenic pillows.*

Shangri-La ★

*89 Soi Wat Suan Plu, New Road,
Bangrak, 10500,* 📞 *02236 7777,
www.shangri-la.com.*

On the banks of the Chao
Phraya right next to Saphan
Taksin BTS station and the
Central Pier, the Shangri-La is
the most conveniently located of
all Bangkok's luxury hotels for
travel around the city. This is
just as well because you'll need
plenty of encouragement to
leave the place. Acres of polished
marble are surrounded by a jungle of tropical plants and flowers. All rooms have river views
but they are better from the
higher, deluxe rooms. Some
rooms also have balconies or
small sitting rooms, making
them close to Junior Suites.
Facilities include two swimming
pools, air-conditioned squash

Views of the Chao Phraya river from the Royal Orchid Sheraton

courts, and outdoor tennis courts, health club and beauty salon. Although right next door to the Central Pier, the Shangri-La also has its own pier on the river from where it runs sunset cruises on a river behemoth equipped with large outdoor decks and a live band.

Rooms 799 including 52 suites in separate wings. *Rates* double 8000B–12,000B, suites 12,000B–20,000B. *Credit* AE, DC, MC, V. *Amenities* six restaurants, spa, laundry. *In room* babysitting/childcare, A/C, TV, in-house movies, tea/coffee facilities.

MODERATE

Asia Hotel VALUE

296 Phayathai Road, Petchburi Ratchathewi, 10400, ☎ *02215 0808,* *www.asiahotel.co.th.*

Almost a Bangkok institution, this is a well-located and very reasonably priced hotel with the unusual advantage of one- and two-bedroom suites, ideal for larger families – though all rooms can interconnect on request. They also offer travellers on a budget basic 'Cabin Rooms' which are as large as the normal guest rooms but look out on to a brick wall or similar. In compensation Cabin Room guests usually get a buffet breakfast included, and with triple Cabin Rooms this is something of a bargain in this location.

Facilities are clean and well kept, with two large swimming pools, one especially for children, a choice of restaurants (not brilliant, to be honest), and if

your children are broadminded (and most are) the Asia Hotel is also home to the very popular Calypso Cabaret, a leading ladyboy show.

Access to the BTS system could hardly be easier, with a walkway leading directly from the hotel to Ratchathewi station, and the hotel is in easy walking range of Siam Square.

Rooms 601. *Rates* twin 4680B, Asia suite 1 bedroom 6435B, Asia suite 2 bedrooms 10,500B, extra beds 700B, cots free, triple cabin room 4460B. *Credit* AE, DC, MC, V. *Amenities* four restaurants, two swimming pools. *In room* satellite TV, A/C, fridge, babysitting (inexpensive, charged according to the number of children).

Holiday Inn ★ ★ FIND

971 Ploenchit Road, Patumwan Road, 10330, ☎ *02656 1555,* *www.holidayinn.co.uk.*

This well-known chain operates at the lower end of the market in the UK, but its Bangkok property is a totally different animal – still inexpensive but also classy and supremely comfortable.

Hassled travellers straight off an international flight will find their family suites provide an immediate haven of peace. These rooms – book ahead, there are only four – have a separate area for children, with bunk beds on one side plus their own TV fitted with games console and supplied with family-friendly films and games. Draw the blackout curtains, dial up one of the excellent child meals, and get over your jet-lag the easy way.

There's a large swimming pool, shaded most of the time, that no one seems to use, and a selection of restaurants. On Sundays they operate a very popular children's brunch club, with face-painting, child entertainers and more, which draws in expat families from all over the capital.

Immediately outside are the Erawan Shrine and Chitlom BTS station, with the Siam Paragon and Central World Plaza a short, elevated walk away.

Rooms 379. **Rates** double 4400B–10,300B, family suite 6800B, room only. **Amenities** western and Thai restaurants, pool. **In room** A/C, satellite TV.

Mayfair Marriott Executive Apartments

60 Soi Langsuan, Lumpini, Pathumwan, 10330, ☎ 02672 1234 www.marriott.com.

The two-bedroom apartments here include small but well-equipped kitchenettes and two bathrooms, and most are fitted with washing and drying machines – though check this when you're making the booking if this is important – as well as LCD televisions and DVD players. Strangely the second, smaller bedrooms are the ones fitted with double beds while the larger rooms have the two singles. Living rooms are huge and include roll-out sofa beds.

The main family action is on the roof, where there is a large swimming pool, spa and children's play area. The location is good, within easy walking distance of Chitlom BTS station.

Rooms 162 units, 82 one-bed, 62 two-bed and 20 three-bed. **Rates** one-bedroom flats from 6000B. **Credit** AE, DC, MC, V. **Amenities** heated rooftop pool with Jacuzzi, four restaurants. **In room** A/C, crib, satellite TV with movie channels, kitchen with dishwasher.

Pathumwan Princess ★ ★
`FIND`

444 MBK Center, Phayathai Road, Wangmai, Pathumwan, 10330, ☎ 02216 3700, www.pprincess.com.

This large hotel is beautifully positioned for shoppers: they can visit the MBK shopping centre and through to the National Stadium BTS station, Siam Paragon and Central World Plaza without ever having to drop down to street level.

The breakfasts are superb, but make sure you aren't charged extra for them if it's meant to be included in your room rate.

Rooms 462 rooms and suites. **Rates** double 5400B, suite 6500B. **Credit** AE, DC, MC, V. **Amenities** 25m salt chlorinated pool, gym.

Pullman Bangkok King Power `VALUE`

8–2 Rangnam Road, 10400, ☎ 02680 9999, www.pullmanbangkokking power.com.

Even in Thailand there aren't that many hotels where the porters, unasked, whisk sleeping children from a taxi and deliver them, still asleep, to your room. And you certainly don't expect that at this very reasonable price point.

The Pullman Bangkok King Power has a swimming pool and

sundeck on the fourth floor, children's pool and spa. Rooms are spacious, and a child under 11 is free if sharing your room. If you have more children you'll have to go for a suite or get interconnecting rooms. There's an all-you-can-eat afternoon tea for 280B which presents a useful challenge if you've got adolescent boys. The location is good, just within walking distance of Phya Thai BTS station, though the hotel runs a free complimentary shuttle *tuk-tuk* for hotel guests.

Rooms *386 rooms and suites.* **Rates** *double 5000B.* **Amenities** *three restaurants, swimming pools for adults and children, spa.* **In room** *A/C, 24-hour room service, flat-screen TV.*

Siri Sathorn ☆

27 Soi Sala Daeng 1, Silom Road, Bangrak, 10500 (between Sathorn and Silom Roads), ☎ *02266 2345,* *www.sirisathorn.com.*

Although designed for long-stay residents – and business people at that – this contemporary apartment hotel provides comfortable and well-located accommodation for families. The suites are beautifully fitted out with an uncluttered, minimalist designer chic, with smooth wood and stone floors. Some come with terraces and a few have bathtubs as well. There is a small, shady pool next to a gym and yoga room. The smart little restaurant isn't really aimed at the family market, but all suites have fully-equipped kitchens and there are

plenty of places to eat nearby. Its location, in the tree-lined Soi Sala Daeng 1, is between Silom Road MRT and Sala Daeng BTS stations, putting you right in the city centre but with easy access to both mass-transit systems.

Rooms *111.* **Rates** *one-bedroom suite 5000B, two-bedroom suite 10,000B, two-bedroom terrace suite 12,000B, two-bedroom deluxe suite 14,000B.* **Credit** *AE, DC, MC, V.* **Amenities** *restaurant, bar, pool, fitness centre, spa.* **In room** *A/C, satellite TV, CD player, full kitchen, WiFi.*

INEXPENSIVE

Bossotel Inn ☆ ☆ VALUE

55/12–13 Soi Charoen Krung 42/1, Bangrak, 10500 (on Soi 42, near Shangri-La Hotel), ☎ *02630 6120,* *www.bossotelinn.com.*

Though it's not an obvious choice for families this hotel does have a pool and is fantastically located, within easy walking distance of Saphan Taksin BTS station and the Central Pier, meaning the city's best transport routes are right at your door.

At a fraction of the price of the nearby Shangri-La Hotel this is a perfectly comfortable, if basic, cheerful choice. Even the lower-grade rooms are of a good size, with plenty of space for an extra bed. It's a justifiably popular hotel, and some of the rooms get snapped up by long-term visitors. Book ahead, preferably by email as not all staff speak English.

Rooms 46. *Rates* double 1800B–2600B, suite 4500B. *Credit* AE, MC, V. *Amenities* coffee shop, swimming pool, laundry. *In room* A/C, satellite TV, fridge, WiFi.

New Siam Riverside

21 Phra Arthit, Chanasongkram, 10200, 📞 *02629 3535, www.new siam.net.*

One of the very few truly river-side hotels still charging budget rates, this is perfectly located. Phra Arthit River Pier is less than 100m away, and once you've got across a busy road you're into a shady set of virtually traffic-free *sois*, a sort of urban city park where cafés spill on to the streets outside count-less budget hostels, that lead to a large tranquil temple and then to the Khao San Road.

The rooms interconnect and are quite acceptable, but the main attraction is the view from the pool, which matches those of the city's prime hotels that charge 10 times as much. Prices are low partly because it doesn't have a restaurant: meals are delivered from the sister prop-erty across the road, and break-fast is included. It would rate several stars but its welcome has been somewhat blunted by too many years' exposure to Khao San Road dross.

Rooms 70. *Rate* double 1450B, triple 1950B, extra bed 500B, cot 250B. Add 500B for river view. Best rooms Deluxe Riverview (with balcony) 2290B. *Credit* MC, V. *Amenities* restaurant, pool with chil-dren's end, laundry. *In room* A/C, modest TV.

New Siam Riverside Hotel

Pranakorn-Nornlen Hotel

★ ★ FIND

46 Thewet Soi 1, Phranakorn, Bangkhunprom, 10200, 📞 *02628 8188-90, www.phrakorn-nornlen.com.*

To the north of Banglamphu, this is a charming boutique hotel in an atmospheric part of the city beyond the tourist belt. It man-ages to be effortlessly elegant without being the slightest bit formal, with walls and furnish-ings hand-painted and individ-ual. Children love the enclosed, shady garden, and everyone loves the staff, guests competing with tales of how impossibly helpful their hosts have been.

There are no family rooms, but it is a small and intimate enough place for most children to feel happy sleeping next door to their parents.

It does seem out of the way when you arrive – you'll need a map to show any taxi driver and

Family-Friendly Accommodation

it isn't close to any mass transit system – but if you intend to spend most of your time following the line of the river, Pier 15, Tha Thewes, is close by.

Rooms 20. **Rates** double/twin 2400B. **Credit** MC, V. **Amenities** restaurant. **In room** A/C.

Silom Convent Garden VALUE

35/1 Soi Piphat 2, Sathorn Soi Convent, 10500, 02667 0130, www.silomconventgarden.com.

Slick, central and convenient, this brand new apartment hotel is suited to longer stays, with daily, weekly and monthly rates. Rooms are clean and contemporary in bright colours and good, modern taste, with kitchenettes and communal laundry facilities. Each room has a small balcony, and there is a rooftop terrace. Eminently affordable, this is in easy reach of Sala Daeng BTS station.

Rooms 44 units. **Rates** 1650B–3650B. **Credit** AE, DC, MC, V. **Amenities** restaurant, communal laundry, wifi. **In room** A/C, satellite TV, kitchenette.

FAMILY-FRIENDLY DINING

Bangkok Sky Restaurant
THAI/INTERNATIONAL

Bayoke Sky Hotel, 222 Rajprarop Road, Rajthevee, 10400, 02656 3000, 02656 3456, www.baiyoke hotel.com.

Thais claim that this is the highest restaurant in the world and eating here is quite an experience. The restaurant is on the 76th and 78th floors of the Bayoke Sky Hotel and features a daily buffet of western and Thai dishes, and special meals for children. Parents with adolescent boys will appreciate the promise 'All you can eat'. Prices, for the setting, are very reasonable. Depending on visibility, views are of all Bangkok.

Reserve your table in advance and bypass the long queues that can build up at reception.

Open breakfast 5.30am–10.30am, lunch 11am–2.30pm, dinner 5.30pm–11.30pm. **Buffet** 600B. **Credit** AE, MC, V.

Silom Convent Garden

The Blue Elephant THAI

233 South Sathorn Road, 02673 9353, www.blueelephant.com. Close to Surasak BTS station.

One of the most elegant, refined and expensive restaurants in Bangkok, this is in a beautiful traditional mansion, standing out from its immediate surroundings. The décor is lavish, the service excellent and the presentation perfection – the fresh fruits for dessert are exquisitely carved. It also runs a cooking school which, though not obviously geared to children, might let them show their appreciation of their holiday by cooking you some Thai food at home.

Open 11.30am–2.30pm, 6.30pm–11.30pm. Main courses 500B. Credit AE, MC, V.

Crepes & Co EUROPEAN

18/1 Sukhumvit Soi 12, 02653 3990. Ten-minute walk from Nana BTS station.

Popular with Bangkok expats – and their children – crepes here are light, fluffy and filled with dozens of combinations, both savoury and sweet: all delicious. They also serve a good range of Mediterranean dishes such as mezze and couscous. The place is very family-friendly, even down to the cat which likes to curl up and sleep next to diners. Great coffee and a good selection of tea.

Reservations recommended. Open 9am–midnight. Main courses 100B–300B. Credit AE, DC, MC, V.

Erawan Tea Room VALUE
THAI/INTERNATIONAL

2nd Floor Erawan Bangkok 494 Ploenchit Road, 10330, 02254 1234. Directly linked by walkway from Chitlom BTS station.

The new Erawan Tea Room at the Grand Hyatt gives you the chance to sample traditional Thai cuisine at its best, escaping the rush of Siam Square, at a very reasonable price. In a five-star setting five-star cuisine is provided at a two-star price. For 150B they serve a platter of some of the most delicious Thai specialities you're ever likely to find including deep-fried prawn spring rolls, minced pork and water chestnuts wrapped with egg noodles, sticky rice with mango, flower-shaped dumplings filled with minced chicken, and sweet bean paste fruit shapes – a meal in itself, with the chance for your children to try a whole new palette of tastes. The meal also includes scones and jam, water sticks, chocolate cake and unlimited cups of tea from Thailand, Sri Lanka, India and China. After you've eaten cross the road to the Erawan Shrine and pray for this crazy promotion to continue for years.

Open 10am–11pm. Meals 150B. Credit AE, MC, V.

Hard Rock Hotel INTERNATIONAL

424/3–6 Siam Square Soi 11, 02251 0797, www.hardrockcafe.co.th.

A *tuk-tuk* hangs from the front façade and a skyline graphic claims – rather spuriously – to be saving the planet. How? It can only be the Bangkok Hard Rock Café. For a blast of American fast food, washed down by live music and an energetic, vibrant atmosphere, this can hardly be beaten. It's not Thai food and it's hardly authentic but who cares?

Those with children are asked not to arrive after 10pm which is wise: customers here may have been drinking three-litre 'Beer Towers' for the previous six hours.

Open *11am until late.* **Main courses** *600B.* **Credit** *AE, MC, V.*

Outback Steak House
`INTERNATIONAL`

2/F, Siam Discovery Center, Rama 1 Road, Pathumwan, 📞 *022658 0202. Two-minute walk from Siam BTS station.*

When only steak will do, this Australian steakhouse chain focuses on beef but also serves chicken, pork and seafood alongside token pasta alternatives.

Open *11am-midnight* **Main courses** *400B.* **Credit** *AE, MC, V.*

Pathumwan Princess
`THAI/JAPANESE/CHINESE`

444 MBK Center, Phayathai Road, Wangmai, Pathumwan, 10330, 📞 *02216 3700, www.pprincess.com. Easy walking distance from Siam Square and directly connected to the MBK Shopping Mall.*

Take a break from the Siam Square retail madness at this relaxing hotel lobby, with

child-friendly Filipino singers and an all-you-can-eat buffet including Japanese, Thai and Chinese cuisines as well as European favourites.

Open *10am-midnight* **Buffet** *399B.* **Credit** *AE, MC, V.*

The Sylvanian Families Restaurant ⭐ `FIND` `INTERNATIONAL`

6th Floor Central World. BTS Chidlom or Siam, Rajdamri Road, Patumwan, 10330, 📞 *02613 1666, www.thesylvanian.com.*

Small children will be captivated by the Sylvanian Families Restaurant. Tables are set in jump-friendly padded booths, amid miniature scenes of Sylvanian life, and all the waitresses are dressed as cuddly Sylvanian characters.

Inside the restaurant there is a playground with a ball pool and various colourful playthings. There is a children's menu with wholesome alternatives as well as sweet treats, and a menu of western options for parents. The location on the 6th floor of a shopping mall means traffic risks are far away.

Central World is a good shopping centre, with a Legoland in the children's department of Isetan. It is very close to Siam BTS, and in the same block as the Siam Paragon Mall, with its Aquarium and IMAX cinema, making it an excellent lunch stop.

Open *10.30am–9.30pm.* **Main courses** *400B.* **Credit** *MC, V.*

Chao Phraya Cruise Meals

A number of tour operators offer lunch and dinner cruises along the Chao Phraya River, ranging from floating discotheques with all-you-can-eat buffets to beautifully restored rice barges, rich with history and a quiet, simple atmosphere. Most have special rates for children, who love the romantic atmosphere and exotic surroundings. Traditional music, live rock bands and Thai dance shows might be provided: see individual websites for details.

Based at the Bangkok Marriott Resort and Spa (📞 02476 0021), the Manohra, Manohra Moon and Manohra Star are elegantly restored rice barges that offer various day, sunset and evening dinner cruises on the Chao Phraya River from 750B. Numbers are limited and boats can be chartered for private functions: see *www.manohracruises.com*.

The gargantuan Grand Pearl cruise (rates from 600B, 📞 *02861 0255*, *www.grandpearlcruise.com*) drifts out from the River City Pier at 7pm for a gentle cruise serenaded by jazz greats, returning at 9.30pm.

Another rice barge option is offered by Loy Nava (📞 *02437 4932*, *www.loynava.com*) with two sailings daily from the Sri Phaya Pier. For families the better one is the earlier 6pm–8pm, from 1295B.

Other cruises start at particular hotels. Click on *www.bangkok. com/dinner-&-shows-tours* for details.

Dinner with Thai Dance

Several venues offer cultural experiences, though children – and their parents – can often find the experience too stylised and slow. These are the shows that will catch – and keep – children's interest.

Siam Niramit ★ ★ THAI

19 Tiamruammit Road, Huaykwang, 10320, 📞 02649 9222, www.siam niramit.com. Opposite Thailand Cultural Centre. Exit 1 Thai Cultural Centre MRT station.

The meal here – delicious, Thai cuisine – is just a sideshow: Siam Niramit is one of the most spectacular acrobatic and theatrical displays in the world. More than 150 performers in 500 costumes make a journey into the enchanted heart of Thai culture, helped by a state-of-the-art sound system and advanced lighting effects. At once dance, theatre and circus, the Siam Niramit is long remembered by young minds.

Show times daily 8pm. Admission show only 1000B adults, 750B children; meal and show 1250B adults, 950B children. Under 0.9m free. Credit AE, MC, V.

Sala Rim Nam ★ ★ THAI

Charoen Nakhorn Road, on the Thonburi side of the Chao Phraya River, 📞 02437 2918.

The Oriental Hotel has re-opened this beautiful riverside Thai restaurant with a glittering new interior and the same impeccable standards of cuisine and entertainment. The drama happens across the river from the main hotel, reached by a magical ferry journey. Dining is an extensive *dégustation* menu of Thai favourites, which can be stripped of spices if required, eaten from either western-style tables or Thai-style on floor pillows. While you eat, classical Thai dancers in full glittering regalia dramatise ancient Thai legends and traditional folk dances. A free shuttle boat crosses from the hotel's private pier. Find it by following signs for the Hotel Shuttle Boat next to Central Pier by Saphan Taksin.

Open *daily 7pm–10pm, performance 8.30pm.* ***Admission*** *1700B.* ***Credit*** *AE, DC, MC, V.*

Supatra River House ★ ★
VALUE **THAI**

266 Arunamarin Road, Soi Wat Rakhang, Siriraj, Thonburi (diagonally opposite Patravadi Theater), ☎ *02411 0305. 15 minutes by boat from the Central Pier, five minutes from Tha Maharat Pier.*

This popular Thai dancing theatre is a good place to relax with excellent fresh seafood, fish cakes, spring rolls, steamed fish and a host of great Thai favourites, usually tamed for tourists, served on outdoor tables overlooking the Grand Palace, or in the rigorously air-conditioned indoors. Dance spectaculars are on weekend evenings, and if you call ahead a little steamer will pick you up from the Central Pier.

Open *daily 11am–10pm.* ***Main courses*** *200B.* ***Credit*** *AE, MC, V.*

4 The Eastern Gulf: Pattaya, Koh Samet & Koh Chang

EASTERN GULF

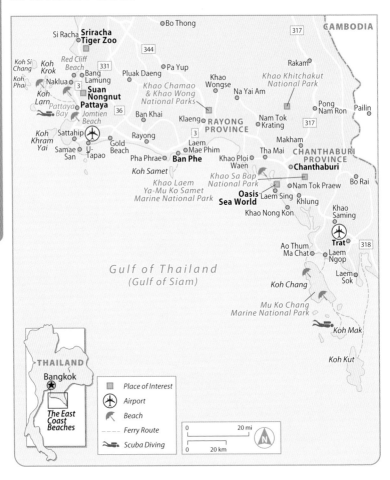

An hour and a half east of Bangkok the coast starts with a bang at the resort city of **Pattaya**. Not so long ago this was just a simple fishing village, but then the Americans chose to use it as a resort to let its Vietnam forces 'relax'. A tourist industry exploded and now Pattaya is one of the largest cities in Thailand: a high-rise seaside palace of pleasure built on exotic titillation and rental sex. The result is rather like Benidorm on Viagra. Since the regular supply of US servicemen dried up Pattaya has made energetic attempts to reposition itself to appeal to the family market and is, to a great extent, succeeding.

Outside Pattaya Centre – known as 'The Strip' – the sex industry fades away. Stay on quieter Jomtien Beach and you'll hardly see it. Restaurants are wildly overpriced but thanks to the sheer number of visitors, mid-market resort rooms are excellent value for money, and a wide selection of family-friendly attractions have been developed over the years.

Two hours' drive further east and the island of Koh Samet represents a wholly different Thailand; a little gem of a National Park surrounded by small coves and larger beaches, each fringed with small, family-run resorts that pack a surprising number of small chalets tightly into the shady forests that cloak the interior.

Koh Samet is especially popular with expats and weekenders from Bangkok and you'll need reservations at weekends, not least because it tends to stay sunny long after the monsoon rains have damped down the western resorts of the Andaman coast. There's little to do on Koh Samet beyond the usual beach games, and getting back to the mainland, whether by expensive speed launch or slow chugging ferry, is always going to be something of an expedition. But for a simple holiday with sand and sea it's ideal. There are virtually no cars, the bays are generally sheltered without dangerous currents, and dining is invariably on the beach: bliss for families with young children.

Further east again and Koh Chang has long been positioning itself as a new, 'undeveloped' Thailand, now with a few upmarket resorts to prove it. Personally, I'd hesitate to take families here because too many people catch dengue fever, a viral disease spread by daytime mosquitoes. An attack is not usually life-threatening but there's no effective treatment and, like many diseases, it can be more dangerous for children. This is also one of the few parts of Thailand where I'd actively recommend malaria prophylaxis.

But if you're in search of a deserted Alex Garland-style 'beach' this is a good place to start. Ferries from Koh Chang reach out to the even more remote islands of Koh Wai, Koh Kood, Koh Maak and Koh Kham where tourism is truly in its infancy.

Koh Chang is Thailand's second-largest island after Koh Samui. And worth considering, for a wild experience of red dirt roads, stilted fishermen's villages such as Ao Sapparot, Ao Bang Bao and Ao Salakphet, and quiet bays where in the cooler months, fireflies light up magical nights. However, from May to October many ferry services stop, resorts close and the seas too rough for swimming.

ESSENTIALS

Getting There

By Air There are two airports on the southeast coast. The airport at the naval base of Utapao was built by the Americans so they could ferry their servicemen to and from their official R&R resort of Pattaya, 30 minutes' drive north of town. These days it doesn't see much traffic but Bangkok Airways (☎ *02265 5555*; *www.bangkokair.com*) flies between Utapao (☎ *03824 5595*) and Samui and Phuket, making this an easy way to skip Bangkok on a journey across the Gulf of Thailand.

By Bus Most travellers reach the southeast coast by road. If flying in to Suvarnabhumi Airport you can avoid the capital completely and start the journey in a taxi, reaching Pattaya in less than an hour (800B) along a fast toll highway. The public 389 bus is a cheaper but much slower way to reach Pattaya: take the Express Route airport shuttle bus to the transportation centre.

There are plenty of operators selling shared services from the centre of Bangkok to Pattaya, but allow a good extra hour to clear the capital. Combined minibus/ferry tickets are sold from Banglamphu in Bangkok to Koh Samet and Koh Chang, but a far more comfortable journey is by the air-conditioned buses leaving from Bangkok's Eastern Ekkamai (☎ 02391 2504) Bus Terminal or Northern Morchit II Bus Terminal. Each has departures every 30 minutes from 5am to 7pm costing 100B. They follow Bangkok's main Sukhumvit Road that leaves the capital and continues along this coast all the way to Cambodia. Travel times from Bangkok are about two hours to Pattaya, four hours to Ban Phe pier for Koh Samet, and six hours to Laem Ngop for Koh Chang.

By Rail There is a single daily train service between Bangkok (Hualamphong station) and Pattaya (☎ 03842 9285), but it leaves at 7am and takes five

hours, so is not remotely convenient.

VISITOR INFORMATION

In Pattaya the main TAT (8.30am–4.30pm, ☎ 03842 8750) is rather out of the way on Cliff Road between Pattaya and neighbouring Jomtien. More convenient is a smaller satellite TAT, open the same hours, at the northern end of Walking Street on 'The Strip'.

Publications

The publishing centre of the coast is Pattaya, where local publications such as *What's On Pattaya* and *Explore Pattaya and the East Coast* can be found in most hotel lobbies and at restaurants. They include good area maps. Alternatively buy a copy of the *Pattaya Mail*, the local English-language paper.

As you head further east local information is limited to local maps surrounded by advertisements. For simple islands such as Koh Samet this is perfectly adequate while on Koh Chang there's little to mark on the map.

Orientation

Pattaya

Pattaya's main tourist area backs 5km-long Pattaya Bay, a strip of water constantly busy with yachts and jet-skis, its narrow

PATTAYA

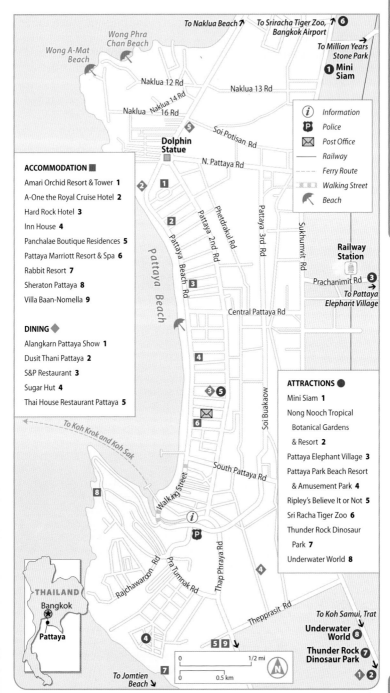

To Naklua Beach

To Sriracha Tiger Zoo, **6**
Bangkok Airport

To Million Years
Stone Park

Mini **1**
Siam

Wong Phra
Chan Beach

Wong A-Mat
Beach

Naklua 12 Rd

Naklua 13 Rd

Naklua 14 Rd

Naklua Naklua
16 Rd

Soi Potisan Rd

Dolphin **5**
Statue

N. Pattaya Rd

ⓘ	Information
P	Police
✉	Post Office
—	Railway
- - -	Ferry Route
▥▥▥	Walking Street
⚓	Beach

Railway
Station

Prachanimit Rd **3**

To Pattaya
Elephant Village

ACCOMMODATION ■

Amari Orchid Resort & Tower **1**

A-One the Royal Cruise Hotel **2**

Hard Rock Hotel **3**

Inn House **4**

Panchalae Boutique Residences **5**

Pattaya Marriott Resort & Spa **6**

Rabbit Resort **7**

Sheraton Pattaya **8**

Villa Baan-Nomella **9**

DINING ◆

Alangkarn Pattaya Show **1**

Dusit Thani Pattaya **2**

S&P Restaurant **3**

Sugar Hut **4**

Thai House Restaurant Pattaya **5**

Pattaya Beach

Pattaya-Beach Rd

Pattaya 2nd Rd

Phetdrakul Rd

Pattaya 3rd Rd

Sukhumvit Rd

Central Pattaya Rd

Soi Buakaow

2 **1**

2

3

4

◆ **3** ● **5**

✉ **6**

To Koh Krok and Koh Sak

South Pattaya Rd

8

Walking Street

ⓘ

P

ATTRACTIONS ●

Mini Siam **1**

Nong Nooch Tropical
   Botanical Gardens
   & Resort **2**

Pattaya Elephant Village **3**

Pattaya Park Beach Resort
   & Amusement Park **4**

Ripley's Believe It or Not **5**

Sri Racha Tiger Zoo **6**

Thunder Rock Dinosaur
   Park **7**

Underwater World **8**

THAILAND

Bangkok

Pattaya

Rajchawaroon Rd

Pra Tummak Rd

Thap Phraya Rd

Thepprasit Rd

4

To Koh Samui, Trat

Underwater **8**
World

Thunder Rock **7**
Dinosaur Park

1 **2**

4

5 **9**

7

To Jomtien
Beach

0		1/2 mi
0	0.5 km	

N

strip of sand packed with wooden sun-loungers shaded by parasols sponsored by local international hospitals. Pattaya Beach Road runs – fast-moving and one-way – north to south, making access to the beach something of a challenge to parents with young children. A neat grid of *sois* (streets) links back to Pattaya 2nd Road, which runs south to north.

At the heart of this is Central Pattaya, known as *Pattaya Klang*, with tour operators, chemists, banks, restaurants and shops. South of this is 'The Strip', packed with hostess bars and strip clubs, giving way eventually to Walking Street. The sex industry is so open here that even the most broad-minded parent might find themselves parrying questions they'd rather not answer.

The bays on either side of Pattaya Beach are quieter. To the south 15km-long Jomtien Beach is lined with high-rise condominium blocks. It is known for its windsurfing but watch the safety flags – at times the water can be dangerous.

To the north Naklua Bay is also blighted by timeshare developments but somehow retains traces of its village past.

The main Sukhumvit Highway – a straight continuation of Sukhumvit Road in Bangkok – runs several blocks inland, and is where most of the major family tourist attractions have been developed.

Getting Around

The narrow pavements in Pattaya, fretted by invariably heavy traffic, make trailing a family around something of a challenge, especially as you're never quite sure what your children's next sideways glance has in store.

By the beach in Pattaya

A majority of visitors seem to be single: for them the shared *songthaews* – known here as Baht Buses – that run up and down Pattaya Beach Road (20B per person within Pattaya, 40B for longer trips, such as to Jomtien) are a useful way to get around. Families will often be better off hailing a taxi that will, for little more, take them exactly where they are going. Unusually for Thailand there are no *tuk-tuks*.

FAMILY-FRIENDLY EVENTS

Crocodile Egg-Hatching

From May to August children can cradle crocodile eggs as they hatch in Sri Racha Tiger Zoo (see p 97). There's little that can match the experience of feeling a tentative baby croc feel its way around your hand.

May to Aug.

Pattaya Music Festival

Thailand's largest music festival takes over Pattaya's beachfront every year and attracts leading artists from all over the world. The latest sounds are on show but most events are rather retro, catering for the ageing population of sex-seeking expats.

Three days in the middle of Mar.

Songkran

Though not as messy as the northern celebrations, Songkran here can last longer. Out of deference to the provincial capital, Chonburi, the celebrations in Pattaya are supposed to start a few days after the official Songran date. Most Thais and no tourists realise this. The result is that the wet mayhem lasts longer than ever and you can never be sure when the next bowl of water, sometimes chilled, might land on your head. Buy water-pistols if you want to look like a tourist. What your children need is a bucket.

Usually from the 13th–16th Apr.

FAST FACTS

ATMs Pattaya is Forex and ATM city because the girls prefer cash. The major Thai banks can be found on Pattaya 2nd Road, one block in from the beachfront.

Car Hire For car rental Avis (℡ 05320 1798, *www.avisthailand.com*) and Budget ℡ 05320 2871 (*www.budget.co.th*) have offices in Pattaya and charge from 2500B per day upwards. You can halve these rates at independent outlets, but they won't always include insurance. One example of this, offering 1500cc Toyotas for 1300B per day, is Car For Rent (℡ 081 1771269, 16/46 Moo 6, Green View Village, Nongprue, Banglamung 20260), which also quotes for airport and long-distance journeys.

Chemists Pattaya has plenty of chemists, usually open until midnight and invariably selling Viagra and condoms.

Dentists Dental care in Pattaya is generally cosmetic – often with

Border Crossings

Thailand's land borders have opened up considerably over the last 20 years to travellers on western passports, and there are several border posts where you can cross over to Cambodia, Burma, Laos and Malaysia. For most you will need passport photographs and some cash dollars to pay for your onward visa, however, there may be other requirements. Local travel agents, accustomed to organising 'visa runs' for foreigners extending their visas, are the best people to ask about their nearest border, as regulations frequently change.

Local disputes can affect some border regions: the security situation in southern Thailand towards Malaysia is poor (Muslim separatists) and relations with Cambodia (territorial disputes about Praeh Vhear) are uncertain.

From Koh Chang the nearest Cambodian border is Hat Lek on the coast with a poor road leading onwards to the capital, Phnom Penh, though from Pattaya it's as easy to head inland to Aranyaprapthet which is closer to Angkor Wat.

---

a five-year guarantee. The Inter Dental Clinic (✆ 03825 1289) and Modern Smile (✆ 03872 0820, *www.modernsmiledental.com*) are two practitioners.

Hospitals Bangkok Pattaya Hospital (✆ 03825 9999, *www. bangkokpattayahospital.com*) has full services – including a recompression chamber for divers who have come up too fast – and an English-speaking staff. The Pattaya International Hospital (✆ 03842 8374, *www.pih-inter. com*) is also recommended.

Internet Pattaya has countless Internet cafés, especially along Pattaya Beach Road.

Post Office Pattaya's post office is on Soi 13/2, known as 'Soi Post Office'.

Safety Pattaya has its fair share of bag-snatchers, gem-scam artists and cons, but the greatest danger is the traffic, especially along the busy one-way roads that cut the town off from the beach. Prime hazards are drunk, middle-aged western men who struggle to control their rental motorbikes, though no one gives much quarter to pedestrians, even if small.

Travel Agents There are countless travel agents in Pattaya and most are good and professional at organising taxis, excursions and air tickets. One is the German-run Sea-Air-Land Tours (✆ 03871 0829-30, 183/2-6 Soi Post Office, Pattaya 20260, *www.sal-thailand-tours.de*) and another is Meeting Point Travel (✆ 038711 1194, Soi 12, 2nd Road, Pattaya) but there is a lot to be said for starting with the nearest operator to your hotel. Even the most modest roadside stall can be a useful resource for local excursions because they keep track of changing opening hours, show timetables and closures.

Don't allow any tour operator to obtain Thai visa extensions on your behalf as this is illegal, but they can help with onward visas and travel arrangements to Cambodia. From Chantaburi routes into Cambodia head across to Aranyaprathet close to Angkor Wat, while from Trat they use the Hat Lek border crossing.

WHAT TO SEE & DO

Children's Top 10 Attractions

❶ **Feed** the crocs and bet on piglet races at a tiger zoo. See p 97.

❷ **Explore** the world in miniature. See p 94.

❸ **Relax** on a family-sized beach on Koh Samet. See p 100.

❹ **Ride** an elephant in an island jungle on Koh Chang. See p 106.

❺ **Fly** down the waterslides of a clifftop water park. See p 96.

❻ **Meet** tropical fish and walk under sharks. See p 98.

❼ **Take** a night safari at a tropical zoo. See p 94.

❽ **Ride** an ATV or buggy on a jungle adventure. See p 99.

❾ **Dive** wrecks and reefs in sheltered seas. See p 100.

❿ **Catch** a breeze with a windsurfer or kite. See below.

Attractions

Pattaya

Golf

This is Thailand's golf Mecca, with 18 top courses within less than an hour's drive, designed by such names like Jack Nicklaus, Robert Trent Jones Jr, Desmond Muirhead and the Royal Thai Navy. This is Asia, so your caddy is likely to be a young woman, but then this is Asia so they're likely to play off 0.

You can arrange your own tee-times and a round usually costs 1000B on a weekday, 1800B at the weekend, with a caddy adding 250B and a set of clubs 500B.

It's easier and no more expensive to use a specialist operator to arrange both transport and green fees. One is Pattaya Golf, ☎ *03842 0824*, *www.pattayagolf.com*, whose website helpfully gives full details of all the courses.

Kitesurfing/Windsurfing ★
AGE 6 AND UP

Club Loongchat, 8km from South Pattaya intersection and about 1km before the Ambassador City Hotel, ☎ *081340 2180, www.clubloong chat.com.*

The different orientation of Pattaya and Jomtien beaches make this a good year-round place to learn windsurfing or kitesurfing – windsurfing being something of a speciality of Jomtien which is also less crowded with motorised vessels.

From November to mid-January the northeast monsoon blows between 10 and 25 knots, creating choppy conditions in Pattaya but leaving Jomtien's waters flat. From mid-January to March the winds are usually 8 to 12 knots from west to southwest – ideal for windsurfing lessons. From March to June southwest-erly winds are usually between 8 to 20 knots and low tides create wide beaches so perfect for learning to kitesurf. The south-west monsoon starts to blow in mid-July but winds get lighter through August, usually between 6 to 12 knots, until the north-east winter monsoon returns in November.

From the earliest days of windsurfing in the 1970s Thailand has been a major pro-ducer of equipment, and Club Loongchat has been a leading school since 1985. When the winds blow hard they rig up small sails and party in the surf.

Equipment rental 350B an hour for windsurfing boards, 1000B an hour for kitesurfing gear, 700B per hour for hobie cats: rates drop with three-hour or daily rentals. Instructor serv-ices from 300B–550B an hour depending on speciality, language skills and nationality.

Comparable rates from the Blue Lagoon Water Sports Club (Baanammao, Chonburi, 20150, 📞 08521 36731, *www.iwindsurf.asia* on Dongtan beach.

Mini Siam ★ ALL AGES

387 Moo 6, Sukhumvit Road, Naklua, Banglamung, Chonburi 20150, 📞 03872 7333, 📞 03872 7666, *www.minisiam.com*. Just north of central Pattaya on the main inland highway, shuttle from downtown Pattaya 9am, 10am, 12.30pm, 3.30pm: call 📞 03872 7333 or e-mail *E: info@min-isiam.com* to arrange a pickup.

If traipsing around Thailand's palaces and temples is just too hot for your children, Mini Siam recreates all the country's greatest cultural and architectural treas-ures shrunk to an eminently strollable 1:25 scale. The Bridge over the River Kwai is there, as is the Temple of the Emerald Buddha, and 80 other Thai exhibits.

While there, why not quickly tour the great buildings of the world? A separate section (endearingly including the Statue of Liberty and the Sydney Opera House in Europe) has scale models of the Arc de Triomphe, the towers of Pisa and Eiffel, Egypt's Abu Simbel, and many more.

Open daily 7am–8pm. *Admission* 100B adults, 50B children. *Amenities* café, gift shop.

Nong Nooch Tropical Botanical Gardens & Resort ★ ALL AGES

18km south of Pattaya, 📞 03842 9321, *www.nongnoochtropical garden.com*. Book ahead to take advantage of a free shuttle from downtown Pattaya at either 8.30am or 1.15pm.

More than just a pretty place, this 600-acre attraction – sup-ported by the Thai Queen – it is said to have Thailand's largest collection of orchids. More than this, it offers elephant shows and rides, cultural dances, musical performances and Thai boxing, pedalos for rent on the lake, bicycles, canopy skywalks and more. There is also a small zoo with tiger for photo opportunities, and a collection of birds.

Open daily 8am–6pm. Shows at 9.45am, 10.45am, 3pm and 3.45pm. **Admission** 420B adults, 210B children. **Credit** MC, V. **Amenities** café, gift shop.

Pattaya Elephant Village
ALL AGES

48/120 Moo 7, Tambol Nong Prue, Pattaya City 20150, ☎ 03824 988, ☎ 03824 9853, www.elephant-village-pattaya.com.

Pattaya's solution to the elephant problem is to collect strays and orphans into the Pattaya Elephant Village. Shows lasting an hour and a half give visitors the chance to help wash the elephants and see displays. Elephant treks through the jungle can be bareback or in howdahs, with river rafting and (uncomfortable) ox-cart journeys also available.

Though somewhat expensive in comparison to other elephant camps around the country, for what it's worth the Elephant Village proclaims itself a not-for-profit organisation. Call ahead for their shuttle service from central Pattaya hotels.

Open Daily 8am-5:30pm. **Admission** Elephant show 2.30pm, 650B adults, 500B under 1m, Elephant rides 60 minutes for 1200B, combination show/elephant bathing/rafting/elephant trekking/lunch or dinner, starting 10.30am or 4pm, 2000B per person. **Credit** MC, V. **Amenities** café.

Pattaya Park Beach Resort & Amusement Park ★ ALL AGES

345 Jomtien Beach, Pattaya City, Cholburi 20150, ☎ 03825 1201-8, www.pattayapark.com. Though prominently perched between Jomtien and Pattaya beaches, it is a long hot walk from the inter-beach road and for such a huge resort it's not that easy to find and little known by locals. Best book a taxi.

Perched on the bluff between Jomtien and Pattaya Beaches,

Pattaya Park Beach Resort & Amusement Park

this large resort has a small adventure park offering some entertaining family activities. At the heart of the resort is a 240m tower with three revolving restaurants at the top. It's not advisable to eat (even the mainly Russian clientele complain about overpriced food). The experience is about coming down again – by sky shuttle to the beach, or 'Tower Jump', dropping the 170m harnessed to a steeply sloping slide line. The Tower Jump is open to anyone over 1.3m tall unless pregnant.

At its base is a small theme park called 'Funny Land' with a monorail linking a selection of attractions including a swing Viking ship, samba tower, carousel and the first 'Tower Shot' to be built in Thailand. There is also a roller-coaster but it wasn't operational on my visit. Paid for individually these rides become hugely expensive, but prepaid tickets for several rides bought at the entrance work out cheaper.

If you're anything like me a few minutes here will leave you clutching your wallet tightly and resentfully. But I'd happily pay for my children to enter Pattaya Park's Waterland, with several quite ambitious slides, a large shallow swimming pool and a whirlpool.

There's an inexpensive chip-n-burger type café attached so you can get plenty of time for your admission fee, the limiting factor likely to be you: there's not a lot of shade and the out-door furniture is basic.

Open Sun–Fri 10am–7pm, Sat 10am–8pm. **Admission** Waterland 100B adults, 50B under 1.2m. Most Happy Land rides 100B–200B paid individually, Happy Land packages (280B adults, 250B under 1.2m) cover about half the rides at a time so you might need to buy two. Observation Tower 300B adults, 120B under 1.2m, includes one soft drink and one trip down, by sky shut-tle or tower jump. **Credit** AE, DC, MC, V. **Amenities** café, gift shop, swimwear shop.

Ripley's Believe It or Not ★★
ALL AGES

Royal Garden Plaza, 218 Moo 10, Beach Road, Pattaya 20260, ☎ 03871 0294-8, www.ripleysthailand.com.

Ideal for a rainy day, Ripley's Believe It or Not is on the top floor of the Royal Garden Plaza shopping centre in the heart of Pattaya. It's hard to miss, as a mock crashed plane is embedded in the side of the centre with cockpit and one wing on display inside. There are plenty of inter-active displays set in 10 themed galleries. Torture devices, optical tricks and scientific pseudo-truths are gathered with an unerring eye for the shocking and downright weird.

On the same floor other attractions include Ripley's Haunted Adventure, complete with live and lavishly made-up ghouls, an infinity maze and a four-dimensional theatre where the extra dimension is provided by moving seats.

Paid for ride by ride the whole thing could become expensive but a group ticket

Ripley's Believe It or Not

gives you reasonably priced access into all the displays.

The whole shopping mall is reasonably child-friendly. On the ground floor local mums send their babies toddling around a timed-jet fountain: occasionally one gets soaked.

Open *11am–11pm.* *Admission* *Ripley's All Play Package 780B adults, 680B children, Ripley's Believe It or Not 380B adults, 230B children, Ripley's Haunted Adventure 380B adults, 380B children, Ripley's Infinity Maze 380B adults, 380B children, Ripley's Moving Theatre 200B any age.* *Amenities* *café, gift shop.*

Sri Racha Tiger Zoo ★★ FIND
ALL AGES

341 Moo 3, Nongkham, Sriracha, 20110, ☏ 03829 6556-8, www.tiger zoo.com. Forty-five minutes from Pattaya and within day-trip range of Bangkok, turn inland off the Sukhumvit Road (Highway 7) at Sri Racha along the small road 3241 to Nongkham: after 8km you'll find the zoo on your left.

Less a zoo than some bizarre mix of farm and theatre, the Sri Racha Tiger Zoo reduces Taiwanese tour-groups to giggling bliss and has a very good chance of doing the same to your children. Thailand's flagship species – tigers, elephants and crocodiles – show off in lively and theatrical presentations. Shows include a tiger circus, elephant show, crocodile display, a Scorpion Queen, and pig races. Along the way you can also drive a pool-full of crocodiles wild by dangling meat over them from fishing rods, see pigs do sums, feed tiger cubs for a photo-opportunity, see sows suckling baby tiger kittens and tigers suckling piglets. All slightly strange but good for children, and the whole site is shady, with plenty of side-sights, such as camels, wallabies, rabbits and a few tame chimpanzees. It is easy to fill a whole day here.

The zoo is also a major crocodile breeding centre with racks

Camels at the Sri Racha Tiger Zoo

of eggs incubating year round and from May to August children can hatch out croc eggs in their hands.

Don't expect a private experience: the zoo is big and slick, packed out with coachloads every day, but your children will be spellbound.

Open *daily 8am–6pm. Shows 9am–5pm, pick up schedule from ticket office.* **Admission** *350B adults, 200B under 1.2m, free under 1.* **Credit** *MC, V.* **Amenities** *café, gift shop.*

Thunder Rock Dinosaur Park
OVERRATED ALL AGES

349\5 Moo 12, Nong Prue, Sukhumvit Road, South Pattaya, ☎ *03870 6055.*

If your children are into dinosaurs they might like this rather strange attraction – a park dotted with life-sized replicas of long-extinct species, some animated to a moderately convincing degree. It is possible to take elephant tours around the park and a rather sad selection of crocs lurk around a grubby pool, but it's a bit of a work in progress. If current plans to add a waterpark and minigolf course proceed the entry fee will represent better value.

Open *daily 10am–8pm.* **Admission** *350B adults, 250B under 1.3m, free under 0.9m.* **Amenities** *café.*

Underwater World ★★
ALL AGES

22/22 Moo 11, Sukhumvit Road, Nongprue, Banglamung, Chonburi 20260, ☎ *03875 6879, www.under waterworldpattaya.com. Central to Pattaya but on the main inland highway.*

'Voyage to the bottom of the sea but not get wet' says the somewhat laboured catchline, which does no justice to Pattaya's aquarium which features a 100m underwater acrylic-walled tunnel. Slick, modern and popular, this is the best of the aquariums in the east of the country. The experience is fully interactive with a petting pool, a shark and ray pool, and you can even dive with sharks for an extra 3000B.

Underwater World is priced for the international market and Thai tourists are more likely to go to the much less expensive aquarium run by the Thai Fisheries Department at Ban Phe, near the ferry piers for Koh Samet.

Open *daily 9am–6pm, last admission 5.30pm,* **Feeding times** *Coral Reef Tank 10am, 2.30pm, Shark and Ray Tank 11am, 3.30pm, Shipwreck Tank 10.30am, 2pm* **Admission** *360B adults, 280B children, under 0.9m free.* **Credit** *MC, V.* **Amenities** *café, gift shop.*

White Elephants

Elephants are hugely significant in Thai culture. They appear on the navy's flags, royal crests and bottles of beer. Albino elephants are even more revered: when born they immediately become the property of the King although it takes several years to authenticate if they are white enough (and genteel enough in character) to be considered truly 'white'.

Previous kings are noted for how many white elephants they accrued during their reigns: the current monarch has 14, one of which lives in the Royal Palace.

Being considered royal, the creatures cannot be put to work, taught to paint or dance, or be made into handbags. Being elephants, however, they eat a great deal and live for 70 years or more.

Should the King of Thailand present you with a white elephant it's a great honour but a financial obligation that will last for generations, giving rise to the phrase's current English meaning of large but ultimately useless.

Other Attractions in Pattaya

There are two venues for bungee jumping. Take a leap from 50m up, day or night, over a lake at **Jungle Bungee** (℡ *07833 6655*, 1600B first jump) near Jomtien, or at **Pattaya Bungee Jump** on Thepprasit Road (℡ *03830 0608*) that also offers reverse bungee and is attached to Pattaya's main go kart race track (with child karts available) and paint ball combat ground. Go kart rental is for 10 minutes at a time, with children's karts starting at 200B and separate courses for different skill and age levels (℡ *03842 2044*, 9.30am–6.30pm).

Tenpin bowling is available at two air-conditioned venues, open 10am until 2pm, prices ranging from 50B–80B per game depending on day and time. **Pattaya Bowl** is in North Pattaya on Pattaya 2nd Road opposite the Palladium and **PS Bowl** is on the 3rd floor, Tops Super Market on Pattaya Central Road near Pattaya 2nd Road.

Five kilometres out of Pattaya at km 150.5 on Sukhumvit Road, **Lakeland Cable Water Ski** offers two hours of cable waterskiing for 300B adults, 250B children.

More spiritual children might find themselves drawn to the **Sanctuary of Truth** (206/2 Moo 5, Naklua, Banglamung, ℡ *03836 7229-30, www.sanctuaryoftruth. com*), an ambitious handcrafted timber building aiming to preserve and revive ancient knowledge, that task possibly aided by the chance to ride an elephant or horse, or take a trip on a carriage. They also have a few trained river dolphins but their show doesn't do much to advance the cause of world wisdom.

The Million Years Stone Park (📞 03824 9347-9, *www.thaistonepark.org*) includes a crocodile farm, head-in-croc displays, elephant rides, fire-swallowing shows and a collection of strangely shaped rocks.

Water-based opportunities are endless as you can hardly move along the beach for rental jetskis, banana boats and speedboats giving parascending rides.

For sailing the most widely available craft is the Laser, a fibreglass dinghy designed as a single hander. For more than one sailor there are Pringles and Hobie Cats, also available for rent at 500B–600B per hour, from **Wong Amat** in North Pattaya near the Ocean View Hotel, Surf House at Jomtien Beach, near Cobra Canata in North Jomtien.

Horseback riding is available at the **Horseshoe Point Resort & Country Club** (📞 03873 5050, *www.horseshoepoint.com*, just off the road to the Siam Country Club at 12km marker) in 1500 tropical acres, including dressage, polo, trail riding and easy ponies for children.

Diving from Pattaya is more rewarding than you might expect, with a number of wrecks just offshore: the most recent a Thai Navy ship scuttled in 2007. Reputable operators include the British-run **Real Divers**, Soi Welcome, Moo 12, Jomtien Beach Road, 20260, 📞 03823 2476, *www.real-divers.com* and **Seafari Diving Center**, 284/19, Soi 12, 20150, 📞 03842 9060, *www.seafari.co.th*.

Koh Samet

After the frenetic traffic of Pattaya – or indeed, Thailand in general – tiny Koh Samet will come as a huge relief. Less than 8km long, it has only a few hundred metres of tarmac road that fade quickly to dirt. With just a handful of taxis the biggest road hazard is rental quad bikes hired out to westerners.

Koh Samet coastline

KOH SAMET

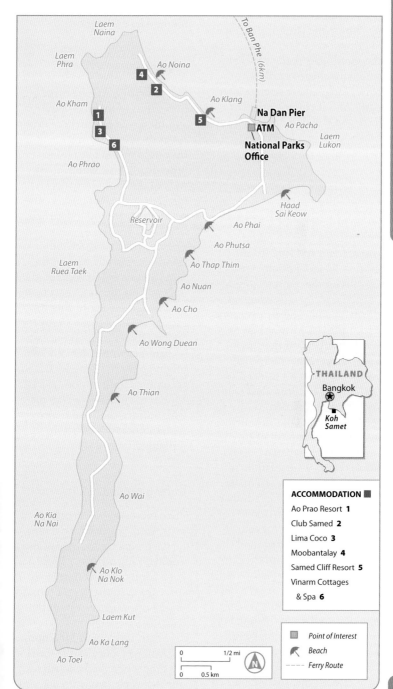

Laem Naina

Laem Phra

Ao Noina

4

2

Ao Kham

Ao Klang

1

5

3

6

Ao Phrao

Na Dan Pier

ATM Ao Pacha

National Parks Office

Laem Lukon

To Ban Phe (6km)

Reservoir

Haad Sai Keow

Ao Phai

Ao Phutsa

Laem Ruea Taek

Ao Thap Thim

Ao Nuan

Ao Cho

Ao Wong Duean

THAILAND

Bangkok

Koh Samet

Ao Thian

Ao Wai

Ao Kia Na Nai

Ao Klo Na Nok

Laem Kut

Ao Ka Lang

Ao Toei

ACCOMMODATION ■

Ao Prao Resort **1**

Club Samed **2**

Lima Coco **3**

Moobantalay **4**

Samed Cliff Resort **5**

Vinarm Cottages & Spa **6**

■ Point of Interest

✦ Beach

----- Ferry Route

0   1/2 mi

0   0.5 km

Getting There

If travelling from Bangkok leave by 2pm at the latest if you hope to get across to Koh Samet. Even the speedboats that greet clients who have already booked at the better lodges don't operate after dark. And if you miss the last ferry you will end up having to find a hotel in a hurry on the mainland.

Visitor Information

If you're looking for tourist information on Koh Samet you've left it too late: its official TAT (8.30am–4.30pm, ☎ 03865 5420) is on the main road 8km outside the city of Rayong on the mainland. There's a National Park Visitor Centre at Hat Sai Kaew, just beyond the check-point that charges 200B park entry fee, 100B for under 14s, under fours free, but can't help with accommodation.

If it is a weekend this might be a problem as most of the resorts will already have been booked out. With a family in tow it is much better to make reservations directly in advance – see the hotel listings below – or as a final resort use the tour operators who hang around the piers where you board the ferry to the island. Their plastic-folder brochures will at least give you some idea of the resort you're booking, and save you long hot walks between potentially full resorts.

There are taxis on Koh Samet, with rather expensive established rates. A friendly driver might be your final opportunity to find a room in an emergency.

Orientation

Not many visitors here make a huge effort to find their way around. Once you've chosen your resort there are few overwhelming reasons to move. The busiest beaches are those within an easy walk of the cheap-ferry dock at Na Dang pier, with bucket rum cocktails on sale around various live-music venues.

Family-oriented accommodation is expensively best on the most remote of the beaches, the only one on the west coast being Ao Prao. There are further less expensive alternatives on Ao Wong Duan Beach on the east.

Families with older children might go for the densely packed accommodation options of Hat Sai Kaew, close to Na Dan pier, with a wider choice of resorts, restaurants and bars within walking distance.

Getting Around

Here most *songthaews* operate as taxis, with expensive fixed rates for each possible journey printed out helpfully on signs. These are good for families as they have space for even the largest brood on the open bench seats at the rear.

There are scooters for rent by Na Dan pier, but the dirt roads are simply not good enough to pile the whole family on one and drive off, and the step mud tracks are lethal when wet. Quad bikes (also available by Na Dan pier), can cope, but you'll end up shuttling your family around in shifts. The British Consulate reports an increasing incidence of accidents on quad bikes which are heavy and dangerous if flipped. If the heat is not oppressive it's a good place to walk.

There are no car rental agencies as the unmade island roads are unsuitable.

Fast Facts

ATM This is on the tarmac road leading from Na Dang pier. It often runs out of cash and the rates given by island resorts are poor, so best change before you arrive.

Health There is a small Health Centre (℡ 03864 4111) on the Na Dan road, which has a limited stock of medicines. In case of any major problem you'll be referred to a mainland Rayong Hospital (℡ 038612999).

Internet Access is limited, though there are two cafés on Na Dan Road that offer slow-speed access, and some of the more expensive lodges offer Internet, though not lightning fast.

Post Office The nearest Koh Samet gets to a post office is a desk at the Naga Bungalows (℡ 03864 4035) south of Had Sai Kaew.

Safety Items have been reported missing from guest house shacks. Strangely it seems to be the cheapest establishments that are most often affected, and it is far from clear that the offenders are always Thai.

What to See & Do

Koh Samet's pleasures are invariably simple, low-key and water-based: sailing Laser boats, heading out in sea canoes, going on fishing expeditions. Most of the beaches have local operators with rates clearly marked on boards by the beach.

Diving is not very rewarding: there's rarely good visibility and what coral there is tends to be shallow: you're better off with a snorkel.

Oasis Seaworld ★ FIND
AGES 5 AND UP

48/2 Moo 5, Paknam Laemsing, Chantaburi 22130, ℡ 03949 9222, www.oasisseaworld.net (in Thai), bookings easier through www.swim withdolphinsthailand.com.

Well off the beaten track on the waters between Koh Samet and Koh Chang, this is a unique refuge for Irrawaddy blue dolphins and pink bottlenose dolphins rescued from the fishing nets off the Gulf of Thailand. Since capture they have been trained to balance balls, catch rings and do other standard dolphin tricks in a display that runs five times a day. Then there is the opportunity for everyone – including children over five if they're brave enough – to swim with these captivating mammals. There aren't many visitors – its location in Laem Sing in Chantaburi Province is not touristic and too far off the beaten track – but the experience is charming, low-key and very Thai.

The water isn't particularly clear but this is for a reason: it is mimicking their natural surroundings and, in clear water, the pink bottlenose dolphins often get sunburn.

If it seems a long way to travel, bear in mind the nearest alternative place to do this is probably in Miami.

Diving Thailand in Pattaya occasionally run day-trips to Oasis Seaworld, leaving at 7am and costing 2300B per person. Contact them on ☏ 06558 7137 or through *www.divingthailand. com*.

Open *daily 9am–6pm. Show times 9am, 11am, 1pm, 3pm, 5pm. Swimming with dolphins 9.45am, 11.45am, 1.45am, 3.45am.* **Admission** *180B per person: swimming with dolphins 400B extra.* **Amenities** *café.*

Koh Chang

Development came late to this island, second only to Phuket in size, comfortably bigger than Koh Samui and the largest of 52 islands set in a marine park near the border with Cambodia. While the finest beaches have attracted a number of guest houses and hotels much of the interior is still untouched and undeveloped. Despite occasional oases of luxury, it's a good place to look for an older style, unspoilt Thailand, albeit with a few mozzies and bugs.

Getting There

For Koh Chang there is an airport at Trat (code TDX, ☏ 03952 5299), served by flights from Bangkok with Bangkok Airways, which saves a gruelling drive from the capital that, especially if leaving in rush hour, would strain most families.

From the airport a minivan service links Ao Thammarat pier on the Laem Ngop coast for the half-hour ferry out to the island.

Which ferry you take will depend on where you choose to stay.

Visitor Information

Koh Chang's TAT (8.30am–4.30pm, ☏ 03959 7259) is on the mainland, on the Naem Ngop coast close to the Old Harbour Pier, with information about the many ferry services out to the island, some seasonal, and accommodation options.

Publications

The *Koh Chang Guidebook*, (*www.koh-chang.com*) is an annual travel magazine.

Fast Facts

ATMs Along with exchange bureaux ATMs are found on all the major beaches.

KOH CHANG

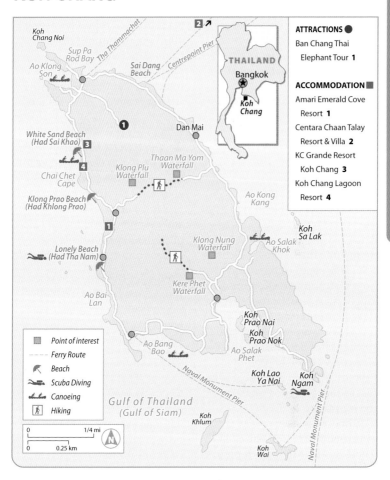

ATTRACTIONS ●
Ban Chang Thai
  Elephant Tour **1**

ACCOMMODATION ■
Amari Emerald Cove
  Resort **1**
Centara Chaan Talay
  Resort & Villa **2**
KC Grande Resort
  Koh Chang **3**
Koh Chang Lagoon
  Resort **4**

Koh
Chang Noi
Tha Thammachat
Sup Pa
Rod Bay
Sai Dang
Beach
Centrepoint Pier
THAILAND
Ao Klong
Son
Bangkok
Koh
Chang
1
Dan Mai
White Sand Beach
(Had Sai Khao) **3**
Thaan Ma Yom
Waterfall
4
Klong Plu
Waterfall
Chai Chet
Cape
Ao Kong
Kang
Klong Prao Beach
(Had Khlong Prao)
1
Klong Nung
Waterfall
Koh
Sa Lak
Ao Salak
Khok
Lonely Beach
(Had Tha Nam)
Kere Phet
Waterfall
Ao Bai
Lan
Koh
Prao Nai
Koh
Prao Nok
Ao Bang
Bao
Ao Salak
Phet
Koh Lao
Ya Nai
Koh
Ngam
Naval Monument Pier
Gulf of Thailand
(Gulf of Siam)
Koh
Khlum
Naval Monument Pier
Koh
Wai

■ Point of interest
--- Ferry Route
Beach
Scuba Diving
Canoeing
Hiking

0   1/4 mi
0   0.25 km

Chemists There are two at Hat Sai Khao and there is a branch of the Bangkok Hospital Group, the 24-hour Koh Chang International Clinic (☎ 03955 1555), south of Hat Sai Khao.

Internet Most of the roadside settlements backing popular beaches on Koh Chang have Internet cafés. Access by Thai standards is slightly expensive at 40B per hour.

Post Office At the southern end of Hat Sai Khao (☎ 03955 1240).

Safety As on Koh Samet, items have gone missing from cheaper lodges.

Orientation

Your experience of Koh Chang will depend on where you stay. The most attractive beaches are generally on the western coast, looking out over the gulf, with Hat Sai Khao the most developed and Khlong Phrao quieter. Watch out for jellyfish on this coast in April and May.

The island's beaches are at their best at high tide, when the postcard pictures are always taken. At low tide it's a long walk to the water and even then more of a wade than a swim.

Getting Around

Koh Chang is simple to navigate: there is only a single road that almost circles the island, though the final 10km stretch across the south of the island has been under construction for so long it must now be regarded as stalled. Shared *songthaews* run round this road (40B per person, surcharge for detours to particular resorts), most commonly from the ferry piers of the northeast to the developed beaches of the southwest.

Some of the ferries take cars, so if you have rented one elsewhere it is easy to bring it on to the island, but 4WD vehicles are preferable.

What to See & Do

The diving is quite good around Koh Chang but it's a dangerous activity, even for adults, with the nearest recompression facilities at Pattaya, four potentially fatal hours along the coast. Visibility is best from November through May.

Snorkelling cruises to outer islands can be arranged from the main beaches, typically costing 400B per person including equipment rental.

Inland there are a number of waterfalls and three elephant trekking camps.

Elephant Tour Camps

● **The Ban Chang Thai**
ALL AGES (📞 *084 863 8185*, 📞 *089 891 7253*, 📞 *03955 1474*). One-hour treks 500B per person, two-hour trek including river and mountain trekking and elephant bathing 900B. Rates include transfer from your hotel.

● **Chang Chutiman Tour** (Near Klong Prao Beach, 📞 *089 939 6676*). Daily 8am–5pm. Two-hour treks 900B, one-hour trek 500B (children under five free).

● **Klong Son Elephant Camp** (Jungle Way, 14 Moo 3 *www.jungleway.com*). Half-day tours 8.30am–11.30am, 900B including transfers, drinking water for riders, and bananas and coconuts for the elephants or possibly shorter rides for children at lower prices.

FAMILY-FRIENDLY ACCOMMODATION

Pattaya

EXPENSIVE

The fading appeal of Pattaya's traditional sex industry, combined with the sheer number of hotel bedrooms that need, somehow, to be filled keeps rates very competitive. You can expect more for your money here than in any comparable Thai resort.

Amari Orchid Resort & Tower ★★

Pattaya Beach: Pattaya Beach Road, Pattaya 20150, 📞 03841 8418, www. amari.com.

This popular resort hotel is at the quiet northern end of Pattaya Bay, with five-star accommodation – all with seaviews and balconies – in the 'Ocean Tower' and four-star rooms in the 'Garden Wing'. The hotel has 15 family rooms in the Ocean Tower which has a cooler, more contemporary feel, but Garden Wing rooms are slightly bigger and also interconnect if required.

The hotel provides children's menus, 24-hour room service and babysitting on request, and there's a children's club, playground and all the facilities you'd expect from a major beach resort.

Beach access is across the rather busy Pattaya Beach Road, but hotel staff are on hand to help stop traffic and keep stray children safe.

Rooms 527 rooms, suites and family rooms. Rates double 9000B–9800B, suite 11,000B. Credit AE, DC, MC, V. Facilities two swimming pools, three restaurants, two bars, spa, salon. In room broadband, satellite TV.

Pattaya Marriott Resort & Spa ★★

Pattaya Beach: 218 Beach Road, Pattaya 20150, 📞 03841 2120, www. marriott.com.

Though it's hard to imagine why families would want to be centrally located in Pattaya, the Marriott, right next door to the Royal Garden Plaza (home to Ripley's Believe It or Not), receives countless repeat family bookings so they must be doing something right.

Rooms are a good size, with wooden floors and balconies, and deluxe rooms have enough space for two adults and two children. Ask for a higher floor to make the most of the views.

The gardens and pools are lovely but often used by non-residents staying at cheaper hotels nearby: this makes it something of a struggle to find poolside space.

Rooms 293 rooms and suites. Rates double 8000B–12,540B, suite 20,140B– 35,720B. Credit AE, DC, MC, V. Amenities three restaurants, two bars, pool, two tennis courts, spa, watersports, games room. In room babysitting, satellite TV, fridge, coffeemaker.

Sheraton Pattaya

Pattaya Beach/Jomtien: 437 Phra Tamnak Road, Pattaya 20150, 📞 03825 9888, www.starwood hotels.com.

Some would maintain this is the only true five-star hotel in Pattaya and it is certainly one of the best in terms of facilities. Beautifully set on a clifftop between Pattaya and Jomtien, it has spectacular views and many swimming pools. This is just as well as the beach, reached by steep buggy-unfriendly steps, is small, fairly rocky and artificial.

Children's pool at Villa Baan-Nomella

With no long walks possible along the shoreline or any obvious pedestrian escape inland some families might start to feel claustrophobic after a while and it's more a hotel than a resort, with no slides on the pool, children's movie rooms or play areas, only a simple children's pool. I've heard teenage girls describing the Business Centre (which has Internet access) as an entertainment highlight in this all-too tranquil refuge from Pattaya City. Mind you their parents were probably very relieved.

Rooms *154.* **Rates** *double 8470B–16,550B, triple 10,400B–18,440B, inc. breakfast.* **Credit** *AE, DC, MC, V.* **Amenities** *three swimming pools.*

Villa Baan-Nomella

Minutes from Jomtien Beach, Pattaya. *www.holidaylettings.co.uk, ref: 32266.*

At some point you're likely to get tired of relentless professional hospitality and this could be the moment to guarantee some family privacy with a rental villa of your own. Villa Baan-Nomella is a four-bedroom property sleeping eight a few minutes from Jomtien Beach. You'll need a car and one is included in the rental. Each bedroom has an en suite bathroom, there is a cot, private child and adult pools, and a further shared adult pool. Linen and towels are provided and there's a fully equipped kitchen. The gardens are fully enclosed with 24-hour security.

Rates *£700–£805 per week or £115–£132 per night, including maid service.* **Credit** *MC, V.* **Facilities** *A/C, satellite TV, wifi, washing machine.*

MODERATE

A-One the Royal Cruise Hotel

Pattaya Beach: 499 North Pattaya Beach Road, Pattaya 20150, ☎ *03825 5560-2, www.a-onehotel.com.*

Children love the nautical theme of this unusual hotel, built in the shape of two ocean-going ships. Set directly on Pattaya Beach (but unfortunately separated from it by the busy beachfront road), it provides full resort facilities for those who don't mind a large-property atmosphere. Good value for its position.

Rooms 466. **Rates** double 2300B–5061B, family suite 5175B–8295B, inc. breakfast. **Credit** AE, MC, V. **Amenities** three restaurants, swimming pool and children's pool, live entertainment, spa, wifi hotspot, karaoke bar. **In room** A/C, TV, in-house movies, fridge/minibar, balcony.

Hard Rock Hotel

Pattaya Beach: 429 Moo 9, Pattaya Beach Road, Cholburi 20260, 📞 03842 8755-9, **www.hardrock hotels.net/pattaya**.

If you've got the sort of children who like to be entertained at all times, the Hard Rock Hotel will suit them – if not you. The large pool has a man-made beach and a child area where there are endless activities like rock climbing, aerobics and ball games, with live music often playing a part as early as three in the afternoon. The Children's Club is energetic and enthusiastic, with a highlight, for many the Saturday Night Foam Party.

On the downside the 1960s 'retro' furnishings can seem simply tacky and it's not the place to stay if you want to relax. To get away from the noise you'll need to cross the road to the beach.

Outside guests can check children aged 3–12 into the 'Lil Rock' children's club for 750B per day, hours are 8am–7pm Sunday to Thursday, 8am–10pm on Fridays and Saturdays.

Rooms 320 themed rooms. **Rates** double 4560B–7410B, triple 6060B–8880B. **Amenities** six restaurants and bars, Lil Rock Animators Club (children's club) (600B per day, 450B per half day), nightly entertainment, spa. **In room** A/C, satellite TV.

Panchalae Boutique Residences

Jomtien Beach: 46 Jomtien Beach Road, Jomtien 20260, 📞 03823 3178.

These spacious luxury two-bedroom, two-bathroom apartments are right on Jomtien beachfront and fully equipped for a family. Four beds are provided, with space for two more, alongside full kitchen facilities, balconies and daily cleaning service. With a contemporary design and furniture these are the perfect alternative to a traditional hotel.

Beyond your apartment there are few facilities beyond a small, somewhat overlooked central courtyard, but walk out of the security gates and the beach, floodlit at night, is just across the road.

Rooms 75. **Rates** 5600B per night. **Amenities** 24-hour security. **In room** A/C, full kitchen, satellite TV, wifi, daily cleaning and weekly linen.

Rabbit Resort ★ ★ FIND

Pattaya Beach/Jomtien: 318/84 Moo 13, Soi Dongtan Police Station, Jomtien 20260, 📞 03830 3303, **www.rabbitresort.com**.

Set in four acres of oceanfront gardens, this boutique property is an unexpectedly peaceful oasis, with Pattaya Beach on one side and Jomtien on the other. In the Rabbit Resort's expansive and peaceful rooms you'd hardly guess Pattaya's red-light frenzy was so close by.

The mainly two-storey villas, most with full kitchens and catering facilities, are beautifully crafted with wood and Thai silk fabrics, in tranquil grounds with a quiet, inexpensive restaurant. The hotel has its own deckchairs and bar service on Dongtan Beach, just across a road closed to traffic through the day. However, many guests spend all their time around the pools and in the resort's lush gardens.

The resort is named after its owners, Mr and Mrs Rabbit, the theme elaborated in porcelain rabbits dispensing salt and pepper in the restaurant, rabbit profiles tiled into the floor of the two pools (one for families, one for adults), and more rabbits embroidered into towels at this family-friendly haven.

It's not easy to find, especially during the day when the beach road is closed, and not all taxi-drivers are aware of its existence so take a card from reception before you go out to save confusion getting home.

Rooms 49. **Rates** double 5900B–6200B, inc. breakfast, Antique rooms sleeping up to four from 6200B–6700B, inc. breakfast for two, two-bedroom villas from 11,500B. **Credit** AE, DC, MC, V. **Amenities** restaurant, pools, babysitting, laundry. **In room** kitchens, silverware, crockery, antique furnishings and modern Thai art.

INEXPENSIVE

Inn House

322/1 Moo 10, Soi 13, Nongprue, Banglamung, Jomtien 20260, ☏ 03841 5717, www.innhousegroup.com.

This bright and modern hotel represents extremely good value, if little in the way of character. Rooms are well-specified, a good size and interconnect, and location is central, 100m from the beach and within easy strolling distance of Ripley's and other city centre attractions. There's even a pool, rather sunblasted on the roof, with great sea views.

Rooms 53 rooms and suites. **Rates** double 1046B–1240B, triple 1450B–1599B, inc. breakfast. **Credit** MC, V. **Amenities** restaurant, pool, gym. **In room** TV, fridge, 24-hour room service.

Koh Samet

Accommodation on Koh Samet seems to operate under something of a cartel: prices tend to match neighbouring properties rather than reflect the quality of rooms. There's a distant possibility that Koh Samet hoteliers are shy about encroaching on what is technically a National Park which might just explain why so many rooms are cramped, squashed too close to each other in dense little developments.

If visiting on important holidays such as Christmas, New Year, Songkran or Chinese New Year, you're bound to be hit with a room surcharge, and may be forced to pay for a compulsory and hideously overpriced 'Gala

Dinner'. Even on weekends and public holidays, some of which you might not have heard of, booking ahead is essential because it's not uncommon for all the resorts to fill up, in which case you might find yourself and your family paying over the odds for a miserable, mosquito-ridden inland shack with laughable toilet facilities in a remote unlit shed.

On Koh Samet the resort you choose should depend on your choice of beach, and for families it is worth picking one of the more remote bays: beaches that look good at dawn may not look so clever at lunchtime when countless speedboats have dumped off pasty day-trippers from Pattaya to ruin your desert-island dream.

All the beaches have something in their favour but there are too many small resorts to list here. Instead I focus on a couple of the best bays and beaches for families, running through the prime alternatives on each.

Ao Prao

Known as 'Paradise Bay', Ao Prao is a small beach set rather away from things on the northwest of the island with two very upmarket boutique resorts either side of a more affordable alternative. All provide complimentary speedboat transfers from the mainland, or it's a 200B private *songthaew* transfer from Na Dan pier on the island.

The bay has a dive centre and Jimmy's stall runs snorkelling trips.

EXPENSIVE

Ao Prao Resort

📞 *03864 4101-3, **www.samed resorts.com**. Once on Ao Prao the path leads down to this resort.*

Rooms are in detached villas, air-conditioned with TV. At the moment Ao Prao guests are allowed to use the pool at the Vinarm Cottages (they're part of

Ao Prao Resort

Vinarm Cottages and Spa

the same collection of Samet hotels), but this may not continue as Vinarm guests do resent it – you can almost hear them sniff.

Rates *double 6500B–11,000B, extra bed 1400B even in low season, more expensive the closer you get to the beach, two-bedroom family suite 18,200B–16,500B, rates including transfers from the mainland and American breakfast daily.*

Vinarm Cottages and Spa

📞 *0384 4104-7, www.sameresorts. com.*

The last resort on the bay, the most upmarket and the only one with a pool. Accommodation is in 20 villas.

Rates *double 9800B–13,900B, 1500B for an extra bed, inc. breakfast.*

> **MODERATE**

Lima Coco

📞 *02938 1811, www.limacoco.com.*

In the middle of the bay, spread up the hill, this is the mid-market

option. You can add extra beds but would struggle to fit one in the standard rooms. Instead you'll be looking at one of the more expensive rooms such as a deluxe.

Rooms *44.* ***Rates*** *double starting (at the back) at 2850B, extra bed 605B fitting in deluxe rooms from 4000B. Be clear on booking that tax and service is included.*

Ao Noi Na

The road from the Na Dan pier funnels travellers across the headland to Hat Sai Kaew, the party beach. Instead turn right and after 25 minutes you will reach Ao Noi Na beach, looking back towards the mainland. This is one of the quietest and nicest beaches, not so cut off that you're restricted to your lodge's restaurant, but with good accommodation as well.

> **MODERATE**

Club Samed

📞 *03864 4341-7, www.samed resorts.com.*

Struggles to fit more than one extra bed into rooms aimed at couples, including two lodges with pools.

Rooms *30.* ***Rates*** *2600B–3200B per bungalow, extra bed 950B, inc. breakfast.*

Moobantalay

📞 *081838 8682, www.moobantalay. com.*

Probably Koh Samet's best mid-market resort, with guest chalets set along or close to the beach.

Rooms 24. *Rates* pond villa 4700B–5500B, deluxe seaview villa 6600B–9000B, extra bed 1000B low season, 1500B high season. *Amenities* swimming pool.

Samed Cliff Resort

☎ 03864 4404, *www.samedcliff. com.*

Bungalows here are stepped up from the beach into the natural forest, and all have spectacular sea views, though the beach itself is a sandy downhill stroll. Newly renovated rooms have floor-to-ceiling glass windows and private balconies cooled by the sea breeze. Apart from the usual doubles, they also offer two-bedroom family suites, sleeping four, and a Kiang Talay Family Room with space for seven: per person per night this is something of a bargain for Koh Samet.

Rates double 1500B-2400B, family rooms sleeping four 3730B–4895B, Kiang Talay 3000B-4000B, all b&b, extra roll-out mats 350B, proper extra bed 500B. *Credit* MC, V.

Koh Chang

With the risks of dengue fever, malaria, sandflies and, from April to May jellyfish on the best, western beaches, I wouldn't recommend families staying in the cheapest beach hut accommodation here. Best choose somewhere that has air conditioning to knock out buzzy pests, believes in insecticides and has a well-trained, motivated staff to ensure your comfort and safety.

EXPENSIVE

Amari Emerald Cove Resort

Klong Prao Beach: 88/8 Moo 4, Tambol Koh Chang, King Amphur, Koh Chang 23170, ☎ *03955 2000, www.amari.com.*

This slick and sophisticated resort is stunningly set on Klong Prao Beach on Koh Chang's western coast. They spray the grounds daily with mosquito killer which is a good idea but doesn't completely address the problem of sandflies on the beach. The 50m main pool and separate children's pool do much to redress the issue. Superior rooms have space to sleep two adults and one child but you will have to upgrade to a deluxe room to get views of the sea, and tea- and coffee-making facilities. Larger families have a choice between renting interconnecting rooms or a suite. Both cost about the same but a suite elicits a more effusive reaction from the check-in staff.

Rooms 165 rooms and suites. *Rates* double 4854B–8932B, two under 12s with two adults max per room. *Credit* AE, MC, V. *Amenities* three restaurants, dive centre, kayaks, spa, fitness room, activity centre, room service, babysitting. *In room* cable TV, cots if required.

MODERATE

Centara Chaan Talay Resort & Villa ★ ★ FIND

Trat mainland facing Koh Chang. 4/2 Moo 9, Tambol Laem Krud, Amphur Muang, Trat 23000, ☎ *03952 1561-70, www.centarahotels resorts.com.*

Centara Chaan Talay Resort

This resort is on the mainland 40 minutes from Trat town and airport. Though it is not on Koh Chang itself, it has views of the island and is too good to be treated just an emergency fall-back for travellers who've missed the last ferry out to Koh Chang. All rooms are suites, with separate living rooms doubling easily as an extra bedroom, and up to two children under 12 eat free if their parents are staying half board. There are two restaurants or families can dine privately in a beachfront *sala* (pavilion).

Rooms 62. **Rates** *family suite villas 4600B–6000B, extra bed from 1100B for adults, 550B for children.* **Amenities** *spa, infinity pool and children's pool, complimentary watersports including windsurfing, snorkelling and sailing.* **In room** *A/C, flat-screen TVs with in-house movies, DVD player, tea- and coffee-making facilities.*

KC Grande Resort Koh Chang

Had Sai Khao Beach: 1/1 Moo 4 Baan Haad Sai Khao, Koh Chang

23170, 📞 *03955 1199*, **www.kckoh chang.com**.

Set on the best stretch of Sai Khao's beach, this is a relaxing traditional Thai beachfront bungalow setup, but with a few mod cons added. The resort has its own pool and well-maintained and equipped air-conditioned chalets. The showers are something of a let-down, but won't inflict too much damage on the island's chronic lack of water. There are plenty of restaurants within a sandy stroll, and if your budget will stretch to it the best rooms are the deluxe bungalows right on the beach, or for larger families there are two bigger buildings, one on the beach and one in the garden, that would fit several extra beds with ease.

Rooms 60. **Rates** *double 1800B–4000B, deluxe beachfront 4000B–7150B, extra bed 700B–900B, cot free.* **Amenities** *pool, restaurant.* **In room** *A/C, satellite TV, DVD, fridge.*

Koh Chang Lagoon Resort

Had Sai Khao Beach: Had Sai Khao, Tambon Koh Chang, Trat 23170, 📞 *03955 1201-2, www.kohchang lagoonresort.com.*

In the relatively busy setting of Had Sai Khao beach on the west of the island, the Koh Chang Lagoon resort is an excellent mid-range resort with comfortable, two-storey bungalows right on the beach and a newly built two-storey resort-style hotel. Unusually for Thai beach resorts, they've had the foresight to design in a few rooms not tailored to the nuclear couple, but large enough to cope with families of any size. At night the restaurant tables are set out on the sands, and children can play in the shallows.

Rooms *83 rooms and bungalows.* **Rates** *hotel room (new building) sleeping four 2500B–3500B, or sleeping six 3100B–4500B, bungalows from 1600B–2200B, with extra bed 500B.* **Credit** *MC, V.* **Amenities** *restaurant, Internet room.* **In room** *A/C.*

FAMILY-FRIENDLY DINING

Pattaya

Many years of sex tourism have focused Pattaya restaurants on romance. Even now children are something of a novelty.

Europeans like to be directly on the beach, so they don't get run over when crossing from their accommodation to the sea.

Thais like the road to run along the beach so there's easy access for snack vendors and mobile restaurants, and care much less about the traffic. Thus almost all Pattaya's hotels and restaurants are cut off from the beach by the busy Pattaya Road.

Alangkarn Pattaya Show `THAI`

Jomtient. 155km Sukhumvit Road, Pattaya, 📞 *03825 6000, www. alangkarnthailand.com.*

This huge cultural spectacular takes place in an auditorium seating 2000 just outside Pattaya, the restaurant alone seating 1000. If you're not scared of crowds this is the place to see dance, music and stylised, ballet-style *Muay Thai* fighting. In Thai *Alangkarn* means 'really big', and you'll understand why as the show proceeds with laser lighting and fireworks exploding on stage. Some children – and this adult – might find the pace a little slow, but unlike most of its equivalents around the country, it takes place early in the evening and condenses the experience into just one hour.

Open *4.45pm–8pm, daily except Wednesday. Show time 6pm–7pm.* **Admission** *900B per person show only, 1100B show and buffet dinner, children under 0.8m free, 0.8–1.2m 70%. 'Golden Seats' 200B extra.*

Dusit Thani Pattaya `THAI`

West Pattaya: 540/2 Pattaya Beach Road, Chonburi 20150, 📞 *03842 5611, www.dusit.com.*

The Dusit is about the only mainstream resort hotel in the

Alangkarn Pattaya Show

city centre to give directly on to the beach, so is a good choice if you want a top-class meal while still being able to let your children play safely in the sand.

Reservations not needed through the day. **Main courses** *400B–500B.* **Credit** *AE, MC, V.*

S&P Restaurant
INTERNATONAL/THAI

Level Two, Royal Garden Plaza, Moo 10, Beach Road, Pattaya, www.sandp.co.th.

Useful if you've just been to Ripley's, this little restaurant is part of a national Thai restaurant chain on level two of the Royal Garden Plaza. Family-friendly, it serves fantastic chocolate brownies alongside smoothies, hot breads and Thai dishes. They even produce their own cookbook, *Patara*, to let you relive the experience at home.

Open *daily 8am–7pm. Main courses from 300B, brownies 25B per plate.*

Sugar Hut **THAI**

Pattaya/Jomtien: 391/18 Moo 10, Tabphya Road, Chonburi, 20260, 0382511686, *www.sugar-hut. com.*

This is a great place to escape the craziness of downtown Pattaya. The Sugar Hut is a hilltop retreat far from any shops, facilities or the sea, where 28 one- and two-bedroom Ayutthaya-style bungalows are scattered around lush gardens. Service is notoriously slow but with three swimming pools for your children to frolic in it's hard to get too upset, and the cuisine, once it arrives, is delicious.

Main courses *from 400B.* **Credit** *MC, V.*

Thai House Restaurant Pattaya **THAI/CHINESE**

North Pattaya: 171/1 M 6 North Pattaya, Naklua, Banglamung, 03837 0579-81.

Music and traditional Thai dance is the central attraction at this 800-seat establishment that serves European, Chinese, Thai and vegetarian dishes.

Open *daily 11.30am–11.30pm. Show times 7pm–10pm.* **Main courses** *from 380B. Credit MC, V.*

5 The Andaman Coast: Phuket, Krabi & the Southern Islands

ANDAMAN COAST

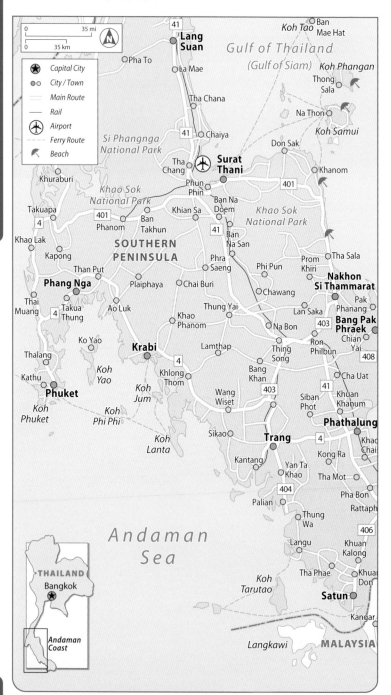

Tear-shaped Phuket is Thailand's largest island, a lush green and mountainous mass linked to the mainland by a causeway. Glorious beaches look west towards the Andaman Sea, and a rugged coastline to the east shelters the sheer rock outcrops of Phang-nga Bay. Once an outpost of rubber-tree plantations and tin mines, Phuket is where tourism started in Thailand, as overlanding backpackers discovered its long sweeping beaches.

Since then development has been rapid. Phuket Town in the east has become a major administrative centre while the western beaches have been intensively colonised by sophisticated beach resorts catering for well-heeled tourists on fly-in package holidays. What they find are a huge selection of world-class watersports, varied restaurants and superb golden beaches. This is not the place to look for simple inexpensive beach bungalows. If you prefer your pace slower then head north from the airport up to Khao Lak on the mainland Andaman coast, a quieter enclave driven back to nature by the 2004 Tsunami and only now rebuilding its tourist infrastructure.

Parallel with Thailand's narrow southern peninsula, the island of Phuket forms one side of one of the world's most stunning natural regions, the sheer limestone islands of Phang-nga Bay. Similar to the landscapes of Ha Long Bay in Vietnam and Guilin in China, they tower over clear, glimmering water with a distinctive greenish tinge.

This sheer, lost-world landscape continues on the mainland on the other side of the bay, between the towns of Phang-nga and Krabi, forming a dramatic backdrop to a series of small beaches, often reached only by boat. Eschewing the jet-skis and speedboats of Phuket, this stretch of coast feels far more tranquil, a relaxing succession of small beach resorts, fishing communities and remote backpacker haunts.

To the south of the bay the landscape softens, with the iconic Phi Phi Islands and the family-friendly wilderness of Koh Lanta fringed by beautiful, white-sand beaches.

Only this area's natural beauty has ensured its commercial success, as it has a very short season. Though the weather is invariably marvellous from November to March, in April the southwest monsoon brings heavy rains and whips up the seas and June to October it is often too rough to swim. Tourists flee to the more sheltered islands of the Gulf of Thailand – Koh Samui and Koh Phangan – and many of Phuket's resorts lie deserted. This can be a good time to visit. It doesn't rain all the time – or every day, and even though swimming in the sea can be dangerous, the climate is somehow gentler and less humid. Most importantly, hotel rates plunge and the frenetic high-season pace slows to island time.

ESSENTIALS

Getting There

By Air Phuket International Airport (☎ 07732 7230, information) is on the island's northwest coast, a modern and efficient place that deals with 15 flights a day from both Don Muang and Suvarnabhumi airports in Bangkok, domestic links to Chiang Mai, Krabi and Koh Samui, and international services from Far Eastern, Australian and European destinations. From Bangkok the flight takes one hour 20 minutes.

Airlines include Thai Airways (☎ 07621 1195 domestic, ☎ 07621 2499 international, *www.thaiair.com*); Bangkok Airways (for Koh Samui, ☎ 02265 5555, *www.bangkokair.com*); Air Asia (☎ 02515 9999, *www.airasia.com*); Nok Air (*www.nokair.com*), and One-Two-GO Airlines (*www.fly12go.com*).

There are banks, foreign exchange desks and car rental agencies at the airport. The meter taxi stand is to the right of the terminal on exiting: it takes between 45 minutes and an hour to drive to Phuket Town or Patong Beach and will cost between 500B and 800B, depending on your bargaining skills and where you are going.

Many resorts will pick you up from the airport. This can save a moment of taxi-rank stress, but usually costs twice the price.

There is now a bus service between the airport and Phuket Town bus terminal, costing 52B per person, from where you can catch buses to all the island's major beaches. From 9am–11pm there is a minibus service that runs to Patong, Kata and Karon, but at 250B+ per person for most families this is likely to cost as much a taxi and is less convenient.

By Bus Long-distance buses link Phuket with Bangkok's Southern Bus Terminal, with prices as low as 275B, but this is only recommended for seasoned travellers. Luxuries such as deafening all-night action films do little to disguise the fact that it is a 14-hour journey. Alternatively you can make the six-hour journey from Phuket to Surat Thani and then complete the journey with 12 hours in a sleeper train, but it is so much easier to fly or take the bus that few take this option. The intercity bus terminal (☎ 07621 1480) is just to the east of Phuket Town.

By Minivan Resort pickups and direct services to Khao Lak, Krabi and Surat Thani (for Koh Samui) make minivans a viable way to travel around the south. Tickets are sold by any tour operator or your hotel's front desk. A ticket to Surat Thani, for instance, will cost in the region of 250B.

By Boat Atmospheric and generally safe in season, the boats that run from the Rassada Harbour to Koh Phi Phi (1 hour 30 minutes–2 hours 30 minutes), Koh Lanta (4 hours 30 minutes) and Ao Nang (for Krabi, November to May only,

2 hours 30 minutes) can be fun for children but more often the trips seem a bit long. In the rough summer weather make sure you know where the life-jackets are.

Though there are timetables they're notoriously unreliable so leave plenty of time if you're using a ferry to connect with a flight, and check the schedule with a local travel agent when you buy the ticket.

VISITOR INFORMATION

The Tourism Authority of Thailand (TAT) has an office in Phuket Town (daily 8.30am–4.30pm, ☎ *07621 2213*) at 191 Klang Road in Phuket Town, but hotel concierges and tour desks also offer brochures and information.

Publications

There are plenty of free maps on offer, surrounded by advertisements. For those driving themselves the most detailed island map is published by Periplus and is available at book stalls and hotel boutiques. Free publications include *Phuket Food-Shopping-Entertainment*, *Phuket.com* (*www.phuket.com*) and *What's On South*.

Orientation

Travelling by car or coach you arrive at the north of Phuket island on Route 402 across the Sarasin Bridge. The road continues to the southeast of the island and Phuket Town.

The prime southwestern beaches of Kata, Karon and Patong are linked by a busy coast road, but this quietens in the north where you usually have to detour down to each beach.

In general, rather than ringing the island, public transport radiates from Phuket Town, so if you want to visit neighbouring coastlines you may end up having to travel right across the island and back.

You don't get a strong sense of Thailand in the western resorts: to experience the country take the time to explore Phuket Town, with its historic Portuguese-influenced heart, and visit the Khao Phra Thaew Royal Wildlife & Forest Reserve in the northeast of the island, renowned for its flora and fauna.

The Western Beaches

Phuket's spectacular beaches are mainly on the west of the island. The southern strands are the most spectacular, with jungled green landscapes dropping sheer down to glorious golden sands. The centre of Phuket's tourist industry is Patong in the southwest, just across the island from Phuket Town. Despite its stretch of beach, these days Patong is a major Thai town and not an obvious choice for families. The beach is busy with jetskis, parascenders and banana boats and the atmosphere frenetic.

Patong Beach, Phuket

Strangely enough there are a couple of good family resorts stuck in the middle of this, and those who stay in them love the experience, returning year after year. And with a wide selection of restaurants, bars and dive shops this is the place for people who like resort facilities without the isolation – a place for an exciting holiday rather than a relaxing one.

Across the headland to the south of Patong and after tiny Relax Bay, Karon Beach is quieter. The big franchise fast-food chains have yet to arrive and it's all the better for it.

Kata Beach, next, is an excellent family choice as the water is shallow for 30m to sea, and an offshore island – Koh Poo, its name raises several giggles with some children – has great snorkelling. If your children are strong enough swimmers to be able to tackle surfing, this is the place, as from May to October the rollers are the best in Thailand.

Finally, deep in the south, Nai Harn Beach is a little gem. It's one of the most beautiful on the island and ideal for families from November through to April. Watch out in low season though, as undertows can be vicious.

The Southern Beaches

Around the island's southern tip on the eastern side are Rawai Beach and Chalong Beach, which catch the sunset views and have some of the best luxury resorts on the island. Their location means they are close to interesting Phuket Town and further from the madness of Patong, but the sea here is muddy and better suited for mooring boats than swimming – no match for the clarity of the open Andaman Sea.

The Northern Beaches

Back on the western side, north of Patong you cross a major headland to reach Kamala Beach, one of the best for families, with a gently shelving beach dipping into azure waters fading to blue.

Surin Beach just to the north is known as 'Millionaire's Row', thanks to the number of high-end resorts and luxury villas, but that's something of a relief compared to the beach that follows. Bangtao Beach is dominated by the huge Laguna Resort complex, an 'integrated resort' of five major resorts that together provide a huge range of international-standard facilities – something between theme-park bliss and holiday hell. The northern end of the beach, where the land slopes more gently, and casuarina trees replace the southern palms, is thankfully undeveloped.

Travelling north, Nai Thon Beach is quiet, with just a few developments so far. The final northwestern beaches are Nai Yang and Mai Khow, backed respectively by the Sirinart National Park and the airport. With the sea tamed by an off-shore reef it's a great place to drive out for a quiet swim and a picnic away from the crowds.

The reef fades away to the north but this is turtle nesting country: development is supposedly banned but a couple of large resort developments, including the Marriott Hotel and the Sala, have built substantial resorts.

The turtles, increasingly and unsurprisingly, seem to be choosing to stay away.

Getting Around

This can become an expensive business in Phuket. Perhaps because it is the richest province in Thailand restrictive practices thrive in public transport, and there even seems to have been an element of inflation in the terminology of transport. Ask for a *tuk-tuk* here and you'll be directed to one of the open-backed, bench-seat vehicles, called *songthaews* everywhere else. Ask for a *songthaew* and you'll be pointed at a brightly coloured, full-sized bus – and even then it won't take you to the next beach along, only to Phuket Town, where you'll have to change and track 20 minutes back.

The short inter-beach hops are sewn up by the open-backed bench-seaters that would, anywhere else in the country, be called baht buses and carry several passengers cheaply. Not here. All charge set, expensive fares and act as taxis, without the meter. Even if you find a *tuk-tuk* the price doesn't budge – and it goes up sharply after dark.

Phuket is not a great place to drive – accidents are common and often there are parking charges – but if you're planning an active visit and want to see around the island, a rental car is much less stressful than being bled dry, several hundred baht at a time, every time you go out.

PHUKET

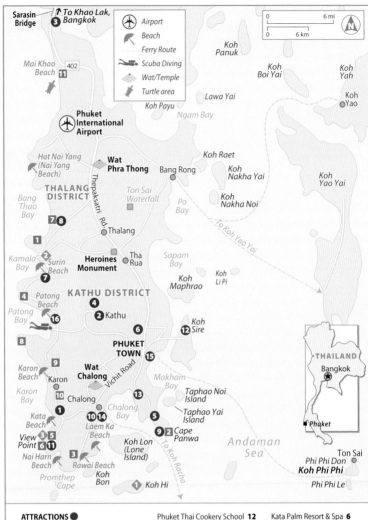

ATTRACTIONS ●

Dino Park Mini-Golf **1**

Jungle Bungee **2**

Khao Sok National Park **3**

Lost Lagoon Waterpark **4**

Phuket Aquarium **5**

Phuket Butterfly Garden & Insectarium **6**

Phuket Fantasea **7**

Phuket Laguna Riding Club **8**

Phuket Pro Dive **9**

Phuket Riding Club **10**

Phuket Surf **11**

Phuket Thai Cookery School **12**

Phuket Zoo **13**

River Rovers **14**

Saphan Hin Stadium **15**

World Bungy Patong **16**

ACCOMMODATION ■

Amanpuri **1**

Cape Panwa **2**

Evason Phuket & Six Senses Spa **3**

Holiday Inn Patong Beach **4**

Kata Beach Resort & Spa **5**

Kata Palm Resort & Spa **6**

Laguna Beach Resort **7**

Le Meridien Phuket **8**

Moevenpick Resort & Spa **9**

Ramada Phuket **10**

Sala Phuket **11**

DINING ◆

Coral Island Beach Club **1**

Da Ali Restaurant **2**

Mom Tri's Boathouse **3**

Car rental companies at the airport include Avis (☎ 07635 1243), Hertz (☎ 07632 8545) and the slightly cheaper Budget (☎ 07620 5396), which also has counters at several hotels. Plan on spending up to 1800B per day to include – and you should – insurance.

Family-Friendly Events

Phuket Vegetarian Festival

'Don't try this at home' might be a good warning before watching the bizarre procession of pierced, bleeding devotees at the end of Phuket's most important religious festival organised by its Chinese temples. After nine days eschewing meat, alcohol and sex, worshippers dress in white and retreat to their temples, where drum rhythms induce a trance state. In this transcendent state they pierce their cheeks with objects – broom handles, fishing rods or flag poles have been tried – walk over hot coals, and climb ladders with bladed rungs. Meanwhile evil spirits are kept away with loud drumming and noisy fireworks. Children with sensitive hearing will be scared off, if they haven't already been traumatised enough by the strange sights they've seen.

This astonishing tradition dates back to many Thai's Chinese roots, though in China itself such practices have long since disappeared. Dancing and singing are key parts of the ceremony, particularly at Wat Jui Tui on Thanon Ranong in Phuket town.

Miraculously, the next day none of the participants seem to bear a mark of their ordeal.

Every year at the start of the ninth lunar month of the Chinese calendar (Sep–Nov). More information on www.phuketvegetarian.com.

Loi Krathong

With the sea on every side, this national festival takes on a slightly different cast in Phuket. As the sun sets and the moon appears in the sky, floating candles are launched on every river, lake and waterway in a spectacular display that children always love. The belief is that if your *krathong* floats away you will have a year of good luck. This means the west coast is the place to be as winds are generally offshore.

The best way to engage the family in this is to let the children buy their own *krathongs* – flower-covered mini boats on sale everywhere at this time of year – and personalise them with a few 'magic' personal items such as nail clippings, baby teeth or strands of hair. Then in the evening head down to the beach. Launching your own little candlelit crafts among the host of others carrying the prayers of thousands of Thais is the ultimate way to bring your family close to this intensely superstitious culture.

Nov, on the night of the full moon.

FAST FACTS

ATMs These abound in Patong and other resort areas. The major banks have their headquarters in Phuket Town along Ranong and Rasada roads, with branches at Chalong, Nai Harn, Kata, Karon and Patong beaches. Money changers are at the airport, shopping areas on each beach and at most resorts.

Hospitals The three major private hospitals all have English-speaking staff. Bangkok Phuket Hospital (2/1 Hongyok-Uthit Road in Phuket Town, 07625 4421) has high-quality facilities, a specialist dental clinic and an outside clinic for tourists in Laguna Canal Village, Laguna Phuket (07632 5442). Phuket International (07624 9400) is next to the Big C Shopping Mall, outside Phuket Town. Mission Hospital (Thepkasattri Road, Phuket Town (07621 2386) also offers good medical services.

Internet Most small cafés and tour agencies offer good Internet access. In Patong they get cheaper farther from the beach. Walk five minutes inland and you'll get access for 1B per minute.

Post Office The main General Post Office is in Phuket Town (07621 1020) at the corner of Thalang and Montri roads.

WHAT TO SEE & DO

Children's Top 10 Attractions

❶ **Power** snorkel amongst the corals. See p 132.

❷ **Catch** a wave at Kata. See p 130.

❸ **Cable**-ski Kathu. See p 129.

❹ **Canoe** through caves into the islands of Phang-nga Bay. See p 133.

❺ **Mooch** round the mangroves. See p 132.

Canoeing Thailand's 'Hongs'

Dino Park Mini-Golf

6 Homestay with a Thai family. See below.

7 Play crazy golf with dinosaurs. See below.

8 See an elephant extravaganza. See p 130.

9 Climb a sheer limestone cliff. See p 142.

10 Chill on a remote castaway island. See p 183.

Attractions

Phuket

Dino Park Mini-Golf ★★ FIND
AGE 5 AND UP

Karon Beach, up the hill heading south towards Kata on the right, 📞 *07633 0625, www.dinopark.com.*

There are plenty of golf courses in Thailand but let's face it, it's just too hot. Mini-golf, on the other hand, is taken seriously, and this slightly deranged course, set on a shady hillside above Karon Beach, is a delight. There's an underlying Flintstone theme that extends to the staff uniform, and 18 little carpeted greens that thread through and around vast fibreglass dinosaurs in a primeval landscape of broad-leafed tropical shrubs and gentle cooling waterfalls and streams. Children under eight will struggle to use the putters provided but infants coming along as spectators are free. If you're still playing at 8pm there's even a volcano that erupts.

After being photographed on a Fred Flintstone car most children love being served by Thelma lookalikes with hearty dinosaur fare – and a local baby elephant often comes round for a snack. Meals include Thai classics and Dinoburgers,

Open 10am–midnight. Rates 200B adults, 120B children under 1.2m. Amenities restaurant, main courses from 200B.

Homestay in a Thai Fishing Village ★★★ FIND ALL AGES

Andaman Discoveries, 120/27 Sukapiban 3 Road, Moo 1, Kuraburi, Phang Nga Province, Thailand 82150, 📞 *087 917 7165,* 📞 *081 243 3848, www.andamandiscoveries.com.*

Homestays, where you stay with a local Thai family and share their meals and daily activities, have been around for a while but what is new is to offer the experience to families. Children are excellent ice-breakers and if you're travelling as a family you will end up trailing a little gang of local children everywhere you go. As the young interact naturally and openly, the atmosphere quickly softens, helping you to relax into the village environment.

This project, set up in a remote area untouched by tourism in the wake of the 2004 Tsunami, is particularly well-run. A facilitator will stay in another village house and will help with translations when and if required, as well as organising a whole host of activities including replanting mangroves, batik painting, cashew shelling (and eating), fishing on the beach and swimming at sunset.

The greatest revelation for me was the food. Each meal was a great Thai feast, with seven or eight dishes of lightly spiced seafood and skinny village chickens – perfect for the heat and the natural, easy lifestyle.

Our homestay here was a highlight of our last visit to Thailand. Kuraburi is three hours drive north of Phuket and at least one from Khao Lak. This is too far for a day-trip and a three- or five-night stay is much more rewarding.

Homestays can be arranged through KohYaoHomestay at http://kohyao travel.com/homestay.htm. Five-day family tours with Andaman

Discoveries start at 26,500B for a family of two adults and two children, including transfers from Kuraburi, a translator/guide and full board accommodation. A taxi from Phuket Airport will cost in the region of 3000B. Other homestays can be arranged in more visited villages on Koh Yao Noi island and involve less travel time. Longtail ferries travel three times a day from Bang Rong Pier on Phuket's east coast, charging 50B per person.

Khao Sok National Park ★
ALL AGES

Siam Safari Nature Tours, 45 Moo 10, Chao Fa Road, Chalong, 83130, ☏ 07628 0107, www.khaosok.com.

Of all Thailand's stunning national parks, Khao Sok is the most dramatically beautiful. In a landscape eerily similar to Guilin in China it rises in sheer limestone outcrops swathed in tropical rainforest.

At its heart is Chiao Lan Lake, dotted with more than 100 sheer-sided limestone islands. It's fantastic for naturalists, with the world's largest flower, the Raffelsia, growing to a metre across and weighing up to 7kg, a huge number of insects, and wild elephant, tiger, gibbon and pangolin all permanent residents.

Best for children are perhaps the brightly coloured frogs and the experience of drifting around on inflatable Zodiacs.

Exploration is by elephant, on foot, by jeep or by canoe. Khao Sok is three hours' drive north of Phuket and one hour from Khao Lak. It can either be visited in a day-trip or, much better, spend three days with two nights in simple jungle-lodge accommodation.

Rates *One-day tours from 3200B adults, 2240B children; three-day tours from 9750B–11,250B adults, 6750B–6950B children.*

Lost Lagoon Waterpark ★★
FIND **AGE 6 AND UP**

Phuket Cable Ski, 86/3 Moo 6, Vichitsongkram Road, Kathu, 83120, ☎ *07620 2525-7, http://phuket cableski.com.*

On a large shallow lake just 2m deep, Phuket Cable Ski offers hours of family fun. Young children might find the take-off too sudden, but older ones will revel in sending up huge tracks of spray as they follow the power around the water, using wake boards, knee boards, ski discs and trick boards. Expert tuition is available and Cable Ski Kathu is just 10 minutes' drive from Patong.

Open *daily 10am–6.30pm.* **Rates** *30 minutes 500B, 2 hours 1000B, full day 1500B.* **Credit** *MC, V.*

Phuket Butterfly Garden & Insectarium ★ ALL AGES

71/6 Samkong, 83000, ☎ *07621 0861, www.phuketbutterfly.com.*

This lovely butterfly farm was a hit with my children, especially the acre of netted gardens, filled with butterflies of every colour and size. There is also a winning display of insects of all kinds, including a fascinating silk museum that showed silkworms at work and the manufacturing process.

Open *daily 9am–5pm.* **Rates** *300B adults, 150B children aged 4–10, under fours free.* **Amenities** *café.*

Phuket Fantasea ALL AGES

99 Moo 3, Kamala Beach, Kathu, 83120, ☎ *07638 5000, www.phuket-fantasea.com.*

There are times when parents just have to defer to their children's (arguably) better taste. Phuket Fantasea is perhaps one of these occasions – a lavish performance involving a cast of

Phuket Butterfly Garden

thousands, processions of synchronised elephants and acrobats flying through the air. Children love it – it firmly established elephants as my daughter's favourite animal – while adults, already reduced in status by having their cameras and phones confiscated at the gate, are more likely to cringe.

There's a buffet meal before the show, but you can save money by missing this: the show itself is expensive enough.

Before and after the main show there is something of a carnival outside, with brightly lit fantasy buildings and handicraft stores. Very little is free, however, and there are plenty of opportunities for parents to fritter away cash. So although the show is slick and spectacular, and no doubt great fun if you have the budget, if cash is in short supply you're likely to feel fleeced.

There's the chance to cheat back a little after the show when a tiger cub, sedated with a baby bottle, will be placed in your child's arms for about five seconds while a company photographer takes their picture. The same goes for elephants draping their trunks over your children's shoulders. If you don't buy the photo – and heaven knows when you'd ever need it – the experience comes free.

*Open daily except Thurs, park 5.30pm–11.30pm, buffet dinner 6.30pm, main show 9pm. Arrive 20 minutes early as the crowds mean it takes a while to get in to both the buffet and show: it also takes time for them to confiscate your camera (although not as long as it takes to get back after the show). The performance is one hour 15 minutes. Reservation required as it sells out in season. **Admission** show only 1500B adults and children over four. Under fours free (no seat). Dinner and show 1900B adults, 1700B children 4–12. Transfers 150B per person. **Credit** AE, MC, V.*

Phuket Surf ★★ AGE 6 AND UP

Kata Beach above the Boat House Restaurant, ☎ 07285 4718, www. phuketsurf.com.

Through the low season, from April to October, Kata Beach is where you'll usually find Thailand's best surf. International competitions take place here and surf schools teach children and their parents. It's hardly Wakiki but that's just as well when it's your family in the water. Take sunscreen and neoprene or Lycra tops for surfers to avoid board rash.

From November to March the surf goes to Samui but there is nowhere there to match Kata Beach's surf culture.

*Open daily. **Rates** beginners 2-hour course 1500B, 4-hour course 2800B per person. Minimum age 5. Family packages available from 3000B.*

Phuket Zoo ★ ALL AGES

23/2 Moo 3, Soi Palai, Chaofah Road, Muang, 83000, ☎ 07638 1227, www.phuketzoo.com.

Don't expect western animal welfare standards from this small zoo between Chalong Bay and Phuket Town, but children love the scheduled shows and you'll also see plenty of animals at close

Phang-nga Bay & the Hidden Hongs

Protected from the open sea by Phuket, Ao Phang-nga is a 400 square kilometre National Park (entry 200B) between Phuket and Krabi, with mangrove-jungled shores and sheer karst mountains jutting from the water.

Geologically young, these were formed by a huge patch of coral seabed being forced up into the air, to erode at its own gentle pace. One of the most dramatic was made famous as the cinematic hideaway of Scaramanga in *The Man with the Golden Gun* before the special effects department made the towering outcrop appear to disintegrate.

There's little James Bond romance left in the experience now as speedboats, longtails and cruise ships cluster round for a better view. Other islands offer a more private experience, but in this iconic landscape you're never likely to have the place to yourself.

The central bay can be explored in all sorts of vessels – large cruise ships, nippy longtails and speedboats all offer day-cruises from Phuket, Phang-nga and Krabi, with tickets sold by tour operators and travel agents, but you can also head out on traditional sailing junks and sleek, fast and comfortable catamarans.

However, seeing the islands only from outside is to miss the bigger picture. Erosion from within has formed long, low caves, flooding interior lagoons which are ringed by sheer karst walls up to 300m high – a secret originally known only to a few Thai fishermen, who climbed these cliffs to collect birds' nests to sell to the Japanese.

In 1989 the American John Gray, a scuba diver since the age of 12 and from a Sierra Club family, researched and mapped the islands, taking advantage of any very low tides, which create space for a low boat to slip through. He used inflatable sea canoes to set up the first operation to introduce westerners to these internal lagoons – the most expensive but best way of exploring.

John Grey's tours out of Phuket (see p 133) are still the safest and best, though there are now otheroperators imitating from bases in Phi Phi, Khao Lak, Krabi or Phuket.

All sea canoe trips operate from large motherships. Leaving from Phuket they concentrate on the western part of the bay, and departing from Krabi they focus on the east.

range. It is never too crowded and is a hands-on experience.

You'll see monkey performances, elephants doing circus tricks, and crocodile trainers putting their heads inside gaping jaws.

The aquarium is something of a highlight, mainly because its lower level is the only part of the complex that is air conditioned, but the aviary and butterfly areas alone reward the cost of entry.

Ignore the photo opportunities with tiger cubs and orangutans: three hours is enough to see the three main shows and most of the animals.

Open daily 8.30am–6pm. Shows: monkey 9am, 2.30pm, 4.45pm. Crocodile: 9.45am, 12.45pm, 3.15pm, 5.30pm. Elephant: 10.30pm, 1.30pm, 4pm. **Admission** 500B adults, 300B children, infants under two free. Parking free. **Credit** MC, V.

Power Snorkel the Deep
★ ★ ★ **FIND** AGE SEVEN AND UP

Coral Island Beach Club, Banana Beach, Koh Hae, 07638 3796, www.sea-scooter.com.

Easy snorkelling has arrived with the Coral Island Beach Club's admirably simple system, ideal for children struggling with snorkels and even swimming. It needs no diving equipment, buoyancy tanks or qualifications. Wearing a life-jacket if required, your air floats in a cylinder close by while a simple tube feeds to a fool-proof regulator. In time this can even lead to easy shallow dives – in pairs for safety. Armed only with a weight belt you can swim at a depth of up to 5m for up to an hour – a perfect introduction for your children to the wonders of Phuket's fish-filled coral world.

There's plenty more to do on this day-trip island south of Phuket, including paddling a glass-bottomed kayak over the reef, riding a banana boat, racing round the reef on a ski scooter, parascending and lunch.

Power snorkelling, snorkelling and sea canoe rentals are included in speedboat or longtail trips.

Open daily. **Cost** tickets including resort pickups and speedboat transfers from Chalong Pier or longtails from Rawai Beach 2900B adults, 2300B children 4–11. Child price negotiable as owner sympathetic to parents. Price covers activities, equipment, meal and soft drinks all day. Extras banana boat 600B, parasailing 600B.

River Rovers ★ ★ **FIND** ALL AGES

1/16 Moo 9, Soi Ao Chalong, Chaofa Road, 83100, 07628 0420, www.riverrovers.com.

Phuket is not totally developed: there's also a world of mangrove swamps and fishing villages the tourist trail has yet to reach. Take the road less travelled with flexible, relaxing journeys into Phuket's rural hinterland along the Tha Chin canal with River Rovers. Not far from Phuket Town – you could drive there in 5 minutes – is a different world where the waterways are too shallow for speedboats and locals are still astonished to see foreigners.

What you do and see depends partly on your interests but options include birdwatching, meeting local fish farmers, dining on a floating restaurant eating fish chosen by yourself, feeding bananas to troupes of wild monkeys, and stopping to meet sea gypsy communities.

Children particularly love meeting local fishing-family

children their own age in this leisurely step aside from commercial tourism.

Rates 2950B adults, 1500B under 12s, under fives go free. Wheelchair accessible. Longer trips (overnight) available. Minimum passenger numbers 4, maximum group size 10.

Sea Canoe Phang-nga Bay's Hongs ★★★ ALL AGES

John Gray Sea Canoes, 124 Soi 1 Yaowarat Road, Taladyai, Muang, Phuket 83000, 📞 07625 4505-7, www.johngray-seacanoe.com.

In Thai *hongs* mean rooms – and that's what you find in the middle of some of Phang-nga Bay's sheer limestone islands. Exploring them is unforgettable. Take a large boat and at the island pick up stable, manoeuvrable sea canoes, with tough inflated rubber tubes running down either side. They are two-person canoes, shared with a guide or your child. When the tide is right, paddle up to a cliff and – just at the last minute – see a chink in the rock.

Carefully you slip into a world of total darkness, with only the faint beam of a torch showing what's ahead – and overhead. Sometimes you have to bend back to avoid low sections: at others you listen to the frantic fluttering of disturbed nesting bats – and snap your mouth shut as you realise what might land on your tongue.

Then there's light at the end of the tunnel and you emerge, blinking, into a stifling, enclosed world, where sheer cliffs rise 300m on every side, fringed with twisted bonsai plants. Mudskippers and frogs skitter around the edges and red-backed sea eagles fly overhead. You can paddle around for a while but not too long: when the tide turns your exit will be cut off.

To avoid the crowds John Grey increasingly avoids the mornings. Hong by Starlight starts with a lavish lunch amongst the islands and uses the evening tides to enter the *hongs*, before dinner on board

Phang-nga Bay

as you motor back through the darkening islands.

Hong by Starlight pickup from your Phuket Hotel at 12.30pm and returns by 9.30pm–10pm. It includes a light lunch, one or two daylight hong expeditions, sunset self-paddle or swim and dinner. Cost 3950B adults, 1975B children 5–11, under fives free.

Other Phuket operators which might be slightly less expensive include Andaman Sea Kayaks, ☎ 07623 5353 and Sea Cave Canoe, ☎ 07621 0434.

Snorkel the Waters of the Andaman Sea ★ ★ ★
AGE SEVEN AND UP

The waters south of Phuket are often startlingly clear, with visibility up to 40m in season, plentiful corals, and the chance to see rays and sharks. A number of companies run day-cruises in various types of boat that include lunch, a bit of snorkelling and some time to explore a deserted beach.

Speedboats cut down your travel time but can be uncomfortable and also, with the cost of fuel, expensive. The larger cruise vessels are the least expensive option but do tend to flood snorkelling sites with lots of people, all at one time. When snorkelling with your family it is easier and safer to be on your own or part of a small group. If your budget will stretch to it a sailing yacht is a good way to go. Catamarans are ideal. They have large shady and stable living areas if you need to get youngsters out of the sun, and all children love seeing the water woosh under the net between the keels.

Alternatively there are several newly built but completely authentic timber sailing boats which are fully equipped and luxurious but blend with their timeless landscape and serenade your journey with gentle timber creaks and quiet flaps of canvas.

The following prices are based on the popular day-trips to Racha Yai Island, 25km south of Chalong Bay, or Phi Phi Island to the east.

Simba Trips (Royal Phuket Marina, Phuket 83150, ☎ 07628 9044, www. simbaseatrips.com) is an excellent operator, running small-group day-trips from 2800B adults, 1800B children 3–10. A day's speedboat charter will cost from 12,000B if you book direct with an operator such as Coral Seekers (PO Box 450, Muang, 83000, ☎ 07635 4074, www.coralseekers.com) for a family-sized vessel with shade.

A good operator running both catamaran and timber boat day-trips is Pro Dive (43/24 Moo 5, Ao Chalong Road, 83100, ☎ 07638 3913-4, www.phuket-scuba-diving.com), which runs day-trips every Tuesday in low season, daily in high season, prices for snorkelling from 1900B adults, 1250B children under 12. Prices include transfers from the southern beaches (7.30am), lunch, water and soft drinks, fins and masks. You can also dive – or take an introductory course – for a small extra fee.

On a budget there's a large public ferry that shuttles between Chalong Bay and Racha Yai, charging 20B per person.

Further Attractions in Phuket

Several worthwhile family attractions can't be fully described here but might strike a chord with your children. These are:

Phuket Aquarium VALUE (Cape Panwa, ☎ 07639 1126 *www.boat housephuket.com*) is run by the Institute of Marine Biology: 100B adults, 50B children.

Elephant rides through **Siam Safari Nature Tours** (45 Chao Far Road, Chalong, 83130, ☎ 07628 0116, *www.siamsafari. com*). Open daily 9am–5pm.

Horse-riding at the **Phuket Laguna Riding Club** (Bang Tao Beach, ☎ 07632 4199) or the **Phuket Riding Club** (Rawai, ☎ 07628 8213).

Bungee jumping at **World Bungy Patong** (Soi Kepsap, 2 Sai Namyen Road, Patong Beach, ☎ 07634 5185). Open daily 10am–7pm. Rate 1400B per jump or at **Jungle Bungee** in Kathu, ☎ 07632 1351.

Bicycle rides with **Action Holidays Phuket** (10/195 Jomthong Thani 5/4 Kwang Road, 83000, ☎ 07626 3575, *www.biketoursthailand.com*). Equipment for all ages provided, half- and full-day tours. Rates 1950B adults, 1600B children.

Thai cookery classes daily at **Phuket Thai Cookery School** east of Phuket Town (☎ 07625 2354, *www.phuket-thaicookery school.com*, 1900B including beach transfers) or on weekends at **Mom Tri's Boathouse Hotel** ★★ on Kata Noi (☎ 07633 0015, *www.boathousephuket.com*, 2000B), which is rather better because if your children get bored it's usually possible to hire a babysitter and send them to play on the beach.

Thai boxing fights at the **Saphan Hin Stadium** south of Phuket Town (☎ 07621 4690, Tuesday and Friday 8pm–11pm, 500B). If you've got active teenagers they also run Thai boxing courses at their Suwit Gym (15 Moo 1, Choa Fa Road, 83130, ☎ 07637 4313, *www.best muaythai.com*).

Fast and plentiful boat links between Phuket, Krabi and the Phang-nga Bay islands mean that most of the excursions around Krabi and the Gulf of Phang-nga are also offered by tour operators in Phuket.

Khao Lak

Phuket was already a busy, established resort long before developers started to clear the mangrove forests at Khao Lak on the Thai mainland's Andaman coast. The 2004 Tsunami washed away almost all the limited infrastructure that had been put in place, and while the community is rebuilding itself, nature is regreening the landscape just as fast.

Currently the resort is beautifully low-key with no high-rise buildings and all accommodation small-scale and low-pressure. A few dive operators head out to the world-class diving of the Similans, three hours' boat ride offshore, and Khao Sok National Park is close by inland, but apart from the natural beauty of the region it's a superbly relaxing family-friendly haven.

KHAO LAK

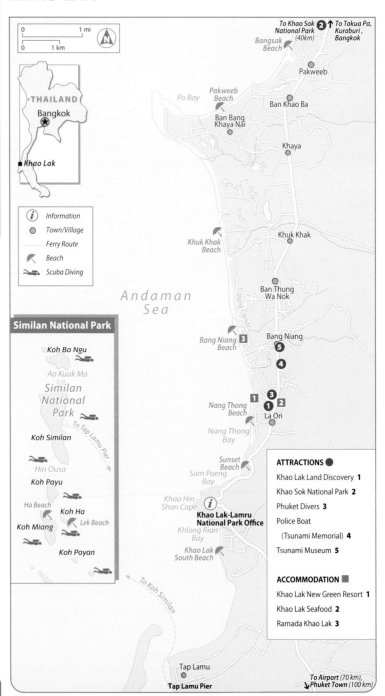

0 1 mi
0 1 km

THAILAND
Bangkok
Khao Lak

(i) Information
◉ Town/Village
---- Ferry Route
🏖 Beach
🤿 Scuba Diving

To Khao Sok 2 ↑ To Takua Pa,
National Park   Kuraburi,
(40km)   Bangkok

Bangsak Beach
Pakweeb
Po Bay
Pakweeb Beach
Ban Khao Ba
Ban Bang Khaya Nai
Khaya
Khuk Khak
Khuk Khak Beach

Andaman Sea

Ban Thung Wa Nok

Potg Canal

Bang Niang Beach 3
Bang Niang
5
4
1 3 2
1
Nang Thong Beach
La On
Nang Thong Bay

Sunset Beach
Sam Poeng Bay
Khao Hin Shan Cape
(i) Khao Lak-Lamru National Park Office
Khlong Rian Bay
Khao Lak South Beach

Similan National Park

Koh Ba Ngu
Ao Kuak Ma
Similan National Park
Koh Similan
Hin Ousa
Koh Payu
Ha Beach
Koh Ha
Lek Beach
Koh Miang
Koh Payan
To Tap Lamu Pier
To Koh Similan

ATTRACTIONS ●
Khao Lak Land Discovery **1**
Khao Sok National Park **2**
Phuket Divers **3**
Police Boat
  (Tsunami Memorial) **4**
Tsunami Museum **5**

ACCOMMODATION ■
Khao Lak New Green Resort **1**
Khao Lak Seafood **2**
Ramada Khao Lak **3**

Tap Lamu
Tap Lamu Pier

To Airport (70 km),
↓ Phuket Town (100 km)

Watch Out for Waves

Along the Andaman coast from Krabi to Ranong, you'll see solar-powered posts, towering above the palms, with sensors looking out to sea. These were built with the aid money that flooded in after the Tsunami of Boxing Day 2004 and take signals from buoys far offshore, hopefully providing early warning of any future tidal waves. Don't hold your breath: the buoys had a high failure rate when first fitted and it's not clear how they have been maintained since. But if the sea suddenly retreats from the beach, leaving fish flapping in pools, you know what to do. Run for high ground!

Getting There

By Air Khao Lak is an hour (70km) north of Phuket Airport by taxi, or two hours north of Phuket Town by car or bus. From Phuket Airport the taxi fare should be 1500B but it might be hard to bargain down.

By Bus Most buses on the Bangkok route go via Surat Thani and Phang-nga, but those generally leave too late at night to be useful. Through the day long-distance coaches from Phuket to Ranong will drop travellers to Khao Lak on the main road, 1km inland, at the bus station, or close by your resort if you are headed somewhere particular.

Regular buses also link Khao Lak with Phang-Nga town and Krabi, as well as Bangkok 12 hours to the north.

The bus station is your best chance of finding a taxi and Budget has a car rental desk by the Nang Thong supermarket (📞 07644 3454, *www.budget.co.th*).

Orientation

The name Khao Lak is used to refer to three separate beaches but the actual beach of Khao Lak is the most southerly, with just a couple of bungalow lodges and a single resort.

The heart of things is 7km further north, along the main road as it runs inland from Nang Thong Beach. This is where you'll find the greatest choice of restaurants, dive shops and boutiques, as well as some good low-cost accommodation. The beach is lovely, with rocky outcrops breaking up long stretches of soft sand.

You can walk north along the beach from here in an hour or so to reach the third beach, Ban Niang. The sands are beautiful but watch out for invisible stinging jellyfish (yes I know that's not easy) at high tide. This stretch was worst hit by the Tsunami but such naturally cleared development space seems to have attracted a rather unimaginative set of developers: rather charmless villa communities, probably destined for the international property market, have taken root in the 2km stretch between the sea and the main inland road.

What to See & Do

Various land tours from here include elephant rides and treks in Khao Sok National Park, and swift transfers mean you can still take part in trips around the islands of Phang-nga Bay. Operators include Khao Lak Land Discovery (07642 0411, *www.khaolakdiscovery.com*).

There are also snorkelling and diving trips to the Similan Islands, but the journey takes three hours by normal boat and two interminable and bouncy hours by speedboat – each way. In one day this is too much for most children (and many adults).

Operators such as Phuket Divers (07642 0628, *www. phuketdivers.com*) are based in Nang Tong and do two-day liveaboard diving trips that also take snorkellers. Advance booking is advisable.

Most of the charm in Khao Lak is simply that there aren't too many things to do.

The Tsunami Museum is a touch disturbing for children, who might very reasonably ask when the next wave was due. More rewarding is the police motor launch, washed 2km inland, that has become something of a shrine to the 2004 Tsunami. Painted grey and the size of a motor torpedo boat, it sits among the palms while enterprising Thais flog t-shirts and commemorative magazines from a trestle table, apparently for charity.

Krabi

Krabi, on the opposite side of Phang-nga Bay from Phuket, was once part of the world's largest coral reef that stretched from Guilin in China, through Halong Bay in Vietnam, and down to Papua New Guinea. Long ago the seabed was forced up into the air, resulting in one of the world's most dramatic landscapes, of sheer karst outcrops, here teetering over shallow, tropical seas and small, sheltered beaches. Around Krabi Town itself these stunning features are uniquely accessible, an everyday backdrop to a world of tropical beauty.

Unlike Phuket, Krabi takes a steady approach to development. Jet-skis and parascending are banned, and life proceeds at a slower, gentler pace. The dramatic landscape is paradise for climbers and canoeists, but also pretty good for people who just like lying on a beach and enjoying the view.

Getting There

By Air Krabi Airport (07569 1940) is 16km east of town and receives daily flights from Bangkok and Tiger Air flights from Singapore. A new terminal building, completed in 2005,

Float Your Boat

Destination Air (📞 *07632 8637-39*, *www.destinationair.com*) runs small float-planes to Krabi (trip time: 12 minutes), Koh Lanta (trip time: 28 minutes) and Koh Phi Phi (trip time: 16 minutes). Operated by foreign pilots, this network is growing fast. Their float-planes can also be used for scenic flights over Phuket's spreading beaches or the limestone islands of Phang-nga Bay, daily 8am–5pm, one plane seating four, the other nine. A 15-minute private charter is from 2999B, Krabi to Phi Phi 13,600B round trip. Infants under two free.

indicates they hope to increase their international capacity. It has ATM machines and a café but little else.

Krabi town is mainly useful as a transit point for nearby beaches and resorts, boat journeys out in Phang-nga Bay or Koh Phi Phi.

Getting Around

Taxis have fixed prices: Krabi Town is 300B, beaches of Ao Nang 500B, Klong Muang 800B, and the ferry terminal for the island of Koh Lanta 1500B: you'll be able to bargain much better rates for the journey back.

Visitor Information

Krabi's TAT office (daily 8.30am–4.30pm, 📞 *07562 2163*) is not very conveniently sited in the north of town but tour operators are everywhere and generally more useful.

Publications

Various advertising-funded maps are available and there is a monthly magazine, *Flyer* (*www. yourkrabi.com*), with general information.

Orientation

The beaches stretch out west of Krabi and the road loops inland behind an impassable karst that blocks land access to Railay Beach.

After 20 minutes or so the road regains the shore at Ao Nang, the busiest of Krabi's beaches. This has some major resorts so no desert island feel, and after dark lots of small stalls open up, selling counterfeit designer goods and handicrafts, while tailors desperately try to persuade those who don't need suits that they do. Prices are inflated so bargain hard.

Next along is quieter Hat Nopparat Thara, stretching to the west. Thais like roads along their beaches to provide easy access for restaurant motorbike sidecars and snack vendors. This means bungalow hotels and restaurants are on one side of the road and the beach on the other. At low tide you can wade out a

KRABI

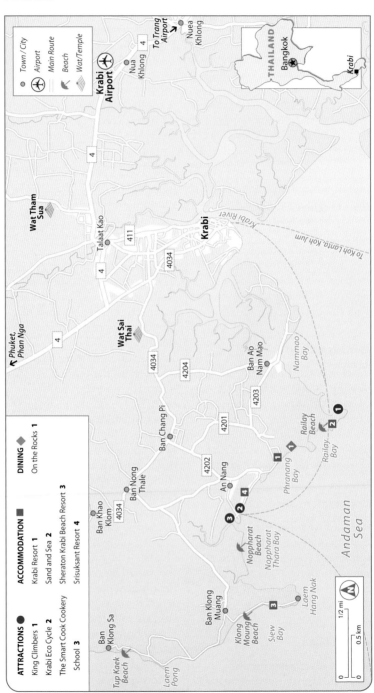

ATTRACTIONS ●

King Climbers **1**

Krabi Eco Cycle **2**

The Smart Cook Cookery School **3**

ACCOMMODATION ■

Krabi Resort **1**

Sand and Sea **2**

Sheraton Krabi Beach Resort **3**

Srisuksant Resort **4**

DINING ◆

On the Rocks **1**

Longtail boat off Hat Nopparat Thara Beach, Krabi

long way so small children are unlikely to drown, but the need to cross the road is off-putting.

Further northwest longtail boats will take you to Klong Muang, the least developed and nicest beach in the area (though you can also reach it, slowly and indirectly, by road). Shaded by casuarina trees, it is perfect for families – calm at high tide and busy with crabs and starfish when the tide is out.

Alternatively double back, by longtail to Railay Beach, also known as Laem Phra Nang. This feels rather like an island because there are no cars or scooters, and it's also the best place to try mountaineering on the sheer limestone karsts (see p 142).

With a lot of bars, resorts and hostels crunched in amongst the mountains, it sometimes feels a little cramped: fine for a day-trip or a few nights away but not somewhere to base yourself for a long family holiday. Fortunately there are not that many rooms so once the evening longtails take the last day-trippers away the atmosphere mellows considerably.

Getting Around

In a region with more water than roads, many routes are best covered by longtail taxi, either because quicker and cheaper, or because the destination (like Railay Beach) can't be reached by road. These days all have life-jackets aplenty hanging on their rails.

Longtail taxi boats run from Ao Nang to Railay, charging 60B per person (100B after 7pm). Boats leave whenever they have enough customers, in theory four or five, but often drivers will wait until they have at least 10. It is quicker to hire one of the longtails that bob hopefully all along the beaches in Ao Nang: the owners will generally approach you.

Longtail boats from Krabi town's Chao Fah pier are less frequent and drop you on the

Rock-climbing at Railay Beach, Krabi

eastern side of Railay beach, so at low tide there's a long walk across the mud-flat to get to your resort.

What to See & Do

Most tour operators and hotels can arrange a speedboat charter, prices depending on the destination but starting at 1200B for a half-day outing to the local islands of Chicken, Poda and Ko Tub, and be ready to pay around 12,000B per day for a 15-seater speedboat to Phi Phi. Try Chokpaisan Andaman Sea, ☎ 07563 7570, *www.chokpaisan daman.com*.

Climb that Karst ★ ★ ★

AGE 5 AND UP

These days climbing operators string lines up sheer cliff-faces all over Krabi's landscape and offer climbing and abseiling courses. In such a dramatic landscape, with so many vertical drops, this is perhaps unsurprising.

Before sending your children up a mountain it's somewhat impractical to check upper-mountain bolt fittings, but watch carefully to make sure all equipment is good quality and safety procedures are observed.

Sport climbing was born in the karst mountains above Railay Beach, with King Climbers among other pioneers, and this climbing school is still one of the leaders. Half-day introductory courses set off from the beach to the base of a sheer karst cliff, where one of your instructors will casually clamber halfway to heaven up a sheer cliff to fix a metal belay pin, feed through a rope and bring it back. Usually you'll be belaying your own child's climbing rope, shouting out helpful words of advice, trying to give them a strategy to climb the sheer rock, possibly stop crying and, once they've got to the top, to help them to learn to abseil back down. It's worth noting that, dangling 30m up a sheer rock face, they hear very little and certainly ignore most of the advice you give.

Neither your children nor the lithe Thai instructors will necessarily be heavy enough to carry your weight in an emergency: bear this in mind if climbing yourself.

Three-day courses and guided climbing trips also available.

Railay: King Climbers, offices by Railay East Beach, ☎ *07569 5286,* ☎ *07562 2581, www.kingclimbers. iname.com.*

Ao Nang: Ao Nang Climber, 307 Moo 2, Tambol Aonang, 📞 08588 72473, www.railay.com.

Prices for both: half-day courses 800B, full day 1500B, includes insurance, equipment, water, fruit and local hotel pickup.

Krabi Eco Cycle ★★

41/2 Ao Nang, Muang, Krabi 81000, 📞 07563 7250, www.krabiecocycle. com.

Take time inland to explore Krabi's Emerald Pool, a spectacular natural freshwater pool in the jungle, and take a geothermal sauna under the Hot Spring Waterfall in this gentle 25km cycle tour of the countryside. Bikes are good-quality mounts with front suspension, and children's bikes are available.

Day tours start with a hotel pickup at 8.30am and end at 4.30pm. **Rates** *1700B adults, 1400B children, including support vehicle, water, lunch, fruit, cycle helmet, National Park entrance fee and insurance.*

Kayaking ★★★ VALUE
AGE 5 AND UP

All tour agents in Ao Nang sell a selection of kayaking expeditions that enter Phang-nga Bay's hollow island *hongs*, similar to John Gray's island *hong* tours from Phuket(see p 133). However, a leisurely day kayaking around the coast doesn't need a guide and can be a great family adventure. Outlets all along Ao Nang beach rent out kayaks for 100B–150B an hour and not much more for the day. The trip to Railay is a gentle hour-long paddle along a spectacular landscape passing plenty of perfect places for a swim and lunch.

The Smart Cook Cookery School AGE 6 AND UP

Ao Nang, 19 Moo 5 Ao Nang, 81000, 📞 06186 3468, www.smartcook thailand.com. Free pickup in Ao Nang.

The Smart Cook School runs daily cooking classes, using picture menus that let you choose the dishes you want to make. Uniquely they also provide Internet support in case you've forgotten the recipes when it comes to recreating the tastes of Thailand back home.

Daily courses 8.30am–1.30pm and 3.30pm–4.30. **Rates** *1600B.* **Credit** *MC, V.*

Koh Phi Phi

One of Thailand's most iconic islands, Koh Phi Phi is actually made up of six islands protected (allegedly) as a National Park. Most are not inhabited and one was made famous as location of the film *The Beach*, while the main island, Phi Phi Don, is where people visit and stay.

Phi Phi Don is a classically beautiful island, with two main mountainous landmasses linked by a narrow strand with beaches on either side. This is where boats from Krabi and Phuket arrive, and since the dawn of the backpacker era this small patch of land has been packed with bungalow lodges, bars and shops, many built illegally by squatters on National Park territory.

All were smashed into history by the 2004 Tsunami as waves converged from either side. Thanks largely to volunteers the beach was cleared, but any hopes that redevelopment would learn lessons from the past have been disappointed. The lure of the tourist dollar means it is just as crowded now as it was before.

Getting There

By Boat Unless you take a sea-plane the only way to get to Phi Phi is by boat. Public boats run three times daily (10am, 2.30pm, 4pm) from Chao Fa pier in central Krabi Town and cost 300B, taking a good two hours, but there is sometimes an express service that cuts transit time by half.

From Phuket boats leave from the Ratchada (Rasada) pier near Phuket Town (8.30am and 1.30pm) and charge 450B. Ferries are neither particularly comfortable nor interesting, so it's well worth looking out for other, faster services that set out from Phuket's western resorts, depending on demand. Speedboats take about 45 minutes.

In season more services are laid on, including boats from Ao Nang and Koh Lanta, and various snorkelling and diving trips from Phuket also visit Phi Phi.

Make sure you make note of where the lifejackets are kept as ferries have been known to sink, especially in low-season storms.

Orientation

Boats arrive at Ao Ton Sa and most backpackers don't stagger too far from here to find their accommodation. Packed with day-trippers through the day and partying through the night, this doesn't really meet most family's expectations and though the island is small, measuring 8km by 3.5km, other, nicer beaches feel a world away.

Getting Around

None of the roads that start from the central village get very far, so access to other beaches is by boat, often charging up to 800B for journeys that, on the mainland, would cost much less.

Fast Facts

ATMs are found in Ton Sai only. Resorts change money but at appalling rates.

Health Clinic Limited medical facilities at Phi Phi Hospital (☎ 08270 4481) at the western end of Ton Sai.

Police There's a police box (☎ 081536 2427) on the track out of Ton Sai towards Leam Hin.

What to See & Do

The main activities on Koh Phi Phi are diving, snorkelling and rock climbing. If diving, bear in mind that the nearest recompression facility is on Phuket – and that not all dive schools are insured to use it. Dive operators include Visa Diving (☎ *087280 1721, www.visadiving.com*).

Best avoid the big-boat snorkelling trips as they are often impossibly crowded. Better to tag along with a scuba expedition, which will usually take non-divers for a reduced fee. While they're diving you'll have the shallows to yourself.

Alternatively for about 1200B you should be able to organise a private longtail snorkelling trip, with equipment provided (check children's goggles fit before you leave).

On most beaches you'll find kayaks for rent for about 800B per day and in this setting of limestone cliffs and sheltered coves a kayaking/swimming/sunbathing day is a relaxed family adventure.

Rock climbing is nearly as big here as in Railay, good operators include KE Hangout (☎ *081958 1820, www.kehangout.com*). Prices are around 1000B for half a day, including harness.

Koh Jum & Koh Lanta

Close to the mainland south of Krabi, the islands of Koh Lanta Yai and Koh Lanta Noi (big and small, further information from *www.lantaresort.com*) are where you go looking for the peaceful beach Thailand of 20 years ago. Even better is lesser-known Koh Jum, a beautifully unspoiled island gem.

Getting There

In season, from November to March, Koh Lanta and Koh Jum can be reached by ferries from Krabi and Koh Phi Phi. From June to October access is by minivan from Krabi to Laem Krunt for Koh Jum, and Bo Muang for Koh Lanta, making for shorter, safer boat crossings. The resorts listed below don't close in low season, but many others do.

FAMILY-FRIENDLY ACCOMMODATION

Phuket

Room rates in Phuket are something of a moveable feast. Hotels pay little notice to rack rates and like cheap-flight airlines raise and drop prices to fill their beds.

The high season peaks from 15th December to 15th January when rates can be hideously inflated. To milk clients further over the key nights of Christmas and the European New Year minimum stays are enforced, along with compulsory 'Gala Dinners' that, in the most expensive resorts, can cost hundreds of pounds.

The general rule in Thailand – that you get what you pay for – doesn't always work here. On a limited budget there is a lot to be said for travelling off-season when published rates, already low, are often discounted by 50%

or more through Internet bulk vendors.

VERY EXPENSIVE

Amanpuri ★

Pansea Beach. 118/1 Moo 3, Srisoonthorn Road, Pansea Beach, Phuket 83000, ☎ 07632 4333, www.amanpuri.com.

This is the place top politicians stay – perhaps not surprising given the cost. Stunningly set over its own private beach, facilities include six tennis courts with coaching, a yacht, sumptuous spa and selection of restaurant. The atmosphere is otherworldly, with a main pool in midnight blue and every blade of grass in its place. Prices are in US dollars, possibly because they find it hard to find space on the credit-card counterfoils to add all the 0s that would be necessary in baht. It's the ultimate place to stay for well-heeled families, with a range of villas offering up to six bedrooms.

Rooms 115. Rates smallest garden pavilion US$750–$1200, two-bedroom garden US$2200–$3100; includes airport transfers. Credit AE, MC, V. Amenities three restaurants, dive school. In room A/C.

Laguna Beach Resort ★★

Bang Tao Beach. 323 Moo 2, Srisoonthorn Road, Cherngtalay, Thalang District, Bangtao Bay, Phuket 83110, ☎ 07632 4352, www.laguna beach-resort.com.

Laguna Beach is the most family-friendly member of the Laguna Resort complex, an 'integrated resort' of five international resort hotels round a series of lagoons. Guests can shuttle between all five hotels, and for a small fee make the most of all the extensive facilities. This opens up 30 restaurants, 15 swimming pools, several children's clubs and three spas. There's an 18-hole golf course, a Camp Laguna club teaching teenagers abseiling, rock-climbing and sports, tennis, horse

Room with a lagoon view at Laguna Beach Resort

riding and more. The Laguna Beach is not the most expensive of the five hotels, but it's probably the best for families. Don't pay extra for Deluxe Sea View Rooms: they're on the ground floor and instead of the sea your view is of a line of beach stalls and shacks. Either pay more for a first-floor Andaman Suite, or less for a Lagoon View Room (or Suite), which is more private.

Facilities are excellent, with a waterslide, marine centre with complimentary Hobie Cats, windsurfers and instruction and a good children's club.

Eating and drinking on the beach costs a fraction of resort dining: Lotus and Lulu's are two recommended shack restaurants.

There can be quite an undertow on this beach, especially in low season, so take care.

Rooms 254. **Rates** superior room 5000B–10,000B, inc. breakfast, extra beds 2100B, up to two children using existing bedding free. **Credit** AE, MC, V. **Amenities** dive school, games room, spa. **In room** daybed, high-speed Internet, satellite TV, minibar.

EXPENSIVE

Evason Phuket & Six Senses Spa ★★

Rawai Beach. Rawai Beach, Phuket 83130, ☎ 07638 1010-7, www.six senses.com.

An outstanding children's club makes this superb hotel rise above its beach which, in Phuket's eastern lea, can't quite match the western strands. To get around this the hotel has a free shuttle running to Koh Bon,

an island 15 minutes offshore, where it has an exclusive beach with *salas* (pavilions) for long lazy days, a beach bar and full dining service. Should you feel like sampling the spa, taking a cooking course, or simply relaxing for a while you can safely leave your children at 'Just Kids': the staff are fantastic and your children play, have adventures and seem absolutely loved.

The two-bedroom Andaman Suites in this beautiful minimalist hotel are just below the main hotel but share all its facilities and are excellent for families.

Rooms 260 rooms, suites, pool suites, pool villas and two-bedroom apartments. **Rates** studio room garden view 8000B–12,000B, two-bedroom Andaman suite 18,000B–27,000B, extra bed 1800B. **Credit** AE, MC, V. **Amenities** five restaurants, spa, three swimming pools, two floodlit tennis courts, dive school, canoes, windsurfers, shuttle to Patong and Phuket Town. **In room** A/C, satellite TV, tea/coffee, DVD on request.

Moevenpick Resort and Spa ★

Karon Beach. (Formerly Crowne Plaza) 509 Patak Road, Karon Beach, Phuket 83100, ☎ 07639 6139, www. moevenpick-phuket.com.

The Moevenpick has one of the Phuket's best children's clubs, tucked away beneath the main lobby and occupying an expansive area of playrooms, computer rooms, games rooms and more. The Play Zone has a DVD lounge, full-size pool and billiards tables, table tennis, a ball-filled play cage and playroom.

Villas and suites are scattered around lush tropical gardens, with a beautiful swimming pool and children's pool at the heart of the hotel. The beach is just across the main coast road from the hotel's outer reaches, but from the heart of the resort it actually feels a long way away, a hot pound along endless flower-strewn footpaths. Most guests prefer the comfort of their pampering resort enclave. The newest and smartest additions are 30 two-bedroom apartments, overlooking the beach, that are smart, slick and – for the right money – for sale.

Rooms 342. **Rates** double 6000B–9750B, two-bedroom suite for up to four 12,000B–20,000B, extra bed 2200B. **Amenities** five restaurants, three bars, two with live entertainment, swimming pool and children's pool, spa. **In room** A/C, satellite TV, tea/coffee, fridge, Internet.

Sala Phuket ★★

Mai Khao Beach. Mai Khao Beach, Phuket 83110, 📞 *07633 8888,* **www.salaphuket.com.**

One of Phuket's leading hideaways is quietly – if not remotely – set far in the north of the island. It's a long way from central Phuket and its child-friendly attractions, but if you're staying here you're likely to rely on the resort for entertainment. Children's bicycles are complimentary, inflatable pool toys are provided in villas and PlayStations are available on request. Pool villas are supplied with baby monitors, and fishing

equipment is provided for children and adults. Overall it's a good family choice for those who want to get away from it all, and a vastly better option than the Marriott just along the unspoiled beach.

Rooms 79, of which 63 have private pools. **Rates** deluxe balcony suite 10,500B–20,000B, two-bedroom pool suites 30,500B–40,000B. **Amenities** restaurant, three beach-front pools, bar, spa, gym, library. **In room** A/C, satellite TV, DVD, wifi, tea/coffee, fridge, private balcony or terrace and (usually) pool.

MODERATE

Cape Panwa ★★★ VALUE

Cape Panwa. 27 Moo 8, Sakdidej Road, Cape Panwa, Phuket 83000, 📞 *07639 1123-5,* **www.capepanwa.com.**

Leonardo de Caprio stayed here while filming *The Beach*, but this outstanding hotel doesn't charge Hollywood prices and is remarkably family-friendly. Countless activities are laid on to fill young (or adult) days, including free scuba lessons in the pool, table tennis, volleyball and Thai soccer on the beach, batik painting, cooking classes, fruit and vegetable carving, and the little-known Thai art of napkin folding. The only drawback is that it is slightly remote. There are no cheap local restaurants in the immediate area, but the hotel's beach bar and restaurants do not overcharge hugely, and the hotel runs shuttle buses into Phuket Town and (less often) to Patong.

Rooms 246. *Rates* superior room 3000B–6100B, superior family (triple) 4200B–7300B, first extra bed for child free. *Credit* AE, MC, V. *Amenities* two pools, tennis court, games room, spa, boat shuttle to Coral Island. *In room* A/C, satellite TV, DVD, Internet, tea/coffee.

Holiday Inn Patong Beach
★★★

Patong Beach. 52 Thaweewong Rd, Patong Beach, Phuket 83150, ☏ *07634 0608-9, www.holiday. phuket.com.*

Patong is not an obvious place for a family holiday and this hotel, in the middle of the action, would seem an unlikely choice but somehow it works. There is a separate 'Busakorn' wing for couples without children but in the main beachfront wing there's an excellent and well-organised children's club right next to a child's pool, with a slide and rocky area for treasure hunts. At the general pool a rainbow coalition of nicely spoken children from all over the world look after each other with unusual courtesy. Older children also get an adult-free 'Club 12' zone with karaoke, Internet access and games.

Guest bedrooms will sleep two parents and two children if required, and also interconnect, but book ahead to secure one of the sought-after family suites that include separate child areas, with bunk beds facing their own TV with PlayStations and DVD recorder stocked with family-friendly films. Parents, across the room, have their own TV.

Enjoying the waterslide at the Holiday Inn, Patong Beach

Blackout curtains let mornings run late and Patong's many shops and, if you want it, nightlife, are just through the hotel's beachfront gate, with staff to usher you and your children across the busy beachfront road.

Rooms 405, 140 in family wing. *Rates* double 4000B–7200B, family suite 8000B–13,800B. *Credit* AE, MC, V. *Amenities* children's menu, spa, four restaurants. *In room* A/C, TV, DVD, tea/coffee, fridge, 24-hour room service.

Kata Beach Resort and Spa
★★★ VALUE

Kata Beach. 1 Pakbang Rd, Tambon Karon, Muang District, Phuket 83100, ☏ *07633 0530-4, www.kata group.com.*

Unusually for Phuket, the resorts at this southern end of Kata Beach have direct access to the beach, with no road or even pavement to cross. This mid-range hotel is right on the beach, with very good standards of

Swimming pool at Le Meridien Phuket

comfort and service in the heart of a quiet, but not too quiet, village setting. Views, of Kata Bay and Koh Poo, are beautiful, from your room or the pool.

Rooms *275 rooms and suites.* **Rates** *superior rooms 5105B–10,000B, junior suite 10,608B–17,183B, extra bed 1300B.* **Credit** *MC, V.* **Amenities** *child and adult pools, three restaurants, spa.* **In room** *A/C, satellite TV, DVD.*

Kata Palm Resort & Spa ★

Kata Beach. 60 Kata Road, Tambon Karon, Phuket 83100, ☏ 07628 4334-8, www.katapalmresort.com.

Take one step back from Kata Beach and prices drop and you get a lot more hotel for your money – as at Kata Palm Resort & Spa, a delightful new hotel where rooms are round a long, freeform pool. Some on the ground floor give directly on to the pool, a facility loved by those children who can swim. Specify

when booking if you want direct pool access.

Rooms *80.* **Rates** *superior 3100B–6500B, deluxe pool access 5500B–8500B, extra bed 1300B.* **Credit** *AE, MC, V.* **Amenities** *three restaurants, two large swimming pools, two children's wading pools, small children's club, spa.* **In room** *A/C, satellite TV, tea/coffee, Internet (specify when booking), babysitting.*

Le Meridien Phuket ★ VALUE

Relax Bay. 29 Soi Karon Noi, Phuket 83100, ☏ 07637 0100, www.le meridien.com.

Dominating the 550m beach of Relax Bay, the Meridien is a well-run resort with trained lifeguards looking after the beach and 16 hectares of tropical gardens. It's a large resort but with good facilities, including two big swimming pools, watersports, four tennis courts, putting green and practice range. It caters firmly for families, with lots of activities and a good daycare centre that children seem to love. Its U-shape layout means 80% of the rooms face the ocean, with the lowest category getting a garden view. All are furnished in rattan and teak, and have private balconies and wooden deckchairs. The many attractions of Patong are close by, as is the family-friendly beach of Kata to the south.

Rooms 470 units. *Rates* superior garden view 4725B–10,325B, terrace suite 8225B–15,925B, one child under 12 sharing stays free. *Credit* AE, DC, MC, V. *Amenities* seven restaurants, three bars with games and live entertainment, two pools including shallow areas, spa, golf driving range, minigolf, floodlit tennis, dive school, children's club, games room. *In room* babysitting, A/C, satellite TV, tea/coffee, fridge.

Ramada Phuket

Karon Beach. 568 Patak Road, Tambon Karon, Phuket 83100, ☏ 07639 6666, www.ramada phuket.com.

On paper and online this hotel appears one of the most child-friendly in Thailand – if not the world. Themed family suites have separate children's rooms done out as spaceships, underwater submarine rooms, or princess' fairy castles. There's a toddler's pool, children's pool with slide, and a free children's club. Reports, however, have not been kind. The fish-tanks in the submarine room are noisy (though to some children it's comforting), the UV lights in the spaceship room highlight strange stains on the sheets, the children's club is not air-conditioned, the food is

not up to Ramada's usual standard, the main pool is cramped, and Karon beach is a hot 10-minute walk away. It is basically an older hotel given a glossy, and not completely consistent, family-themed paint job. Children often love it though, and to be fair it's not hugely expensive for Phuket.

Rooms 121 units. *Rates* double/twin 5900B–8800B, two-bedroom adventure suite 14,300B–19,900B. Children's club free for residents or 1650B per day. *Credit* AE, MC, V. *Amenities* two restaurants, swimming pool, children's pool with slide and toddlers' pool. *In room* A/C, satellite TV, tea/coffee.

INEXPENSIVE

Out of season all the hotels listed above as moderate will drop their rates and many will fall into the 'inexpensive' category – but take care to choose one within easy reach of local restaurants and bars as food and drinks prices will remain unchanged.

In season you'll struggle to find anywhere inexpensive to stay on Phuket. A good place to look is on Pakbeng Road on Kata Beach, inland from the spreading bulk of the Club Med resort.

In an emergency there are cheapish places in the back streets of Patong. Although they're more geared towards 'short-time' customers, they represent your best chance of getting your family inexpensively off the streets.

However, it has to be said that if you're in Phuket in high season on a tight budget you're in the wrong place. If it's early in the day catch a boat to Krabi or any island without an airport. Alternatively – or if it's late – look for a bus and head north: two hours will get you to Khao Lak where knowledgeable and usually kind local taxi-drivers will make it most unlikely you and your family will be left stranded. Here limited funds stretch much further and – shhhh – it's nicer.

Khao Lak

Accommodation in Khao Lak is almost all new, so standards are high. Most are sturdily constructed in concrete as the memories of thatched wooden dwellings wiped from the landscape are still fresh. Prices, however, are still low. Real budget travellers will have to retreat from the beach to the main road, a long hot walk away (or brief wobbling ride on a rental scooter), but even in high season this is a place where good accommodation comes cheap.

EXPENSIVE

Ramada Khao Lak ★★ VALUE

Kukkak Beach. 59 Moo 5, Tumbon Kukkak, Takuapa District, Phang Nga, Khao Lak 82190, 📞 *07642 7777,* **www.ramadakhaolak.com**.

Though it doesn't lay on anything special for children, this rather lovely hotel takes them in its stride. The children's menus are delicious, rooms do interconnect, and there's a benign regime for charging for children. The freeform beachfront pool is huge and well equipped with shade and sun loungers, and it's not a large hotel so the staff soon get to know each member of your family. If your budget can stretch to it the Ocean Front Villas are palatial. If your family are happy playing together on a beautiful stretch of stress-free beach, this is a very good choice.

Rooms 84. Rates deluxe 3520B–11,400B, ocean front villas 14,070B–24,500B, under fours free, 4–12 2250B, extra bed 900B, cot free. Credit AE, MC, V. Amenities four restaurants, two bars, spa, pool and children's pool. In room A/C, satellite flat-screen TV, coffee/tea, babysitting.

MODERATE

Khao Lak New Green Resort
FIND VALUE

Nang Thong Beach, Khao Lak. 📞 *07648 5845,* **www.green beach.de**.

Delightfully simple, this beachfront development of single and interconnecting double wood-and-rattan bungalows are shaded by casuarinas on a beautiful stretch of beach. There are golden sands ahead, with two rocky shoals on either side, often covered in crabs and good for rockpool explorations. None of the rooms are large enough for an extra bed, but discounts are given for renting two interconnecting rooms. The restaurant is on the beach, with sand between your toes, and charges local prices for well-cooked local food.

It's quiet, but if you've got younger children they'll always find Thais their own age to play with.

Rooms 34. **Rates** family rooms 750B–1500B, two interconnecting family rooms 2800B even in high season. No Christmas or holiday surcharges. **Credit** MC, V. **Amenities** restaurant, Internet café. **In room** A/C, no phone.

INEXPENSIVE

Khao Lak Seafood VALUE FIND

Khao Lak. 19/1 Moo 7 Petkasem Road, Kuk Kak, Takuapa, Phang Nga, 82190, ☎ 07648 5318, www.khao lakseafood.com.

The least expensive place to stay in Khao Lak is a new development behind the area's busiest (and probably best) local restaurant on the main road through the village. For the money it is fantastic, though the beach is a long hot walk away (30 minutes, better accomplished in a rentacar or scooter). Rooms are large, clean, modern but unpretentious, and set round a quiet garden well away from the road. The restaurant staff are helpful, and their children will play with yours while fantastic Thai meals are prepared. Many rooms are large enough to fit four or five beds and some have kitchens as well. There are also some fan-cooled rooms but they are smaller.

Rooms 35. **Rates** fan double 600B, A/C family 1200B high season, at other times discounts possible. Airport pickups from Phuket 1500B. **Amenities** restaurant, tour desk. **In room** A/C, fridge, TV (local channels).

Krabi

EXPENSIVE

Sheraton Krabi Beach Resort ★

Klong Muang Beach. 155 Moo 2, Nong Thale, Muang, Krabi 81000, ☎ 07562 8000, www.starwood hotels.com.

The real star of this resort is Rara the elephant, who turns up twice a day to give children rides, play the harmonica and dance. Otherwise it's a well-fitted resort hotel on a beautiful beach. At high tide it's calm and shallow for hundreds of metres offshore, perfectly suited to learning how to windsurf or sail (both complimentary). At low tide it's busy with hermit crabs and starfish. Most hotels in this class are besieged with scrapwood restaurants and massage shacks: this one isn't, being relatively quiet and remote. The children's club is good and the place works like clockwork. Even baby milk is free. What's not to like?

Rooms 246. **Rates** superior room 5500B–17,000B, family packages reduce the price of two interconnecting rooms. **Amenities** six restaurants, spa, dive school, floodlit tennis, table tennis, outdoor children's pool, pool, live entertainment, watersports. **In room** A/C, babysitting, tea/coffee.

MODERATE

Krabi Resort, Krabi ★★ VALUE

Ao Nang Beach. 232 Moo 2 Tambol Ao-Nang, Krabi 81000, ☎ 07563 7030, www.krabiresort.net.

As about the oldest in Ao Nang, the Krabi Resort has a prime position – almost the only one on the beach and still within easy walking distance of the shopping and restaurant area, plus the longtail boats going to other beaches.

In spite of this it feels quiet, private and secluded. It also secured huge grounds with gardens covering 18 acres, something few more recent developments can hope to match.

The hotel has a large pool, a children's playground, a beach-front restaurant, plus direct beach access: family bliss. Rooms are acceptable and good value in the main hotel buildings, but better in bungalows. There is one two-bedroom family suite.

Rooms 108. **Rates** deluxe room 2350B–4440B, under 4 free without bed, extra bed for child up to 12 7000B, includes breakfast, child cots free, two-bedroom suite 9500B–13,300B. **Amenities** billiards, tennis, table tennis. **In room** satellite TV, A/C, fridge, coffee/tea.

INEXPENSIVE

There's nowhere very cheap to stay near the coast in Klong Muang or Ao Nang: on a tight budget you're better off taking a *songthaew* or longtail to Hat Nopparat Thara and trawling the scruffier beachfront establishments.

Sand and Sea ★★

Railay Beach, 39 Moo 2 Aonang, Krabi 81000, ☎ *07382 4627,* ***www. sandsearesort.com.***

This little bungalow resort is right in the heart of Railay West, the swimming beach. Rooms are comfortable, though sometimes you wish they'd taken a bit of the generous lobby space and designed it into the rooms instead. There's a good restaurant and a very child-friendly shady central pool. Alleys lead back across the peninsula to Railay East for endless adventures among the trees and beached boats of the low-tide mudflats.

Sheltered by the towering karst outcrops on every side, this is a good place to stay for a few nights. The best accommodation is in privately rented timeshare bungalows, but in all rooms facilities stop when the generator is turned off.

Rooms 21. **Rates** superior A/C 2282B–3576B; one cot, complimentary. **Credit** MC, V. **Amenities** pool, restaurant, day spa. **In room** A/C, local TV.

Srisuksant Resort ★★ VALUE

145 Moo 3, Nopparatthara Beach Road, Ao Nang, Krabi 81000, ☎ *07563 8002-4,* ***www.srisuksant resort.com.***

One of the first hotels you come across on the eastern end of Hat Nopparat Thara, at the price this is a surprisingly slick boutique property, close to a wide selection of beachfront bars and restaurants, and also a few hundred metres from the longtail taxis to Railay. Rooms are pleasant and easily large enough for one extra bed, and all have private terrace or balcony.

Rooms 68. **Rates** 950B–21,000B, extra bed 500B. **Amenities** swimming pool with child area, restaurant. **In room** A/C, TV, fridge.

Koh Phi Phi

MODERATE

Holiday Inn Phi Phi Island ★

Laem Tong, Phi Phi Island, ☎ *07562 7300, www.phiphi-palmbeach.com.*

This is a good resort hotel on a quiet east-facing beach. Some bungalows interconnect but all are furnished with a double and separate single beds, and have enough space for an extra bed. If resort catering prices get you down there's a sea-gypsy village just along the coast where you can eat and drink more cheaply. Best of the bunch on the island.

Rooms 80. Rates garden bungalow 3650B–8550B, extra bed 850B. Credit AE, MC, V. Amenities four restaurants, spa, swimming pool, dive centre, complimentary snorkels and kayaks, table tennis, table football, TV room. In room A/C, CD player, fridge.

Phi Phi Island Village

Ao Loh Bakao, Phi Phi. 49 Moo 8, Aonang, Muang Phuket 81320, ☎ *07621 5014, www.ppisland.com.*

Arguably the best resort on Phi Phi, this smart property is set on a private beach on the island's western coast. It's a little cut off but there is a small village with a couple of bars and restaurants just inland from the resort – although the hotel staff make every effort to stop you finding it. There are two swimming pools and a waterslide. Water heating is solar which is perfectly adequate in the climate.

Rooms 84. Rates superior room 4700B–7700B, extra bed 700B in a superior room, 2400B in a beachside junior suite or hillside pool villa. Credit AE, MC, V. Amenities three restaurants, pool, spa, dive shop (expensive) In room tea/coffee, satellite TV.

Koh Jum

MODERATE

Koh Jum Lodge ★ ★ ★ FIND

Golden Pearl Beach, Koh Jum. 286 Moo 3, Koh Siboya, Nua Klong District, Krabi 811300, 89921 1621, www.kohjumlodge.com.

French-run and friendly, Koh Jum Lodge is the ultimate place if you and your family just want to experience a peaceful beach break with nothing to do.

Holiday Inn Phi Phi Island

Pimalai beach and jetty

Electricity only runs in the evenings, there are no excursions to make or people to see. It's just you and the sea – and even that goes quite a long way out twice a day; just as well the resort has a decent swimming pool.

The bungalows are very spacious, with room for up to four children as well as two adults, and while it's not the cheapest restaurant you'll find on the island, it's probably the best. Open year-round.

*Rooms 16. **Rates** 3000B–4500B, extra bed 1000B child 13 and up, 500B for a child 4–12, under fives free, inc. breakfast. **Amenities** beach. **In room** no phone, no A/C, no fan, no TV.*

Koh Lanta

VERY EXPENSIVE

Pimalai

Ba Kan Tiang Beach. 99 Moo 5, Ba Kan Tiang Beach, Koh Lanta 81150, ☏ 07560 7999, www.pimalai.com.

By far the most luxurious property on Koh Lanta, the Pimalai offers exceptional accommodation that struggles to satisfy its target market, who find the 2½ hour transfer from Krabi takes the gloss off their luxury experience. This means that Internet rates can bring this superb property into your range. There's nothing so crass as children's clubs, but if you take a two-bed villa you're sitting on 250 square metres of beautifully provisioned beachfront real estate, bigger than most European farmhouses but much better kitted out. TV screens are flat, fabrics silk, the wood solid teak. They even have kitchens, and the hotel buggy will drive you down to the beach to make it easier to reach the nearest 7/11. That they're prepared to do this shows class.

The dive school is one of the best in southern Thailand so this could be a good place to introduce your children to the deep.

*Rooms 121. **Rates** doubles 10,000B–20,000B, two-bedroom beach villa 42,000B–75,000B. **Amenities** five restaurants, four bars,*

50m infinity pool, dive school, tennis, kayaks, windsurfers, spa, library with family DVDs. *In room* A/C, DVD, TV.

MODERATE

Lanta Sand Resort & Spa

Ao Khlong Dao, Koh Lanta. 279 Moo 3, Saladan, Koh Lanta, Krabi 81150, 📞 07568 4633-4, www.lantasand. com.

This deluxe bungalow operation has plenty of children's toys for the pool and larger rooms ideal for larger families – though prices go up accordingly. Open year-round.

Rooms 78. *Rates* deluxe villas 3500B–11,000B, extra bed 1600B, children 3–12 800B, under threes free, inc. breakfast, two-bed junior suite 8000B–21,000B. *Credit* AE, MC, V. *Amenities* restaurant, beach and pool bars, two swimming pools, spa, Internet access. *In room* outdoor bathtub, indoor shower, A/C, coffee/tea, TV, DVD.

INEXPENSIVE

La Laanta Hideaway Resort
★★★ FIND

Bamboo Beach. 188 Moo 5, Ao Mai Phai, Koh Lanta 81150, 📞 07566 5066, 📞 07566 5122, www.lalaanta. com.

This small and friendly resort is the perfect place for families to get away from the touts and hustlers who seem to have taken root in Koh Lanta over recent years. Beautifully decorated, with Thai-style platform beds and murals sketched by a leading Bangkok artist, the rooms are simple but comfortable: bring your own clutter if you want to spoil the rustically minimal lines. The staff are friendly and in such a small beachfront resort will soon get to know your children: it won't be long before you struggle to get them back.

Rooms 20. *Rates* enchanted villa 1200B–3300B, sand castle villa 2800B–6800B, extra bed 500B–800B. *Amenities* two pools plus toddlers' wading pool, restaurant, bar, Internet corner, generator. *In room* A/C, satellite TV, fridge, coffee machine.

FAMILY-FRIENDLY DINING

Phuket

Coral Island Beach Club FIND
THAI

Coral Island Beach Club, Banana Beach, Koh Hae, 📞 07638 3796, www.sea-scooter.com.

The seven-course lunch served on the beach is perhaps not the most compelling reason why this is an excellent dining option. More to the point are the countless outdoor activities put on by this adventure operation, 15 minutes by speedboat from Phuket. Power snorkelling, glass-bottomed kayaks, banana boat rides and parasailing adventures are just some of the things on offer, with batik painting lessons perfect excuses to bring children in from the sun.

Open daily. *Prices* Tickets including resort pickups and speedboat transfers from Chalong Pier or longtails from Rawai Beach 2900B adults,

2300B children 4–11, including a seven-course Thai lunch. Child figure negotiable as owner sympathetic to parents.

Da Ali Restaurant VALUE
ITALIAN/THAI

Laem Singh Beach. No phone.

This gem of a sand-floored shack provides just the excuse you need to explore Laem Singh Beach, a small and beautiful hideaway down a steep path on Thailand's west coast. Of the seven restaurants on the beach this is the best, with a strong Italian influence. While it doesn't have highchairs you can stack two plastic chairs together to raise the level, and lower the table by pressing its legs firmly into the sand. No need to trouble with the Chinken Soup or Boiked Egg that feature on the picture menu; a full selection of Italian and Thai dishes are on offer.

Open *daily in daylight hours.* **Main courses** *180B. No alcohol served.*

Mom Tri's Boathouse ★ ★ ★
THAI/FRENCH

Kata Beach, Phuket. 📞 *07633 0015,* **www.boathousephuket.com**.

At the southern end of Kata Beach, this is that rarest of establishments: a relaxed beachfront setting where a French-trained Thai chef is given free rein to two of the world's finest culinary traditions. There's no road between restaurant and beach, so children can play in the sand – or even eat more economically at a nearby beachfront café while parents stretch out on well-spaced tables and work their way through four-course *degustation* menus, with both Thai and French alternatives, with the option of a carefully chosen glass of wine with each dish. At weekends the restaurant runs cooking classes 10am–2pm, costing 2000B including lunch. This might seem expensive but elsewhere in the world chefs of this calibre would be fiercely protective of their

Mom Tri's Boathouse

secrets – and the lunch itself would cost nearly as much. Children are welcome at the beachfront restaurant until eight in the evening, at which point the management fear they might induce their more romantically inclined clientele to start thinking about birth control.

Open daily 6.30pm–11pm. **Main courses** 600B, four-course degustation menu 1930B per person, with wine 4680B. **Credit** AE, MC, V.

Khao Lak

New Khao Lak Green Beach Resort THAI
See 'Where to Stay', above.

Thai Seafood Restaurant THAI
See 'Where to stay' above.

Krabi

The best meals in Krabi are often served from makeshift kitchens bolted on to motor-cycle sidecars. They set up on the road heading north from the west of Ao Nang Beach, towards Nopparat Thara. Most dishes are priced by weight.

All lodges along the Krabi coast have their own restaurants attached: travelling with children, these will usually be your first, and possibly best, choice for your evening meal. We twice had great Italian evening meals at the tiny Da Ciccione (☎ 085783 3625) on Hat Nopparat Thara: my daughter played Connect Four with the hookers at the deserted

hostess bar next door while my son made friends with mangy and possibly rabid stray dogs on the street. Somehow it just seemed right for this beach.

On the Rocks ASIAN FUSION
Centara Hotel, Krabi, Ao Phai Phlong Beach, 396-396/1 Moo 2, Ao Nang (formerly Central Krabi Bay Resort), Krabi 81000, ☎ 07563 7789, www.centralhotelsresorts.com.

If Railay Beach is too crowded, kayak instead to Ao Phai Phlong Beach, just up the coast to the east of Ao Nang. Just getting there is a great family expedition. You can be there in minutes by kayak or longtail from Ao Nang or Hat Nopparat Thara, or from Ao Nang wade at low tide (though avoid the rocks and preferably wear shoes) or walk in half an hour (wear trainers) along the 'Monkey Trail'.

There is only one hotel on this beach, the Centara, where the best of the three restaurants is 'On the Rocks'. The Australian chef has perfected an Asian fusion cuisine ideally enjoyed as your children play on the quiet empty sands, in the children's pool, or even the children's club. Highlights include white snapper served with asparagus and sun dried tomatoes, and Indian chilled chicken tikka wrapped in roti. With uninterrupted views of Krabi's dramatic limestone karsts this is an unforgettable place to while away a long lunch.

Open daily. **Main courses** from 500B. **Credit** AE, MC, V.

Iced coffee at a Railay Beach Café

Koh Lanta

Same Same but Different THAI

Ba Kan Tiang Beach, Koh Lanta,
📞 *01787 8670.*

Ever wondered where people spending a thousand dollars a night on their hotel bed choose to eat? For guests at the Pimalai it is often at this inexpensive beachfront restaurant right next to their hotel. The name comes from street-vendor patter when selling counterfeit goods but is also a fairly notorious bit of bar-girl slang. There's nothing ambiguous about the food though, with large servings of superfresh seafood spicily flavoured. Ideal for relaxed beachfront cuisine, but reservations are becoming advisable.

Open *daily.* ***Main courses*** *from 300B.*

6 Koh Samui, the Gulf Islands & Coast

KOH SAMUI COAST

Kanchana Buri
Kamphaeng Saen
Don Tum
Pathum Thani
Lam Luk Ka
Ban Sang
Pan Pong
Tha Muang
Tha Maka
Nonthaburi
Nong Chok
Bang Khia
Nakhon Pathon
Chaisi
Sam Phran
★ **Bangkok**
34
Chachoengsao
Photharan
Ban Phrae
Krathum Baen
3
Bang Bo
Phanat Nikhom
Ratcha Buri
Bang Khonthi
35
Samut Sakhon
Samut Prakhan
Chon Buri
Ban Bung
Wat Phleng
Pak Tho
Samut Songkhram
Si Racha
331
Suan Phung
Ban Laem
4
Bay of Bangkok (Ao Krung Thep)
3
Nong Ya Plong
Petcha Buri
Pattaya
36
Bang Chang
Kaeng Krachan
Tha Yang
Sattahip
Rayong
Kaeng Krachan National Park
Cha-Am
✈ **Hua Hin**

Palaw

Mergui

Tenasserim

MYANMAR (BURMA)

Pran Buri
4
Kui Buri
Prachuap Khiri Khan
Thap Sakae
Bang Saphan
Bang SaphanNoi
4
Gulf of Thailand (Gulf of Siam)
Pathiu
Tha Sae
Chumphon

La-un
Sawi
41
Koh Tao
Ban Mae Hat
Lang Suan
Ranong
Pha To
La Mae
Koh Phangan
Thong Sala
4
SOUTHERN PENINSULA
Tha Chana
Na Thon
Koh Samui
Kapoe
Si Phangnga National Park
41
Chaiya
Don Sak
Tha Chang
✈ **Surat Thani**
Khanom
Phun Phin
401
Khao Sok National Park
Ban Na Doem
401
Khian Sa
Khao Sok National Park
Phanom
Ban Takhun
41
Ban Na San

THAILAND
Bangkok ★

Koh Samui ■

★ *Capital City*
●○ *City / Town*
— *Main Route*
— *Rail*
✈ *Airport*
--- *Ferry Route*
🏖 *Beach*

0 — 40 mi
0 — 40 km

It has been said that Koh Samui's biggest problem was falling **coconuts:** I heard 17 people a year died this way. Certainly it's a centre for the fruit, said to have more species than anywhere else on earth. But instead of worrying about them falling on your head it's better to buy one from a roadside vendor, drink its juice and then, if it's the right type, open it up and eat the flesh.

These days many of Koh Samui's coconut plantations have given way to tourist development. An island that had no cars in 1940 and its first concrete road in 1973 now has a busy international airport, a huge Tesco Lotus hypermarket, and a substantial network of roads, villages and towns. Resorts, lodges and hotels crowd every beach but thankfully development has been mainly in low-key, smaller resorts, due in part to a sensible island bylaw that bans any building higher than a coconut palm.

Three-quarters of the population were born in other parts of the country and what was traditionally a backpacker haven is relentlessly drifting upmarket. In Thailand the pattern is familiar. A bamboo hideaway rebuilds beachfront shacks with concrete, plugs in air-conditioning units, digs a swimming pool and then adds a spa: all of a sudden you have a mid-market resort. The smartest developments sidestep this evolution and go straight for Asian chic at its most refined – and expensive. It is still possible, however, to find quiet, family-friendly beaches with good accommodation at a reasonable price.

Koh Samui's position, on the sheltered Gulf of Thailand, does a lot to protect it from the southwestern monsoon rains that drench Phuket through the European summer, though it loses out in high season, from November to May, when its western coast gets roughed up by the northeastern monsoon. All the better for kitesurfing says the tourist board – though very strong riptides come and go on Chaweng Beach and every year people drown. If there's a red flag out stay away.

November is usually Samui's wettest month, though the rain is fitful and still leaves the island basking under seven or eight hours of sunshine every day. Those who prefer a coconut-island paradise – at least when they're not falling on their heads – might decry the flights that flush tourists in from the capital on an almost hourly basis but for families, these are invaluable, shaving hours from the journey from Bangkok, making it easy to bring children to an island that still has a wild and appealing charm.

If you prefer your beaches less developed and a slower pace of life it's easy to take an inter-island ferry to Koh Phangan. Koh Samui's smaller neighbour is best known for its Full Moon Parties, but these take place in one corner of a substantial island. Elsewhere you'll find plenty of quiet, backwater beaches with just a smattering of developments. The third island in the group is Koh Tao, with excellent diving and snorkelling but a disappointing selection of resorts and fewer family beaches.

Often overlooked by overseas visitors, the mainland resorts of Hua Hin and Cha Am, half way between Samui and Bangkok, present great family opportunities. Easily reached overland from the capital, tourism here was sparked by Thai nationals. Holidaymakers here are often expats and the King of Thailand is a prominent resident. Though they can't match the glamour of a paradise island of small palm-fringed bays, this part of the coast does offer huge sweeping white-sand beaches and the towns provide a smooth experience of the Thai culture at its most sophisticated and relaxed.

KOH SAMUI

Essentials

Getting There

By Air Although most of Thailand's airports are owned by the State, Koh Samui's airport (☎ 07742 5029-30), in the north-east of the island, is different. It is owned by Bangkok Airways, which runs an array of routes into the island while keeping the atmosphere friendly and low-key. Direct international flights touch down on the flower-bordered runway from Singapore and Hong Kong, and domestic routes fly direct from Bangkok (Suvarnabhumi), Chiang Mai, Krabi, Pattaya (U-Tapao) and Phuket. Their routes are detailed on *www.bangkokair.com* or you can call them on ☎ 02265 5555 (Bangkok) or ☎ 07724 56000 (Koh Samui). Traditionally Bangkok Air has been able to charge what it likes, but now Thai Airways has also started running flights from Bangkok, usefully denting a monopoly. You can shave a few baht off the price by flying to Surat Thani and then taking a ferry, but there

are more atmospheric boat journeys in Thailand: this one is more hassle than adventure.

At the airport, taxis and minibuses wait for flights and charge fixed rates, between 150B–300B, depending on distance.

For families taxis will work out cheaper than the air-conditioned minibuses that run routes to the various beaches, charging 100B per person. The major hotels will arrange shuttle buses for their clients but often charge for the service.

There are also car rental desks (including Sixt, ☎ 08350 44459, *www.sixt.com*) but bear in mind that Thailand's southern islands have the highest road accident rates in the country.

By Boat Coming from other parts of Southern Thailand the shortest crossing with the mainland is from Surat Thani. Two main operators run boats from Nathon, the principal port on the island's west coast: Songserm Travel (☎ 07742 0157) and Seatran (☎ 07742 6001-2). There is also a slow overnight boat (once again, not recommended).

KOH SAMUI

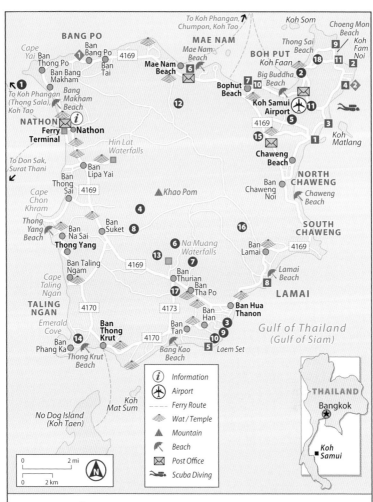

ATTRACTIONS ●

Ang Thong Marine Park **1**

Big Buddha **2**

Kiteboarding Asia **3**

Magic Statue Garden **4**

Monkey Theatre **5**

Na Muang Elephant Camp **6**

Na Muang Falls **7**

Paradise Park Farm **8**

Samui Aquarium & Tiger Zoo **9**

Samui Butterfly Farm **10**

Samui Crocodile Farm **11**

Samui Quad Motor **12**

Sky Fox Cable Ride **13**

Snake Farm **14**

Tesco Lotus **15**

Treetop Tour Cable Ride **16**

Wat Khunaram **17**

Wat Plae Laem **18**

ACCOMMODATION ■

Amari Palm Reef Resort **1**

The Boat House **2**

Chaba Cabana Resort & Spa **3**

Karma Samui **4**

Laem Set Inn **5**

Maenam Resort **6**

Peace Resort **7**

Rocky's Boutique Resort **8**

Sala Samui **9**

The Waterfront **10**

White House Beach Resort & Spa **11**

DINING ◆

Babylon Restaurant &
   Bouncy Castle Park **1**

Padma **2**

Few hotels will meet passengers on the boats that pull in to the main port, Nathon, because their schedule is too unreliable. If you're carrying a family quantity of luggage and trailing tired children it is a long walk to public transport. *Songthaews* run a circular route around the island's ring road at 5B0 per person but they don't leave until they're full and then stop frequently. Families will find taxis a lot more convenient and not much more expensive as a direct ride to even the most distant part of the island should cost no more than 400B.

By Bus If coming from Bangkok, combined coach/ferry journeys take 12 hours in state-run luxury coaches, longer with rail–ferry tickets. The last part of your journey is two-plus uncomfortable hours on a ferry when you all badly need a rest. If you go for this make sure your ticket includes all legs of the journey: otherwise you might find yourself having to spend a night in Surat Thani.

Coming from Chumpon, Koh Phangan and Koh Tao, most boats arrive at piers on Koh Samui's northern coast.

Visitor Information

There is a tourist information desk in the airport, also owned by the airline. The advice favours the Samui Palm Beach, another Bangkok Airways enterprise. The main TAT office (370 Moo 3, Nathon, ☎ 077420720, daily 8.30am–4.30pm) is tucked away in a side street in Nathon just to the north of the ferry terminal. They are helpful but by the time you've sought it out most of the transport meeting the ferry will have left.

Publications

Useful ad-backed monthly publications include *Passport*, a small glossy with money-off coupons and tear-out postcards, *Essential Samui* (**www.essential-magazine. com**), a pocket-sized publication for party-hunters, and *Samui Dining Guide* that amplifies marketing hype. More useful are the bi-monthly *Map Guides* (**http://siammap.com**) that reliably show the road layout and beach locations, with the advertisements little more than a decorative fringe.

Orientation

Koh Samui is Thailand's third-largest island, after Phuket and Koh Chang.

Best put some thought in early as to where you want to be based: the communities that have grown up around the various beaches are all quite different in character and most of your time is likely to be spent near your chosen resort.

Travelling clockwise from the port of Nathon, after about 12km you reach the small northern beach of Ao Bang Po and then the more developed beach of Ao Maenam. The sand is fairly coarse but the beach is sheltered and this is a good place to find inexpensive family accommodation. Next on the north is Bophut, a charming village still largely built of traditional wooden Samui houses. The beach is narrow – especially in the monsoon season – but the range of character restaurants and small hotels make it a good family choice.

Next travelling east is Big Buddha Beach (Bangrak), the closest to the airport, with several new resorts looking out over calm waters towards the huge seated Buddha, built on an island, which gives the bay its name.

Round the Choeng Mon headland on to the island's eastern side there's a beautiful stretch of coast with small, sheltered beaches, including Choeng Mon itself, which open out to the island's largest and most developed beach, Chaweng. This is good for families because in many parts an offshore reef keeps water shallow so children can wade far out with little risk. Inland Chaweng seethes with restaurants, bars and tailors, along with chain outlets such as McDonald's and Starbucks, as well as services such as medical facilities and even a drop-in day-care facility.

Lamai Bay, 10km further south, curves back to the west with a beautiful beach of its own. Free from the bustle of Chaweng it's easy to see why many upmarket resorts are moving in, but the brochure pictures don't show that often the seabed is rocky underfoot, especially at

the northern end, and it is also where you'll see the island's greatest concentration of sleazy hostess bars.

Samui's southern coast has small, stony beaches and is much less developed, although this is where you'll find the Butterfly and Snake Farms and a few quiet, worthwhile resorts. On the west coast Ao Phang Kha is a pretty little beach, but from there back up to Nathon the coast is generally rocky and the coast flat and featureless. Despite sunset views, the area has little to offer families except the modest bouncy-castle playground of the Babylon restaurant.

Getting Around

You can drive around the island's 'ring road', highway 4169, through the forested mountains in as little as 21/2 hours, but with the plethora of advertising billboards and absence of useful signs it's easy to get lost and it can take much longer.

Taxis are relatively expensive and it is not easy to persuade them to use their meters. Flagfall is 90B, then 50B per kilometre for the first two kilometres, then 11B per kilometre after that. This means the minimum charge is 140B for even the shortest hop – and that is when the meter is on.

Songthaews run round the 'ring road' through daylight hours, rates depending on how far you are going and what they think they can get away with. They'll stop where you like and make small detours from their route. Though they're an economical way to cover long distances families find the savings less significant than solo travellers as most taxi journeys should cost 250B or less.

The Thais often carry whole families on a scooter and you can too – by law it is only the driver that has to wear a crash helmet, leaving the rest of the family to take their chances – but accidents are common. It is safer to rent a car. Budget Car Rental (☎ 07742 7188) and Avis (☎ 084700 8161) have offices at the airport, and Hertz (☎ 07723 0500) has a desk at the Central Samui Beach Resort: all offer a range of vehicles starting from 1500B and will deliver and pick up from your resort.

Planning Excursions

Given the issues with getting around, it's easy to see an argument for using a local tour operator who will package different activities into a well-practised itinerary.

Mr Ung's Magical Safari Tour (Moo 3, Chaweng Beach, 84320, ☎ 07723 0114, www.ungsafari.com) has a range of day trips that start at 1400B including lunch, that can feature quad biking, elephant rides, zip wire rides and waterfall swims all in one day.

Rafting Safari Adventure (☎ 07625 4501-3, www.island safaritour.com) packages together ATV riding, elephant trekking, a

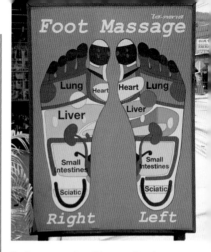

Foot massage sign, Chaweng Beach

monkey show, a ride in an ox-cart and a Thai boxing match in a 2½ hour tour for 900B adult, 700B child.

Independently you'd struggle to pack that number of activities into a day. In the first instance it's best to take advice from your own resort or lodge's tour desk as you'll have more leverage in case of problems. If you get on with them there's no real reason to look further.

Fast Facts

ATMs The major banks have branches in most main towns, including Nathon and Chaweng, and ATMs are everywhere. Even in Bophut, with its ancient wooden buildings, an ATM is provided, circumventing planning restrictions by being fitted into a converted minibus.

Emergencies Dial ☎ 1155 or ☎ 07742 1281 for the Tourist Police.

Hospitals There are excellent health facilities in Chaweng, including decompression chambers and 24-hour rescue and evacuation services if required. It's all private, so be insured. Bangkok Samui Hospital (℡ 07742 9555) and Samui International Hospital (℡ 07723 0781-2) are excellent, while Bandon International Hospital (℡ 07742 5382) has English-speaking doctors who make house calls.

Internet Cafés Most hotels and resorts offer Internet access, along with innumerable cyber-cafés. Chaweng has the highest concentration, with Multi Travel and Tour (164/3 Moo 2 Chaweng, ℡ 07741 3969) one of many.

Post Office There are post offices in Chaweng, Mae Nam and Lamai, all on the main Samui ring road. The main post office (℡ 07742 1013) is on Chonwithi Road in Nathon.

What to See & Do

Children's Top 10 Attractions

❶ **Visit** a monkey theatre. See p 171.

❷ **Blush** for the butterflies. See p 173.

❸ **Zip** through the trees. See p 175.

❹ **Snorkel** Ang Thong Marine Park. See below.

❺ **Quad** bike inland jungle tracks. See p 172.

❻ **Cool** off in a waterfall. See p 175.

❼ **Troll** for sailfish from a traditional boat. See p 169.

❽ **Raft** a mountain river. See p 168.

❾ **Take** in a temple. See p 175.

❿ **Squirm** at a snake show. See p 173.

Attractions

Ang Thong Marine Park
★ ★ ★ AGES 6 AND UP

Even if you plan to spend your entire time on the beach and shun all excursions, make an exception to take a boat trip around Ang Thong National Park. This area includes more than 40 beautiful limestone islands northwest of Samui and their surrounding coral reefs. Many rear up more than 400m from the sea, clad in tropical rain forest and fringed by deserted beaches. One of these islands, containing a sheltered salt-water lagoon, is thought to have inspired Alex Garland's novel *The Beach*.

There are a number of walking nature trails – bring a sturdy pair of walking shoes if you plan to explore inland – snorkelling trails (make sure equipment is provided if you don't have your own) and the chance to canoe through eroded channels to discover the lagoons.

A main operator with a large vessel is the Seatran Discovery boat (☎ 07742 6000). Speedboat operators include Blue Stars (☎ 07723 0497, *www.bluestars. info*) in Chaweng and Grand Sea Discovery (☎ 07742 7001, ☎ 07724 7668, *www.grandseatours.com*) in Maenam. Prices vary from 1800B to 2500B per day depending whether you're just snorkelling or also including island walks and kayaking expeditions.

Buddhist Temples and Shrines ★★ ALL AGES

Although it's not strong on old monuments Koh Samui has several temples that will enthuse young minds. The most dramatic is new. Built on an islet linked to the island by a causeway, the Big Buddha is an island icon 12m tall: chances are your children will have seen it from the flight in, or will catch a glimpse on the flight out – the best views of it. The statue attracts coachloads of Thai tourists but there's not that much else to see.

Instead drop into Wat Plae Laem, just inland on the 4171 Ring Road, where huge, almost cartoon-like sculptures of mythological gods and creatures have been built: 18-armed gods and giggling fat men, towering over gilt-and-crimson temples.

Other sites that might interest children are the two temples that hold bodies of mummified monks. The most popular is Wat Khunaram, along the main road (4169) south of Lamai as it shoots inland to Nathon. Here a monk who died while meditating 20 years ago is still stuck, though now paper-dry, in the same pose.

Kiteboarding Asia ★★
AGES 10 AND UP

Samui Orchid Resort, Tiger Zoo and Aquarium, Hua Thanon, south of

Wat Plae Laem Temple, Koh Samui

Lamai, ☎ *0815 914 592; also at Hua Hin, just to the south of the Marriott Beach Resort,* ☎ *0815 914 593,* ***www.kiteboardingasia.com****.*

November to March is kiteboarding season in Koh Samui, with onshore or cross-shore winds on the beautiful western beaches. Children love the sense of the power of the wind and the race of the board over the waves. Kiteboarding Asia is one of the country's leading schools, with offices at the southern end of Lamai Beach. They don't stop teaching at the end of March, but move round the island to follow ideal conditions. They also have a school at Hua Hin where they use waterproof intercoms in your helmet. The best equipment is very expensive and ages quickly in the sun and salt water, which might explain the somewhat alarming cost.

Cost *beginner's one-day course 4000B, three-day beginner package 11,000B.*

Magic Statue Garden ★★
ALL AGES

No phone. Top of Kao Yai.

In 1976 a well-respected local farmer decided, at the age of 77, to build an open-air sculpture gallery deep in the jungled mountains on the top of Kao Yai, the island's tallest peak. With a selection of Buddhas, demons and gods on display, scattered on unkempt walking trails around a derelict timber-built chalet, this is an interesting alternative to a day on the beach and if your children are sunburned, it would give them the chance to wander round an unspoiled patch of jungle without being taunted all day by the sight of the sea.

Unfortunately the direct tarmac road is through a military zone and the alternative route is tough dirt, so it's best to take a tour in a four-wheel drive with a company such as Jungle Safari (☎ 07723 0144).

Admission *free – something of a welcome novelty on Koh Samui.*

Monkey Theatre ★★ ALL AGES

31/7 Moo 6, Tambon BoPhut, 84320, ☎ *07796 0128-9. On the back road between Chaweng and Bophut close to Bandon Hospital.*

Before tourism Koh Samui's economy revolved around coconuts, and for this they relied on monkeys to help. Over the centuries monkeys have been trained to climb the plants and pick ripe nuts. A good monkey, probably trained on the mainland near Surat Thani, can pick 800 a day.

Though there is less money in coconuts these days, you can see monkeys at work in several places: just look out for scrappy roadside signs saying 'Monkey work coconut' and your arrival will galvanise a sleepy farmer to spur his monkey into action.

Better by far for children is to go to the island's Monkey Theatre. Here you will see at close range how monkeys loosen the nuts before an idiosyncratic show that will include monkeys riding bicycles, doing maths, playing instruments or swimming, depending on the monkeys' available skills.

Shows *daily 10.30am, 2pm, 4.30pm.* **Admission** *150B adults, 80B children.* **Amenities** *simple café.*

Na Muang Elephant Camp
★★   ALL AGES

25/11 Moo 2, Tambon Na Muang, Koh Samui 84140, ☎ 07742 4098. By Na Muang Waterfall.

If your children have never ridden an elephant this could be their chance: there are 50 on Koh Samui. Elephant rides are often included as part of a tour, but to do a stand-alone elephant ride head up to the Na Muang Elephant Camp in the south of the island for a 30-minute journey through the jungle. Small children can also ride on a baby elephant called Spunky.

Open *daily.* **Rates** *700B adults, 500B children.*

Paradise Park Farm OVERRATED
ALL AGES

☎ 07741 8351, www.paradisepark farm.com.

Experiences of Samui's latest attraction aren't favourable, which is a shame as otherwise it would be ideal for families. Set in the mountainous interior it is a private park of waterfalls, small rivers, canyons, wildlife animals and exotic birds, where you can learn about rubber tapping and local flora and fauna.

There are walking trails with aviaries, animals to spot, an infinity pool, spa and a restaurant where the staff often leave the prices blank so they can inflate your final bill. There are a few animals around – including a baby unfriendly emu, and at least one people-hostile monkey – and though the pool and restaurants have fantastic views over the island few people think it justifies the long drive from the coast.

Open *daily 7am–5pm.* **Rates** *300B adults, 100B children, under fours free.*

Quad Bike in the Jungle ★★
AGES 5 AND UP

Children with a taste for speed should steer clear of Samui Go Karts which charges an eye-watering 300B for 10 minutes in the slow lane. Instead head to the hills where Samui Quad Motor runs tours through the jungle lasting two hours or more and can combine that with zip wires or elephant rides.

Rates *Samui Quad Motor (☎ 08484 26081) from 1500B for a driver of a 250cc quad that can take children pillion. Over 12s can rent a 125cc automatic for two hours, taking in a waterfall dip, for 2000B. Namuang ATV Park (☎ 07742 4729) has a circuit opposite Wat Khunaram with a range of quad bikes from 90cc to 700cc.*

Samui Aquarium & Tiger Zoo
OVERRATED   ALL AGES

Hua Thanon, 33/2 Moo 2, Tambon Maret, 84310, ☎ 07742 4017-8, ☎ 07723 2198.

Samui's only aquarium and tiger zoo is a somewhat underwhelming experience. The tanks in the aquarium are too small for the fish they contain, the tigers look miserable, and in the tiger show, where they jump through burning hoops and do other circus tricks, they look bullied. The only ray of light is the bird show, where parrots, macaws and cockatoos perform flying displays, along with birds of prey such as red and sea eagles.

Open daily 9am–6pm, show 1pm. **Admission** 250B adults, 150B children 6–12. **Credit** MC, V.

Samui Butterfly Farm ★
ALL AGES

Centara Villas Samui. 111 Moo 2, Tambon Maret, 84310, ☎ 07742 4020-2.

Get up close to many of Thailand's 520 butterfly species and learn about their life stages at this relaxing farm set in tropical foliage. There are also moths, a bee house and other insects. Views are of the island's southeast coast: it's a pleasant outing but you're unlikely to dally too long.

Samui Butterfly Farm

Open daily 9am–6pm. **Admission** 120B adults, 60B children under 12. **Credit** MC, V.

Samui Crocodile Farm ★
ALL AGES

Bang Rak, 30/24 Moo 4, Tambon Bophut, 84320, ☎ 07723 9002, ☎ 0892 899 613, behind the airport.

More than 100 animals of various kinds, including Siam crocodiles, saltwater crocodiles, snakes, lizards and monkeys form the residents of this cross between zoo, farm and theatre. Crocodile shows feature the standard displays of trainers putting their heads between their jaws. It's a good way to vary the pace of yet another day on the beach.

Open daily 9am–6pm, shows 2pm, 4.30pm. **Admission** 250B adults, 150B children 6–12. **Credit** MC, V.

Snake Farm ★★ ALL AGES

Thong Krut, 88/3 Moo 4, Tambon Talingngam, 84140, ☎ 07742 3247, ☎ 07741 5100.

Drop-in Childcare

From Tuesday to Sunday Kate's Kids Club in Chaweng takes in children by the day or hour. British-run, it has a qualified UK teacher on the premises at all times, a shady outdoor play area and an indoor learning/fun zone. Light meals and snacks are served and they can even arrange local pickups. Prices from 50B per hour, 750B per day. 152 Moo 2, Chaweng, 84320, ☎ 08371 00115, ☎ 083172 8901, *E: katieliz walsh@yahoo.co.uk*.

All kinds of snakes and reptiles have been collected at the Samui Snake Farm at Talingngam on the south of the island. Daily displays demonstrate snakes in action at entertaining – and somewhat hair-raising – shows featuring cobras, centipedes and scorpions that are guaranteed to make your skin crawl. There are also exhibition rooms and snakes houses to visit.

*Shows daily 11am, 2pm. **Admission** 250B adults, 150B children.*

Snorkelling ★★★ AGES 5 AND UP

Snorkelling is something even quite young children love to do. Almost every beachside mini-mart sells child goggles and flippers, and if you want to take it further countless dive schools will rent out masks and fins for 100B per day.

There's good snorkelling in the rocky area between Chaweng Noi and Lamai Beach, but whenever the sand gives way to rock you'll find something going on underwater.

For serious snorkelling take a boat over to Ang Thong Marine Park or Koh Tao. Rather than piling on to a crowded snorkelling boat you might prefer to tag along with a dive school, which usually take non-divers at a reduced rate.

Start Diving
★★★ AGES 10 AND UP

If you are going to start your children diving there are worse places to do it. There are recompression facilities, but check your operator is insured to use them: call ☎ 07742 7427 for further information.

The open water around Samui can be squally so choose an operator familiar with prevailing conditions. Good ones include Samui International Diving School (at the Malibu Resort, Chaweng Beach, ☎ 07742 2386, *www.planet-scuba.net*); Easy Divers with branches in Chaweng (☎ 07741 3373, *www. easydivers-thailand.com*) and other beaches; and Big Blue (☎ 07745 6415, *www.bigbluediving. com*) on Koh Tao for customised trips.

The minimum age is usually 10 and most operators offer bubble-maker courses for the young, getting children to accomplish one dive in relative safety. This will take most of a day and cost in the region of 1500B in a pool (which is neither exciting nor easy) or 2000B in the sea.

To qualify as a PADI Open Water Diver can be packed into as little as four days, though passing is not guaranteed, and will cost in the region of 12,500B.

Tesco Lotus

Between Chaweng and Bophut.

It hardly sounds adventurous, but if the rains sweep in this is a good place to stock up with comfort food and visit the tenpin bowling alley and the cinema. To find out what English-language films are showing call ☎ *07742 7299.*

Wash in a Waterfall ★★
ALL AGES

Thais aren't always too keen on the sea, but love the clean feel of a freshwater waterfall, where they tend to focus on the natural swimming pool at the base. The most popular on the island is the Na Muang Falls, 5km up a dirt track from Route 4169. Take care during heavy rain: in 2007 there was a fatal accident here, caused by a sudden landslide.

Zipwire through the trees

Zipwire Through the Trees
★★ AGES 8 AND UP

Canopy Adventures, ☎ *07741 4150-1,* *www.canopyadventuresthailand. com.*

The Treetop Tour Cable Ride, ☎ *01968 4806, E: treetoptour@yahoo.com.*

Sky Fox Super Ride, ☎ *07742 2667.*

Several operators have set up in Samui's mountainous, jungle hinterland with zip wire playgrounds. Canopy Adventures has established itself in the middle of the forest inland from Maenam, stretching 500m in easy stages across the 'Secret Falls' river with no climbing involved. They have hourly shuttles leaving from the Best Beach Bungalows in Chaweng 9am–4pm, though

FUN FACT ≫ **Snakes Alive** ≪

Thailand has about 163 species of snake, 85 of which are venomous. The largest snake ever discovered was a python found in the jungle: it was nearly 10 metres long. If you find a stray snake call the Samui Snake Rescue and Relocation Centre on ☎ *0966 35085.*

White Elephants

The English phrase 'white elephant' originated in Thailand, where albino elephants are extremely revered. These days there is little space for elephant to roam wild and mechanisation has robbed them of any useful role for logging or on farms. Elephant get through a massive amount of grass, sugarcane and bananas every day (250kg) plus 150 litres of water, and whatever their colour they represent a huge financial burden. You will often see elephants begging for alms in major Thai cities and on beaches – though they've recently been banned from Bangkok because of the traffic – and they are a worthy cause: they often outlive their owners and have nowhere to go. Tourist shows and trekking rides are their best chance of a useful commercial life.

they call the service a 4×4 safari perhaps because the access road is terrible. Exploring the circuit, with experts helping clip you on and off the wires and making sure you stop before hitting any trees, takes around two hours, but you can also fish around in the shady river pools of Secret Falls and breathe in the cool mountain air.

In the mountains above Chaweng the Treetop Tour Cable Ride has 300m of cabling and Sky Fox Super Ride has 600m. Although Canopy Adventures says it takes children as young as six, it largely depends on the child's height and temperament.

Open daily. Rates from 1700B adults, 1200B children under 12: Treetop and Sky Fox are often combined with Namuang Waterfall and Namuang Safari Park. Amenities simple café (Thai food only) in a jungle hut.

KOH PHANGAN

Just to the north of Koh Samui, the island of Koh Phangan is world-famous for its Full Moon Parties, but the lunar madness is restricted to one part of the island and in any case is much diminished. Full moon celebrations have dissolved into a series of commercial events as blackmoon, quarter-moon and halfmoon parties. These days plainclothes police enforce Thailand's strict drug laws at lacklustre affairs that have been sold to death.

But there's a great deal to like about the rest of the island. Beyond the 'Party Beaches' of Had Rin in the south it is beautifully calm and peaceful. There's not much to do here aside from a couple of small elephant camps, but that's all part of its charm. Activities are swimming, snorkelling, sailing, kayaking and trekking, and that's about it.

The beaches are every bit as good as those on Koh Samui but totally different in atmosphere: each has just a few, well-spaced resorts, and some can only be reached by boat.

KOH PHANGAN

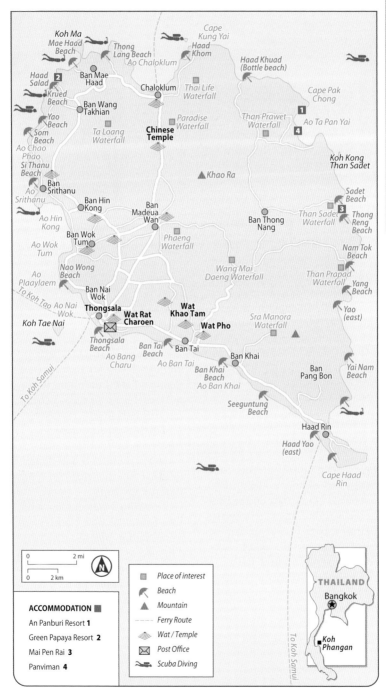

Koh Ma
Mae Haad
Beach
Thong
Lang Beach
Ao Chaloklum
Cape
Kung Yai
Haad
Khom
Haad Khuad
(Bottle beach)
Haad
Salad
2
Ban Mae
Haad
Chaloklum
Thai Life
Waterfall
Cape Pak
Chong
Krued
Beach
Ban Wang
Takhian
Ao Ta Pan Yai
1
Yao
Beach
Som
Beach
Ao Chao
Phao
Ta Loang
Waterfall
Paradise
Waterfall
**Chinese
Temple**
Than Prawet
Waterfall
4
Si Thanu
Beach
Koh Kong
Than Sadet
Ao
Srithanu
Ban
Srithanu
▲ Khao Ra
Ban Hin
Kong
Ban
Madeua
Wan
Sadet
Beach
Ao Hin
Kong
Ban Thong
Nang
Than Sadet
Waterfall
3
Thong
Reng
Beach
Ao Wok
Tum
Ban Wok
Tum
Phaeng
Waterfall
Nam Tok
Beach
Ao
Plaaylaem
Nao Wong
Beach
Wang Mai
Daeng Waterfall
Than Prapad
Waterfall
Yang
Beach
To Koh Tao Ao Nai
Wok
Ban Nai
Wok
Thongsala
**Wat
Khao Tam**
Yao
(east)
**Wat Rat
Charoen**
Koh Tae Nai
⊠
Wat Pho
Sra Manora
Waterfall
▲
Thongsala
Beach
Ban Tai
Beach
Ban Tai
Ban Khai
Ban
Pang Bon
Yai Nam
Beach
Ao Bang
Charu
Ao Ban Tai
Ban Khai
Beach
Ao Ban Khai
To Koh Samui
Seeguntung
Beach
Haad Rin
Haad Yao
(east)
Cape Haad
Rin

0	2 mi
0	2 km

(N)

■ Place of interest
🏖 Beach
▲ Mountain
--- Ferry Route
🛕 Wat / Temple
⊠ Post Office
🤿 Scuba Diving

ACCOMMODATION ■

An Panburi Resort **1**

Green Papaya Resort **2**

Mai Pen Rai **3**

Panviman **4**

THAILAND

Bangkok ★

■ Koh
Phangan

To Koh Samui

Boats to Koh Phangan from Chumphon Pier

From Samui's northern piers it only takes 30 minutes to reach Koh Phangan by boat, but this short journey gets you away from the fly-in crowds, accommodation prices drop dramatically, and hassle levels plummet. If your family like simply relaxing on a beach the journey is well worthwhile.

Essentials

Getting There

Boats to Koh Phangan from Koh Samui arrive either at the principal town, Thong Sala on the west of the island, or the party beaches in the south at Haad Rin. For families Thong Sala makes a better landing place, but if you're coming from Koh Samui's airport or one of the northern or western beaches the shortest crossings, from Maenam or Big Buddha Bay, will drop you at Haad Rin. Fastest is the twice-daily Lomprayah Catamaran (on Samui ☎ 07742 7765-6, on Koh Phangan ☎ 07723 8412, *www. lomprayah.com*), which leaves from Wat Na Phra Larn on Maenam. The crossing takes about 30 minutes and costs 250B.

Lomprayah also makes daily sailings on to Koh Tao and the mainland at Chumphon, north of Surat Thani on the way back towards Bangkok.

The Haad Rin Queen also runs a service four times daily from Big Buddha Beach directly to Haad Rin Pier that takes 30 minutes for 150B.

Travelling from the south of Koh Samui head to Nathon and from Nathon pier the trip to Thong Sala in Koh Phangan takes 45 minutes with the Songserm Express Boat (☎ 07742 0157) and costs 130B, while the Seatran car ferry leaves daily from Bang Rak.

Frequent boats link Koh Phangan with the mainland towns of Chumphon and Surat

Thani, but crossings can be scary and dangerous (rough seas) between June and December.

Visitor Information

Publications

Useful publications include the monthly *Phangan Explorer* (**www.phanganexplorer.com**) and bi-monthly *Phangan Info* (**www.phangan.info**), which also produces a guide/map.

Orientation

Two thirds the size of Koh Samui, Koh Phangan is far less developed. No road goes all around the island and tarmac stretches are the exception, not the norm. Thong Sala is on the island's southwest, while Haad Rin, party central, is on the southeast. There's a reasonable road with frequent transport linking these two centres but elsewhere there's little traffic. Unless you intend to charter a taxi across – or a boat around – the island you need to plan journeys in advance. There are any number of beaches, few of them crowded, including Haad Salad and Haad Noi Yao to the west and Thong Nai Pan in the north, that are well worth seeking out.

Getting Around

Regular *songthaews* run between Had Rin and Thong Sala, but to get to the best beaches, such as Haad Salad, Ao Thong Nai Pan Noi or Thaan Sadet you'll need to be lucky – and to start early in the day – to catch shared transport.

With a family the obvious option is to rent a *songthaew* of your own, costing 800B or so to get from one side of the island to the other. It will take around an hour because the roads are terrible. Getting back is generally cheaper as you'll be able to plan your departure to fit in with a local driver already making the journey.

A more comfortable way to reach out-of-the-way beaches is to hire a boat, if the weather is calm, from Haad Rin or Thong Sala. Koh Phangan's expensive resorts will arrange speedboats transfers from Koh Samui, but often only one a day, and many passengers paying resort prices for the journey resent what is effectively a scheduled service.

Fast Facts

Emergencies The tourist police operate a small information kiosk (☎ *07742 1281* info, ☎ *1155* emergency) on the north end of Thong Sala Pier.

Internet Service is slow and expensive but available at even remote beaches: prices are generally 120B an hour.

Money Thong Sala has branches of the main Thai banks and you'll find ATMs here and in Had Rin.

KOH TAO

'Turtle Island' is best known for its diving which has become so popular that in high season from December to March, it can be impossible to find anywhere to stay. Outside these months it might be an acceptable family choice, especially for those with a special interest in diving or snorkelling, but accommodation is overpriced and the welcome variable. Certainly there's nowhere that can be whole-heartedly recommended.

Essentials

Getting There

Ferries arrive at Ao Mae Hat and Mae Hat village, with the greatest concentration of bungalow resorts just north of here on Hat Sai Ree.

HUA HIN

The King of Thailand has his country palace – and a grocery shop – in Hua Hin and it's easy to see why he likes the place. Developed in the 1920s as a sort of 'Thai Riviera', it can be reached from Bangkok in four hours by train, arriving in the perfectly preserved wooden-built 1920s' station.

Through the 1970s Pattaya, with its longer summer season and party-going atmosphere, siphoned off any sleaze from this royal resort. Along with the slightly staid Cha Am, 40km

north along the coast, and the Thai yuppie hangout of Pranburi 40km to the south, Hua Hin is a very good family choice for those who want to blend a traditional beach experience with a vivid taste of 21st-century Thai culture.

The climate is best between November and May, but through these months hotels are often full, especially at weekends. Midweek many hotels have to drop their rates or introduce special deals. From June to November there is more rain, peaking in October, but this is rarely incessant.

Essentials

Getting There

By Bus From the south regular buses leave Surat Thani (arrival point from Koh Samui) or Chumpon (arrival point from Koh Tao) heading towards Bangkok. Most if not all will drop you off in Hua Hin, though probably just by the side of the main road rather than at a station. If coming from the islands buy combined boat/bus tickets (200B–250B) or risk being stranded on the pier.

Buses leave Bangkok's Southern Bus Station (📞 02434 7192) every 20 minutes (155B) and take a little longer to reach Hua Hin Bus Station (📞 03251 1230).

By Air From Bangkok the fastest way to arrive is by air, with four daily connections to Suvarnabhumi Airport in 12-seater Cessna 208B Caravan

HUA HIN

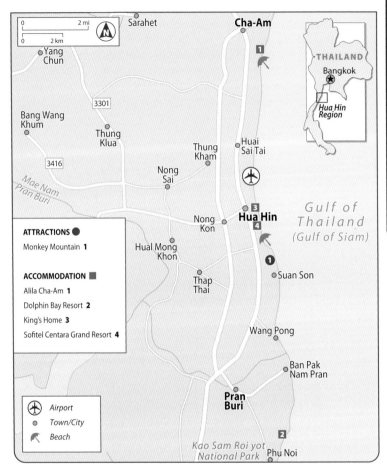

ATTRACTIONS ●
Monkey Mountain **1**

ACCOMMODATION ■
Alila Cha-Am **1**
Dolphin Bay Resort **2**
King's Home **3**
Sofitel Centara Grand Resort **4**

⊕ Airport
● Town/City
↖ Beach

planes operated by Siam General Aviation (📞 02664 6099, *www.sga. co.th*). The flight takes 40 minutes and costs 5200B.

By Car Less expensive is to charter a taxi, which should cost no more than 3000B from Bangkok's airports or centre, and (outside rush hour) take only three hours.

By Rail The best way to travel is to catch one of several trains a

day that rattle slowly out of Bangkok's Hualamphong Station (262B, 📞 02223 7010) and make leisurely progress to Hua Hin's beautiful toytown timber station (📞 03251 1073).

Visitor Information

The Hua Hin TAT (8.30am–4.30pm, 📞 03251 1047, 📞 03253 2433) is tucked behind the city shrine at the corner of

Teetering Squid Piers

Central to Hua Hin's character are the timber Squid Piers that hang off the side of the modern city over the beach or, at high tide, the sea. Most are now used as guest houses and specialist seafood restaurants, but few have any legal title. There's a constant pressure from land-hungry developers for this prime piece of real estate and at any time this important vestige of Thailand's past could be bulldozed away in the race to modernity.

Damnoenkasem and Petchkasem roads.

Publications

Local ad-led publications include *Hua Hin Pocket Guide* and *Inside Hua Hin*, and there are several free local event calendars and maps.

Orientation

Thanks to the straight line of the coast and the main route from north to south, Petchkasem Road, which runs parallel four blocks inland, Hua Hin is easy to navigate. The road to know is the wide Damnoenkasem Road that runs from the railway station, across the Petchkasem highway, and continues straight to the beach and the original Railway Hotel, now the Sofitel Grand.

Walking distance north of here are the main restaurant, shopping and hotel areas, and the atmospheric stilted wooden Squid Piers.

Getting Around

Songthaew pickup trucks follow regular routes in Hua Hin, passing the railway station and bus terminals at regular intervals, with fares from 15B– 30B per person. The journey to Cha Am costs 100B– 200B.

Tuk-tuks and three-wheeled *samlors* ply the streets, and rides within town start at 30B if you bargain.

Avis has a car hire desk at Hua Hin's Sofitel Centara Grand (03251 2021), as does Budget at the Grand Hotel (03251 4220) and self-drive rates start at 1500B. However, inland from the Squid Piers, central Hua Hin is a labyrinth of small streets and alleys best explored on foot.

Fast Facts

Emergencies The tourist police are on 1155 and 03251 5995.

Hospitals The Hua Hin Hospital (03252 0371) is on the Petchkasem Road to the north of town.

Money Banks are along Petchkasem Road and there are

Toy planes on sale at Hua Hin Beach

forex desks and ATMs through-out town.

Post The main post office
(📞 *03251 1350*) is on
Damnoenkasem Road near the
Petchkasem intersection. There
are Internet cafés on most city-centre shopping streets.

What to See & Do

The pleasures of Hua Hin lie on
the beach, with horses as well as
kites for hire, and a plethora of
sandy shacks selling super-fresh
seafood.

In the centre, where the stilted
Squid Piers provide atmospheric
dining, colourful night markets
display the daily catch and
restaurants rub shoulders with
occasionally seedy bars.

Other activities include set-ting out on lunchtime cruises,
playing golf or visiting an ele-phant sanctuary.

Monkey Mountain ★★
ALL AGES

Khao Takiab.

The most popular excursion
from Hua Hin for families is
5km south of the centre where
an isolated hill rears up over the
beach, covered with Buddhas of
all shapes and sizes. Its Thai
name means 'Chopstick
Mountain' but everyone calls it
Monkey Mountain because it's
crawling with the little critters.
Vendors sell hands of bananas to
give to the monkeys, but if your
children are handing them out
too slowly the primates will soon
gang up for a mugging that will
be as violent as it has to be:
many visits end with a burst of
monkey violence and sudden,
shocked tears.

In consolation the statues are
varied and beautiful, with stun-ning views of the gulf coast.

Karma Samui

FAMILY-FRIENDLY ACCOMMODATION

Koh Samui

VERY EXPENSIVE

Karma Samui ★

Koh Samui, near Choeng Mon. 80/32 Moo 5, Bo Phut, 84320, 📞 *077234500,* **www.karmasamui.com**.

Tucked away over a private beach (small with rocks and coarse sand) the Karma Samui has tiered pool villas in a range of configurations to accommodate any size of family. The three-bedroom villas are huge: each bedroom en suite, the whole place air-conditioned and the vast living room decorated in a cosmopolitan, minimalist style. One of the villas has been converted into a small but beautifully-run children's club.

The only problem for families is that there is no way of keeping children out of the pool (without locking them in their rooms)

and the restaurant is ringed with unprotected drops. It's also quite remote: if the hotel's excellent (but expensive) restaurant starts to pall, you'll have to drive or get a taxi. Apart from that it's bliss.

*Rooms 36. **Rates** luxury pool villa 20,300B–28,700B, three-bedroom pool villa 36,750B–50,050B including gourmet breakfast and airport pickup. **Amenities** two pools, restaurant, Chakra spa. **In room** fully-equipped kitchen, incl. dishwasher, fridge/ freezer, washer/dryer, A/C, flat-screen TV/DVD with film library, in-villa dining, outdoor pavilion with day bed.*

Sala Samui ★★

Koh Samui, Choeng Beach. 10/9 Moo 5, Baan Plai Lam Bo Phut, Koh Samui 84320, 📞 *07724 5888,* **www. salasamui.com**.

The first thing parents with young children have to do here is sign a disclaimer because the vast majority of the rooms are pool villas. If you're happy to keep an eye on your offspring this is a fantastic place to stay. One- and two-bedroom villas are beautifully equipped, comfortable in a fresh, contemporary Thai style, and focused on your own private pool. Balcony Suites are also perfectly large enough to fit a child as well.

Children are welcomed with colouring books and toys, child lifejackets are available, baby monitors provided for parents who want to leave their children sleeping, and children's bicycles and fishing equipment are available. Right on one of Samui's best quiet beaches, this is a good upmarket choice.

Rooms *69 units, including 53 pool villas in seven configurations.* ***Rates*** *double balcony 11,000B–12,300B, two-bedroom pool villa suite from 35,000B–43,500B, room only.* ***Credit*** *AE, DC, MC, V.* ***Amenities*** *restaurant and villa dining, two beachfront pools with bubble beds, Mandara spa.* ***In room*** *Satellite TV, A/C, fridge.*

EXPENSIVE

Amari Palm Reef Resort ★

Koh Samui, Chaweng Beach, Samui 84320 (north end of the main Chaweng strip), 📞 *07742 2015,* ***www.amari.com/palmreef***.

This fun family resort has sea-facing suite rooms that are slick and contemporary, with a hint of traditional Thai décor, while the main block has less luxurious rooms. Family rooms – with two single beds on a mezzanine reached by steep wooden stairs – are in a newer selection of mid-range units, set around their own pool on the wrong (inland) side of the main Chaweng Road. This is less dangerous than it might sound, because staff are

on duty 24/7 here, stopping the traffic and helping you – and your children – across.

The central beachside pool area is shady and appealing, as is the dining terrace overlooking it, and the resort is far enough from Chaweng's central strip to be quiet, but close enough to walk there.

Rooms *187 units.* ***Rates*** *superior double 7200B–9000B, family suite 13,100B–15,300B, suite 24,120B–31,500B, extra bed 1640B.* ***Credit*** *AE, MC, V.* ***Amenities*** *three restaurants, two outdoor pools, squash court, spa, children's' club, tour desk.* ***In room*** *A/C, satellite TV, fridge, coffeemaker, babysitting.*

The Boat House

Koh Samui, Choeng Mon. 83 Moo 5, Choeng Mon Beach, Samui 84320, 📞 *07742 5041,* ***www.imperialhotels. com***.

The Boat House is a most unusual resort with a boat-themed design that pervades every detail. The pool is boat-shaped, with cannon, and the most interesting rooms are set in converted timber rice-barges, giving suite accommodation with skylit bathrooms and separate living rooms. They're not necessarily the most comfortable though – the resort's modern wings are lighter with fewer bugs.

The property as a whole is a natural for children, but the hotel insists on marketing itself to honeymooners, wedding planners and even – horrors – conference groups. Take your family anyway, the staff love children, who in turn enjoy swinging on the cannons that point over the main pool, playing endless rounds of table tennis, and making the most of the complimentary watersports on the beach.

Rooms 210, including 34 boat suites. *Rates double 4300B–8500B, boat suite 6800B–11,200B, extra beds 1300B.* *Credit AE, DC, MC, V.* *Amenities spa, two swimming pools, two restaurants, two bars, free windsurfers and canoes, dive school, free table tennis.* *In room A/C, tea/coffee, satellite TV.*

Chaba Cabana Resort & Spa ★

North end of Chaweng Beach, Koh Samui. 160 Moo 2, Bo Put, Koh Samui 84320, ☎ 07723 1350-9, www.chabanet.com.

Set at the quiet, northern end of Chaweng Beach, the sands here are smooth and fine and catch the sun well into the evening, long after other resorts have been drawn into the shade. Conversely, and just as important for children, there is always shade around the pool which is itself right on the beach. Rooms are rather dated but all have balcony or terrace, and the resort's waterfront position means you can stroll into town along the beach, avoiding traffic.

Rooms 80 rooms and suites. *Rates deluxe rooms (sleeping two adults and up to two children) 9360B–11,115B, extra bed 1200B. Junior suites and deluxe villas also available.* *Credit AE, DC, MC, V.* *Amenities canoes, mountain bikes, children's play area, two pools, table tennis, spa.* *In room A/C, satellite TV with in-house movies, fridge.*

Laem Set Inn, Laem Beach
★★★ FIND

Laem Set Beach, Koh Samui. 110 MU 2, Hua Thanon, Koh Samui 84310, ☎ 07723 3299, ☎ 07742 4393, www.laemset.com.

The kayaks leak and the goggles are perished: in several unimportant ways this hotel is on the slide, but it's still a total favourite with families. Thanks to a range of accommodation from simple bungalows knocked up out of recycled wood to lavish pool villas sleeping 10 – it can suit a range of budgets. Unusually for Thailand many rooms are also furnished with bunk-beds.

Facilities include two supervised playgrounds, with a padded play area for young children, and another playground where there is a 10m Ferris wheel (the 'Laem Set Eye'). Child-minding is available at any time of day, there are toys all over the place, and child bikes to rent alongside adult models.

Each evening there's a special early supper sitting so children can be sent off to bed.

Set on a quiet beach it's a long way from Chaweng, but there are plenty of small restaurants within walking distance, and the peace is sublime. Generally it's full of savvy expat families who fly in from all over the Far East to holiday here, so book ahead.

Rooms 65. *Rates fan-cooled bungalow 900B, standard room 2250B–3263B, studio suite 4350B–6113B, room only.* *Credit MC, V.* *Amenities spa, swimming pool and bubble pool, restaurant, kayaks, pedal boats, supervised playgrounds, baby-minding*

Rocky's Boutique Resort

service. **In room** *in the cheapest fan only, in most A/C, fridge, several fitted with bunk-beds, no phone.*

Rocky's Boutique Resort ★★

Lamai Beach, Koh Samui. 438/1 Moo 1, Lamai, Tambon Maret, Koh Samui 84310 (near Lamai Beach), 📞 *07723 3020-1, www.rockyresort. com.*

This relatively new resort brings boutique luxury and flexible, family-friendly accommodation to Koh Samui, with one- to four-bedroom villas on a rocky hillside above a private sandy beach. There are two pools, one in the gardens and another (down a steep, rocky pathway) on the beach. It's five minutes to the north of Lamai (free hotel shuttle) which makes it quiet and peaceful, though perhaps a little remote. There is a hotel longtail that can, for a price, whisk you to private beaches or to explore Ang Thong National Park.

Service is often excellent in Thailand but here it is exceptional, the proportion of staff to guests being one to one, and you'll find they quickly recognise – and keep a careful eye on – your children.

Rooms *33 units.* **Rates** *deluxe gardenview 6100B–9400B, family beachfront villas 14,625B–16,400B.* **Credit** *AE, MC, V.* **Amenities** *two pools, restaurant, complimentary canoes, boat for fishing and snorkelling trips, tour desk, wifi.* **In room** *A/C, TV/DVD.*

MODERATE

Peace Resort

Bophut Beach, Koh Samui. 178 Moo 1, Bo Phut, Koh Samui 84320, 📞 *07742 5357, www.peaceresort. com.*

This family-run resort in Bophut has four types of free-standing bungalows set in lush, peaceful gardens. Villas are spacious, with sunny yellow interiors and private

Sea Wrap Beachfront restaurant at the Peace Resort

verandas. There is a playground and a large central pool with a separate children's pool. The least expensive villas are smaller and although they represent quite good value, they are a fair way back from the beach and not places you'll want to hang around in all day. The extra distance might also cost you dear in the morning race to reserve a sunbed, which is something of a battle here. The beachfront villas are nicer – and extra bed costs stay the same.

Rooms 122 units. *Rates* double 4000B–5100B, beachfront villa 9000B–15,000B, extra bed 1200B–1400B inc. breakfast. *Credit* MC, V. *Amenities* restaurant, bar, pool with children's pool, spa, playground; tour desk. *In room* A/C, satellite TV, fridge, babysitting.

The Waterfront ★★★ FIND

Bophut Beach, Koh Samui. 71/2 Moo Bophut, 84320, ☎ 07742 7165, www.thewaterfrontbophut.com.

If there is one village centre that's worth staying in on Koh Samui, it's the wood-built straggle of bars, shops and restaurants that make up Bophut. This British-run boutique property, right on the beach, with a central pool at the heart of just 12 guest rooms, is often filled with repeat clients.

Apart from standard guest rooms there are two-bedroom beachfront suites, family rooms and family apartments. Most unusually for Thailand, one of the guest rooms even has disabled access and there are plenty of toys around the pool for children to enjoy. You're encouraged to eat out in the evenings, and the hotel restaurant shuts at 6.30pm, but the staff are always happy to babysit.

Rooms 12. *Rates* double 2,1500B–3150B, family beachfront bungalow 4600B–6650B, extra bed 500B. *Credit* MC, V. *Amenities* pool, beach café, Internet and wifi. *In room* A/C, tea/coffee, TV, DVD.

White House Beach Resort & Spa ★

Choeng Beach, Koh Samui. 59/3 Moo 5, Choeng Mon Beach, Samui 84320, 📞 07724 5315, www.samui thewhitehouse.com.

Right next door to the glitzy Sala Samui on beautiful Choeng Mon Beach, the White House is a good, inexpensive option a taxi-ride away from the bustle of Chaweng. Spacious guest cottages with traditional Thai décor each have separate bedroom and seating area, furnished with teak. Deluxe rooms and suites are larger than the 'standard' Superior rooms and a suite means you can be at ground level close to the pool and beach.

The resort is set in tropical gardens with a path leading directly past the small swimming pool to the sea. This beach has a scatter of inexpensive local restaurants to give you a variety of dining options but, for Samui, it's very quiet and peaceful.

The Waterfront's swimming pool

Rooms 40 units. Rates double 3110B–4500B, suites 4400B–5600B, extra bed 1200B, including breakfast. Credit MC, V. Amenities spa, restaurant. In room A/C, satellite TV, DVD, house movies, tea/coffee.

INEXPENSIVE

Inexpensive accommodation is increasingly hard to find in up-and-come Samui. Key is finding resorts that have not yet installed swimming pools and that still have rooms without air-conditioning. Some inexpensive hotels have air-conditioning units which they can switch off and lock, knocking up to 500B off the nightly rate.

Maenam Resort FIND VALUE

Meanam Beach, Koh Samui. 1/3 M.4 Maenam Beach, 84330. 📞 07724 7287, www.maenamresort.com.

Belying its rates, the Maenam is a family-friendly resort that stands out from its backpackery neighbours. The cheapest rooms are fan-cooled but still adequate, while the two-bedroom beach-front family villa is something of a bargain. There is no pool, but with a 250m stretch of gently-sloping, child-friendly beach right outside your door, families on a budget rarely complain.

Rates fan-cooled double 1000B–1200B, extra bed 200B, family two-bed beachfront A/C bungalow 2500B–2700B. Credit MC, V. Amenities restaurant, tour desk, Internet café, laundry service. In room fridge, most rooms A/C.

Koh Phangan

EXPENSIVE

Panviman ★★

Thong Nai Pan Noi Beach, Koh Phangan. 22/1 Moo 5, Thong Nai Pan Noi, ☎ *07744 5101-9, www.panviman.com.*

The best resort on Koh Phangan, the Panviman is incredibly pricey by island standards but compares well with the overrated Santhiburi, and would cost much more if it were across the water in Koh Samui.

They have taken note of family accommodation requirements, providing very comfortable family suites, and though they don't offer any other special facilities for children, the shallow-sloping beach is ideal for the young. The hotel's own restaurant is expensive but there are plenty of alternatives a few sandy paces away, with tables and cushions on the sand.

Rooms 73 including four family suites. Rates double 7062B, family suite 17,067B. Credit AE, MC, V. Amenities swimming pool, restaurant, speedboat transfers from Koh Samui. In room A/C, satellite TV, fridge, tea/coffee.

MODERATE

Green Papaya Resort ★★
FIND

Haad Salad Beach, Koh Phangan. 64/8 Moo 8, 84280, ☎ *07737 4230,* ☎ *07734 9280, www.greenpapaya resort.com.*

Set on one of Koh Phangan's most beautiful beaches, this beautiful and well-respected resort has spacious and delightful bungalows where polished woods and shady verandas set a classic tone. Avoid the least expensive rooms as they're cramped and a bit gloomy.

The pool has sunny areas for tanning and shady pergolas for sun-sensitive children, and the beach, protected by an outer reef, is endlessly shallow: not so good for swimmers but great for youngsters. The beach has a selection of other restaurants and resorts, but all are quiet and calm.

Rooms 7. Rates double 3600B–5900B, family garden villa (king and single beds) 6000B–9600B, extra bed 1000B, free baby cot. Credit MC, V. Amenities beachfront restaurant, infinity pool, wifi. In room A/C, satellite TV, fridge, tea/coffee.

INEXPENSIVE

An Panburi Resort

Thong Nai Pan Noi, Koh Phangan. 84280, ☎ *077445074-5.*

Classic rattan and timber bungalows set on low stilts directly on or within 20m of the beach make this a classic Thai beach hut paradise, intermittently improved by air-conditioning in some bungalows. There are no special family suites but the huts are inexpensive enough to rent a couple, or if you're planning to park the children out on the hammocks that drape your personal verandas remember to bring a mosquito net.

The restaurant is probably the best on this beach and is always

Mai Pen Rai

busy, not least with economic refugees from the Panviman along the shore.

Rooms *63 bungalows.* **Rates** *fancooled room 600B, a/c oceanfront 1800B, extra bed 300B, room only.* **Credit** *MC, V.* **Amenities** *Internet café, restaurant.* **In room** *bed, some rooms A/C.*

Mai Pen Rai ★★ FIND

Thaan Sadet, Koh Phanga. Thansadet Beach 84280, 📞 *07744 5090,* **http://thansadet.com***.*

On one of Koh Phangan's most remote beaches, this charming little lodge recreates a Thailand of yesteryear. Idiosyncratic thatched bungalows are all individually designed to suit different requirements: some set right on the beach.

Family bungalows are twinlevel properties, designed for four but with place to sleep six, teetering above the beach on the rocks. Run by a long-established English–Thai couple (unusually she's English, he is Thai), this is the place to introduce your children to the Thailand of your youth – even the prices have changed little.

Rooms *40 bungalows.* **Rates** *bungalows on the beach 500B–650B, family bungalows 750B–850B.* **Credit** *MC, V, PayPal.* **Amenities** *big trampoline, restaurant, wifi.* **In room** *four-poster beds, fans (until the power stops at midnight), mosquito nets.*

Hua Hin

VERY EXPENSIVE

Alila Cha-Am ★★

Hua Hin. 115 Moo 7, Tambol Bangkao, Amphur Cha-Am, 76120, 📞 *06735 8300,* **www.alilahotels.com/chaam***.*

If you've ever wanted to experience the ultimate expression of contemporary Balinese chic, this

Alila Cha-Am

Thai outpost is a great place to do it – and you can take your children too. A symphony of style, the super-luxury features guest bedrooms that make your home seem obsolete. It's not near any beach restaurants, or local bars, or even very near Hua Hin – but if you can afford to stay here you're not likely to stray. Families with older children love the pool villas with two bedrooms, infinitely adjustable mood lighting, and bathrooms centred round huge rain showers.

Rooms 79, including seven pool villas. *Rates* double 9400B–1200B, pool villa 26,500B–33,200B, extra bed 2000B. *Credit* AE, DC, MC, V. *Amenities* two restaurants, pools, spa, library, cooking courses. *In room* Apple 42-inch plasma TV, built-in Bose speakers.

Sofitel Centara Grand Resort ★★

Hua Hin. 1 Damnernkasem Road, Hua Hin, 77110, 📞 *03251 2021,* **www.sofitel.com**.

Romp into another era at this classy hotel that first opened in 1922. Thailand was never colonised so this is a sort of mock-colonial design, with immaculate gardens filled with topiary animals, broad shady verandas and fine wooden details.

Along with a small museum dedicated to the resort's early years, the 14 original guest rooms from the hotel's launch have been preserved. They're not that large, however – many won't even fit an extra bed. The modern ones are brighter, more comfortable and spacious. Of particular interest to families are the 42 villas of the Centara Hua Hin Village, just across a road from the main hotel, with various configurations including some very smart pool villas. These are, however, somewhat isolated from the main hotel, and in the shade of the huge Hilton hotel nearby.

The three outdoor pools are finely landscaped and have sun decks under shady trees that lead down to the beach. Children are in heaven, with a children's club, play area and miniature golf. With its huge grounds it hardly feels like a city centre hotel, though once you get to the beach, with its food stalls, hawkers and urban pollution, you will be reminded you're right in the middle of a major town.

Rooms *248 rooms and suites (including Centara Hua Hin Village).* **Rates** *double 6400B–9250B, deluxe pool villa 10,700B–17,850B , extra bed 1800B.* **Credit** *AE, DC, MC, V.* **Amenities** *five restaurants, pools, putting green, floodlit tennis, spa, daily craft lessons, watersports equipment, nature tours, billiards room, tour desk.* **In room** *A/C, satellite TV, babysitting, laundry/dry cleaning.*

MODERATE

Dolphin Bay Resort ★★★
FIND

Hua Hin. 227 Moo 4 Phu Noi, Sam Roi Yot, 77120, ☎ *03255 9333,* ☎ *03255 9360, www.dolphinbay resort.com.*

Well to the south of Hua Hin, this magical resort is remote from the city but in easy range of few small, authentically Thai establishments. It is immensely child-friendly, the main complaint by some guests being that the staff won't leave their babies alone. The beach is just across a (very quiet) road and is beautifully unspoiled, and from here you can canoe out to Monkey Island or go out on local boats.

The resort is within the little-visited Sam Roi Nod National Park, so there's plenty to explore. The resort itself has enough attractions to keep most families happy, including table football, a large grassy play area, play buildings, swings and two large pools, one shallow and with a waterslide that is in constant, happy use. The children's menu is extensive and rivals the huge variety offered to parents. Even the bungalow rooms have space to accommodate small families, while two-bedroom apartments have kitchenettes so it's easy to cook comfort food if required, ingredients available from the on-site mini-mart. Three-bedroom apartments share private gardens, pools and Jacuzzis, and there is also a six-bedroom villa.

Rooms *52.* **Rates** *bungalow room 1290B–1590B, two-bed apartment 3400B–3800B, three-bed apartment 5500B–6000B, extra bed 200B, cot 100B.* **Credit** *MC, V.* **Amenities** *playground, children's pool, swimming pool, restaurant, table tennis, massage, billiards.* **In room** *A/C, TV, fridge.*

INEXPENSIVE

King's Home, Hua Hin ★★

VALUE FIND

Hua Hin. 9/1 Poonsuk Road, Soi Sampan, ☎ *089 0520 490, http:// huahinkingshome.blogspot.com.*

Children accustomed to a limited budget are often those least interested in deserted beaches and child meals. If that's true for your tribe, the heart of historic Hua Hin is a perfect place to stay and King's Home, set in the narrow alleys a quarter-block away from the Squid Piers, is a great base for total immersion in a Thai city.

The entire house is cluttered almost to the point of being a museum, and so are the rooms, with artworks and knick-knacks arranged around deep, soft beds, uncommon in Thailand at this price. It has a homely, helpful atmosphere, and the location is just 100m from night-market restaurants serving fish so fresh it's alive.

The manicured beaches outside the Sofitel hotel are also within easy walking distance, but the price of a gin and tonic there will get you a family room for the night in this small, Dutch-run hideaway.

There's a gate to stop children straying out on the alleyway which, in any case, is only tracked by the occasional puttering scooter and stray cat.

Rooms Seven. Rates double 380B– 500B, family room 500B–1050B. Amenities plastic above-ground plunge pool squished into tiny garden, bar. In room fan, TV, fridge, WiFi.

FAMILY-FRIENDLY DINING

Koh Samui

Whatever the hype generated by local publications that rely on advertisements, apart from the few exceptions below it's rarely worth travelling far across Koh Samui – and even less Koh Phangan – in search of particular restaurants. The finest tend to be the least family-friendly, preferring instead an atmosphere of theatrical chic, designed to attract besotted foreigners treating local girls, and upscale honeymooning couples.

With a family you will be better off – and have more fun – strolling down your nearest beach, glancing at menus and judging the crowds before choosing a restaurant that suits your needs. Thai cuisine is invariably excellent, with western alternatives often differing charmingly from what you'd expected.

One region bucking this trend is the Bophut area, especially around the restaurants that dot the street that runs along the beach and cram next to each other on the old timber buildings of Fisherman's Village. Outstanding examples include Seaweed (Swedish), Fifty-Six (Asian fusion), the Shack (blues music and steak) and Coffee Junction (Mexican/ Mediterranean).

If you're in the Bophut area on a Sunday afternoon it is well worth heading to the Secret Garden Pub ★★ on Big Buddha Beach (just under the vast sign saying BBC, 📞 07724 5253) for barbecue food, cheap beer, and a succession of local and guest musicians performing blues and rock songs. The crowd is split between tourists and expats and it's all very relaxed and family friendly.

Chaweng is where you'll find the western stalwarts, such as British pubs serving fish and chips, McDonald's (though the burgers bear little relation to their UK equivalents) and Starbucks. The seriously home-sick can go to Tesco Lotus, where they'll find a lot of meals they recognise from home – and quite a few they don't.

Babylon Restaurant & Bouncy Castle Park ★★★
`VALUE` `THAI`

Bang Por Beach, 📞 08 5792 8806 or 📞 08 7876 6068.

The closest Samui gets to an Adventure Park, the Babylon Restaurant has a playground with six bouncy castles fenced off in an enclosure (50B per child) and a newly built swimming pool with plenty of floaty toys. Though somewhat out of the way on Bang Por Beach, it is worth a detour with young children. They can play while you sample good island-class Thai cuisine in simple, *sala*-style dining pavilions. On Sundays it puts on live music from 3pm, with barbecue buffets and fireworks.

Open 10am–10pm. Prices Sunday concert buffets 300B adults, 150B children including bouncy castles and pool. Weekday meals currently 100B for an adult main course, 50B child menu, but seem to be rising since the pool has been finished. Credit currently no.

Padma `THAI CONTEMPORARY`
Karma Samui, between Chaweng and Choeng Mon beaches, 📞 07723 4500 ext 71.

Rather than a resort restaurant, Padma is a restaurant within a resort. Reached by a chauffeur-driven golf cart through an exclusive enclave of pool villas, it creates unforgettable flavours, dreamt up by the Italian-born, Canadian trained and Thai transformed chef Stefano Leone. Open through the day, it provides the best gourmet breakfasts on the island, lunch, cocktails and dinner. The child menu alone would pass muster for an adult meal.

Open 7am–11pm. Main courses 600B. Reservations recommended.

Hua Hin

There's no need to dig out your credit card to eat well at Hua Hin. A hundred years of upmarket tourism and immediate access to seafood has honed the city-centre restaurants to a razor-sharp standard.

Though the beach is colonised by countless small restaurants, setting out wooden furniture to mark out their patch of sand, in the evening the food scene moves to Naretdamri Road, with restaurants on one side and the guest house/restaurants of the Squid Piers on the other. Arguably these are somewhat overpriced, but the setting is unbeatable: children love playing around the stilted wooden pontoons under dangling Chinese lanterns, and the locals like seeing the young enjoying themselves. Chao Lay (15 Thanon Naretdamri) is deservedly one of the most popular.

Track 100m inland and you'll find all shapes and sizes of fish and crustaceans lit by fluorescent tubes in makeshift displays outside white-tiled inexpensive restaurants: choose your meal and it will be cooked on site.

The Hua Hin Thai Show THAI

67/2Dechanichit Road, ☎ *03251 1423, www.huahinthaishow.com.*

If you're hesitating whether to introduce your children to the Thai *katoey* experience, this could be the place to try. There are elements of Thai dancing and a splash of cabaret, more often than not to the background sounds of western hits, and a brief bout of Thai boxing in this spectacular but informal performance that accompanies a decent Thai meal.

Open 5pm–10pm, show time 8pm–9pm. Admission 450B adults, 350B children under 12.

7 Chiang Mai & the North

NORTHERN THAILAND

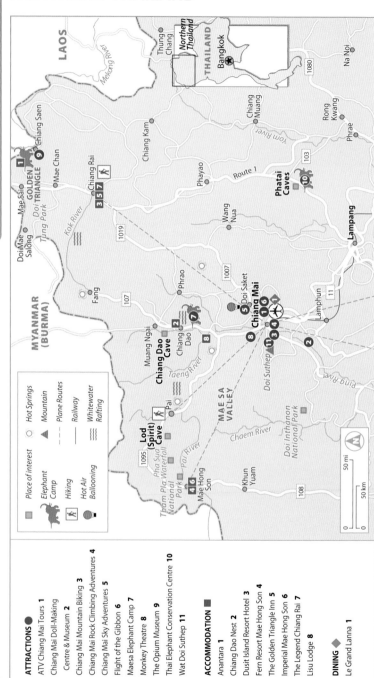

ATTRACTIONS ●

ATV Chiang Mai Tours **1**
Chiang Mai Doll-Making
   Centre & Museum **2**
Chiang Mai Mountain Biking **3**
Chiang Mai Rock Climbing Adventures **4**
Chiang Mai Sky Adventures **5**
Flight of the Gibbon **6**
Maesa Elephant Camp **7**
Monkey Theatre **8**
The Opium Museum **9**
Thai Elephant Conservation Centre **10**
Wat Doi Suthep **11**

ACCOMMODATION ■

Anantara **1**
Chiang Dao Nest **2**
Dusit Island Resort Hotel **3**
Fern Resort Mae Hong Son **4**
The Golden Triangle Inn **5**
Imperial Mae Hong Son **6**
The Legend Chiang Rai **7**
Lisu Lodge **8**

DINING ◆

Le Grand Lanna **1**

Although Chiang Mai is Thailand's second-largest city, it certainly doesn't feel it. The atmosphere is relaxed, the pace of life slower, the temperature cooler, and the main attractions are clustered in a comfortably compact historic centre. Even the pavements are better: this is about the only city in Thailand where you can comfortably push a pram.

The city was founded in 1296 as the capital of the Lanna Kingdom that united the many fiefdoms scattered over the mountainous region, and wasn't fully integrated into greater Thailand until the 20th century. Before 1920 it could only be reached from Bangkok in a long journey involving sections by boat and elephant, and culturally it was closer to neighbouring Burma and Laos. When I first visited in 1981 it was still a breathtakingly quiet place, with dusty streets thronged with flocks of bicycles and few cars in sight. The roads are now tarmac and much busier, but traces of its remote charm remain. There are countless western-friendly restaurants, and new boutique hotels, charging very reasonable prices, that let you settle in to Thai life in comfort and style.

Chiang Mai is still the best place in the country for buying handicrafts. The bargaining is not fierce by Thai standards, and at the night market and on the weekend 'Shopping Streets' you occasionally see prices displayed and suddenly realise you've been paying over the odds for items you'd previously thought a bargain.

Beyond the walled and moated old city centre there are child-friendly attractions on every side and you can quickly escape from the city into the surrounding mountains for elephant shows and rides, bamboo rafting adventures and hilltribe treks.

With an international airport and air links with the islands to the south, a good family itinerary might be to spend some city time here and then fly south to the beaches, side-stepping Bangkok altogether.

ESSENTIALS

Getting There

By Air The most convenient way to get to Chiang Mai is by air. Although the airport is now an international hub, it is still a calm and well-organised place, with bank, car hire bureaux (including Avis and Budget) and even a Pizza Hut. Taxis wait outside for the 3km shuttle into town. Buy a ticket (100B) from the taxi booking counter – for a family this is likely to be cheaper than waiting around for the Thai Airways shuttle bus.

Direct flights link Chiang Mai with Laos, Burma, China and Singapore, plus provincial airports and the islands, the most comprehensive service provided by Thai Airways. Other airlines (currently) include Air Asia, Nok Air, Bangkok Airways, Oriental Airlines and One-Two-GO.

By Rail Sleeper trains take between 12 and 15 hours from Bangkok, a family adventure in its own right. Second-class sleepers (881B upper berth, A/C; 791B lower berth) are comfortable if communal; first-class private but, of course, more expensive (1353B). Seats and fold-out beds need to be reserved, and well in advance on and around public holidays, directly at Hualamphong Railway Station (02223 7010) in Bangkok, Chiang Mai's railway station (05324 5363) or, for a small surcharge, through any local travel agent registered as an SRT reseller.

The quickest rail service is the daily 'Sprinter' but even this takes 11 hours – too long for most families.

By Bus VIP coaches, often showing DVDs and with reclining seats, take 10 hours to Bangkok and can be booked at the Arcade Bus Station (05324 2664) 3km east of the centre. From there you should be able to get a *tuk-tuk* into town for 80B but will often have to pay more.

Beware minibus tickets sold by travel agents going direct from central Chiang Mai to Khao San Road in Bangkok. It's generally a long, squeezed journey with no guarantee of vehicle age or roadworthiness.

INSIDER TIP ▷▷

Though you can't actually book rail tickets online, the State Railways of Thailand posts its

timetables at *www.railway.co.th/ English*. You can even check the number of spare seats or sleeping berths on any given train if you drill through the Thai-language section. This is surprisingly easy if you follow the instructions on *http://www.seat61.com/ Thailand.htm*.

VISITOR INFORMATION

The TAT office (daily 8.30am– 4.30pm, 05324 8604/5) is at 105/1 Chiang Mai-Lamphun Road, on the east side of the Ping River south of Nawarat Bridge. They can provide details of local activities and hotels, although their determination to be unbiased means it's hard to get an opinion out of them. They do have a small forest of brochures, but when it comes to booking it's usually easier to just sign up with an independent who will pick you up from where you are staying.

Publications

Several free magazines – *Guidelines Chiang Mai*, *What's On Chiang Mai* and *Welcome Chiang Mai* – can be picked up from hotel lobbies, restaurants and travel agents, with useful information about upcoming events, interesting cultural insights, plus highly partisan reviews of local restaurants. There is also a weekly English-language newspaper, the *Chiang*

CHIANG MAI

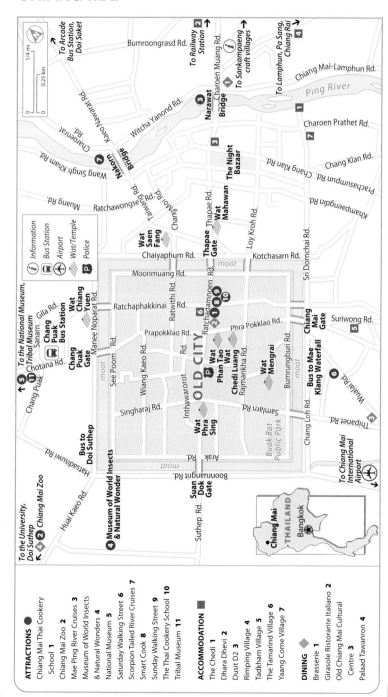

ATTRACTIONS ●

Chiang Mai Thai Cookery School **1**
Chiang Mai Zoo **2**
Mae Ping River Cruises **3**
Museum of World Insects & Natural Wonder **4**
National Museum **5**
Saturday Walking Street **6**
Scorpion Tailed River Cruises **7**
Smart Cook **8**
Sunday Walking Street **9**
The Thai Cookery School **10**
Tribal Museum **11**

ACCOMMODATION ■

The Chedi **1**
Dhara Dhevi **2**
Dusit D2 **3**
Rimping Village **4**
Tadkham Village **5**
The Tamarind Village **6**
Yaang Come Village **7**

DINING ◆

Brasserie **1**
Girasole Ristorante Italiano **2**
Old Chiang Mai Cultural Centre **3**
Palaad Tawanron **4**

Mai Mail, which can also be read online at *www.chiangmai-mail.com*. Several free maps backed by advertising are freely available around town, but for more detail buy a copy of *Nancy Chandler's Map of Chiang Mai* (100B: make sure you're being sold the latest version, 17th edition or later), a colourful and informative map/guide.

Orientation

After Bangkok's formless sprawl, Chiang Mai is refreshingly easy to navigate. At its heart is the Old City, a square 1.5km across, neatly enclosed by a moat. At each corner the remnants of the old city walls (don't get too excited, they date back only to the 19th century) are clearly visible, and mid-way along each wall is a city gate, some restored but all identifiable by a bridge.

Of course it is still easy to get lost as narrow winding alleys and unmarked roads have somehow insinuated themselves into what started out as a simple city plan. But Wat Doi Suthep, on top of a mountain to the west of town, is usually clearly visible, and using that along with a few distinctive temples, roads and the four-sided moat you can usually find your way home.

The Old City is surrounded by two one-way ring roads. The inner ring runs counter-clockwise, while outside the moat another runs clockwise. Using the sun to sort out east and west gives you a decent steer on the roads out of town, and there are frequent U-turn points if you overshoot. The majority of the most important sites are within the old city walls, while much of the traffic seems to stay outside them, which makes wandering around remarkably relaxed. Most tourist facilities are concentrated on the eastern side, inside and outside the walls, around the restored eastern Tha Pai Gate, and stretching down Tha Pai 2km east towards the Night Market and the Mae Ping River.

Getting Around

There are five bus routes around town, charging 15B per person and 5B for a child under 1.3m tall. They run every 15 minutes between 6am–10pm daily. Getting small children on these can be fiddly (there's no space for buggies) but they are air-conditioned. For longer journeys, to craft villages or outlying towns, head to the Chang Puak Bus Station. *Songtaews* (known here as *Seelor* meaning 'four wheels' are red pickups with bench seats in the back. If they already have passengers these can be flagged down in the hope they are going your way, but if they're empty they will behave – and charge – like unmetered taxis or the three-wheeled *tuk-tuk,* so expect to bargain hard.

For most families metered taxis are the best way to get around. They run 7am–midnight and the flag fare is 50B which will cover the first 2km. Most drivers prefer to negotiate a rate (no surprise there) and the meter rate only applies to trips within the outer ring road – beyond that you'll be forced to bargain in any case. Taxis can occasionally be flagged down on the street but more usually can be found outside hotels or called (for a further 50B) on the central taxi co-operative number, ☏ 05327 9291.

Tuk-tuk charges start at 40B and go up with distance. Pedalled rickshaws start at 30B. If planning a family excursion, perhaps to an elephant show, it is easiest and probably cheapest to design a route with one of Chiang Mai's many travel agents to link in several different attractions, negotiate a fare, and let them book a taxi accordingly.

Family-Friendly Events

Bo Sang Umbrella Fair & Sankampaeng Handicrafts Festival

The western New Year's Day, on 1st January, is celebrated by the Bo Sang Umbrella Fair just outside Chiang Mai. The main street is transformed by gaily painted paper umbrellas while contests, exhibition and craft stalls form a lively background to the selection of Miss Bo-Sang.
1st Jan.

Flower Festival

Chiang Mai's spectacular feast of flowers, where lavish floral sculptures are paraded through the streets.

Usually the first weekend in Feb.

Poy Sang Long

Mae Hong Son's most colourful festival sees Thai Yao boys from the age of seven to 14 ordained as monks for the length of the King's long summer holiday. Their heads are shaved and they are done up in lavish costumes, heavy with jewellery, garlanded with flowers, and their faces plastered with makeup. Two days of processions and parades culminate in a quieter, family celebration as they tuck into what will probably be their last meal for the duration.

Usually the first weekend in Apr, Mae Hong Son.

Valentines with a Difference

Bring out the girl in your pre-teen with this romantic pageant. Lanna-style wedding ceremonies take place on Valentine's Day starting with an elephant procession to the bride's parents and proceeding to a sacred setting where newlyweds are symbolically linked by a length of sacred white cotton. Nuptials are followed by traditional Lanna food and drink.

12th–14th Feb, Lampang.

Songkran

Thailand's famous water festival is at its most exuberant in the north and in Chiang Mai celebrations continue for days – so you should expect to get soaked. The idea is to wash away sins and bad luck. For days before Songkran water pistols of various sizes appear on sale, but even the largest – and some are huge supersoakers – will not match

Handmade flower soaps on sale

the buckets, jugs and power-hoses that are brought into service when the festival proper starts. The city-wide waterfights climax with a parade of Buddhas through the streets. If you don't want to get wet stay away – otherwise buy a supersoaker water pistol and join in.

Usually from 13th–16th April.

Loi Krathong

This nationwide festival of fireworks, floating candles and paper balloons is at its most spectacular in Sukothai, but Chiang Mai comes a close second, calling the ceremony *Yipeng*. The skies light up as each and every Thai – and any visitor within easy range – lights their own little candles inside paper hot-air balloons. The heat of the flame lets them rise through the air like a million drifting fireflies, taking with them a year's worth of sins and bad luck. Spectacular.

Nov, on the night of the full moon.

FAST FACTS

ATMs You won't have to look far for an ATM in Chiang Mai: there's one outside most 7/11s, and there are plenty of exchange bureaux. The major Thai banks have machines on Chang Klan and Charoen Prathet roads around the Night Bazaar, and around Tha Pai Gate.

Car Hire For car rental Avis (℡ 05320 1798, www.avisthailand. com) and Budget ℡ 05320 2871 (www.budget.co.th) have offices at the airport and charge from 2500B per day upwards. You can halve these rates at many bureaux that thrive in the more competitive streets of the city centre: try North Wheels, 70/4–8 Chaiyaphum Road (℡ 05374 0585), which also offers a pickup or drop-off service, or Mr Mechanic, 4 Soi 5, Moon Muang Road, just north of Tha Pai Gate, (℡ 05321 4708), an excellent motorcycle agency which also does other vehicles.

Chemists Chemists in Chiang Mai are generally open 7am–midnight. There are two good ones in the Old Town within 50m of Tha Pai Gate, on Moon Muang and Ratchadamnoen streets.

Consulates The British Consulate is at 198 Bumrungraj Road, ☎ 05326 3015.

Dentists Chiang Mai's family specialist is Dentaland, Nimmanhaemin Soi 17, A Muang, ☎ 05322 4578, with child-friendly waiting rooms and laughing gas on tap – though not free. They will deal with emergencies and also, quite possibly, outfit your whole family with braces and crowns. There is also a dental clinic at Ram Hospital.

Hospitals Chiang Mai's hospitals do not currently have a great reputation for clinical performance or ethical behaviour. If you or your child become seriously ill long-term residents sometimes suggest heading directly to a more sophisticated hospital in Bangkok. Even in Chiang Mai, however, the standards of care easily shame their UK equivalents. The Christian-run McCormick hospital on Kaeo Nawarat Road, ☎ 05326 2200-19, out toward the Arcade Bus Terminal is old but has a good reputation, and the facilities to deal with major trauma.

Internet There are thousands of Internet cafés in and around the Old City charging between 30B–40B an hour. Best perhaps is the Smart Café, underneath the Lanna House Hotel, 267 Thapae Road, Changklan Muang, 50100, ☎ 05327 0200, just outside Tha Pai Gate, with sofas for the children, excellent coffee, a fast connection, and plenty of keyboards.

Police For police assistance, call the Tourist Police on ☎ 1155, or visit them in their offices at the TAT office.

Post Office The most convenient branch is at 186/1 on Chang Klan Road, ☎ 05327 3657, although the main Post Office is on Charoen Muang, ☎ 05324 1070, near the train station. The Overseas Call Office, open 24 hours, is upstairs from the GPO and offers phone, fax and telex services.

Safety As in most Thai cities, the risk of violent crime is low – though incidents of bag-snatching and mugging have been reported in dark alleys at night. Gem-scam artists have recently appeared so don't believe anyone selling you cut-price stones. The worst dangers are motorised – take care when driving and when herding your family across busy roads.

Travel Agents Though it's perfectly possible to rent a car and map read yourself, a good travel agent can take the stress out of planning a family outing – tracking the changing times of elephant displays and monkey theatres, how long to allow each attraction, and so on. Start with the agent colonising the lobby of your hotel and, if they're not particularly helpful (and they rarely are) start asking round the travel agents that operate from outside offices. It doesn't take long to find one who is engaging and informative, and these are the ones who rarely disappoint. For key arrangements such as flights and train tickets, Transworld Travel, 259-261 Tha Pae Road, ℡ *05327 2415* or Queen Bee, 5 Thanon Moonmuang, ℡ *05327 5525*, are long-established agents.

WHAT TO SEE & DO

Children's Top 10 Attractions

❶ **Watch** elephants paint. See p 211.

❷ **Stroll** the Walking Street Market. See p 209.

❸ **Trek** amongst the hill tribes. See p 216.

❹ **Light** a candle at Wat Doi Suthep. See p 214.

❺ **Ride** a bike down a forested mountain trail. See p 211.

❻ **Visit** the Golden Triangle Opium Museum. See p 217.

❼ **Meet** the giant pandas at Chiang Mai's Zoo. See below.

❽ **Float** a bamboo raft down the rivers of northern Thailand. See p 211.

❾ **Fly** through the treetops on a jungle zip-wire. See p 212.

❿ **Take** to the track in a top-of-the-range go kart. See p 212.

Attractions

Chiang Mai

Chiang Mai Zoo ★★ ALL AGES

100 Huay Kaew Road, 3km from the city centre: follow signs for Doi Suthep and the zoo is on your left. ℡ *05322 1179*, ℡ *05335 8116*.

Two giant pandas are the main draw at Chiang Mai Zoo, but there's plenty more to do and see and it would be easy for a family to spend a whole day here. Set on the lower flanks of Doi Suthep it was originally a missionary's private collection of family pets. Now it is a 200-acre park containing more than 8000 animals. The experience is interactive: you can buy beans to feed the zebra, there's a children's interpretive centre, a walk-through bird park, a canopy-height monorail, and although some cages are small most of the animals seem to have plenty of space. You have to pay extra to visit the giant pandas in their air-conditioned home (100B adults, 50B children), and also to use the open-sided service vehicles that help you get around the park (20B). Through the hot months a good time to visit is in the evening, when 'Twilight Zone' tours (200B adults, 100B children) after 6pm show you the pandas and let you watch the animals being fed: The tours start either at the front gate or the Palaad Tawanron restaurant (see p 229) at the park's upper boundary.

Shuttle *songthaews* collect outside the zoo gates for the steep, 6km climb up to Doi Suthep, making it quite practical to see both sights in one day using public transport.

Don't confuse Chiang Mai Zoo or its 'Twilight Zone' with the heavily touted 'Chiang Mai Night Safari': a much more expensive operation controversially imposed on the community close by.

Open *8am–6pm, last entry 4pm, Twilight Zone 7pm–9pm.* **Admission** *200B adults, 100B children.* **Credit** *MC, V.* **Amenities** *restaurant, café, children's zone, camping area.*

> **INSIDER TIP** ›
> Bowling is big in Thailand and there are three bowling alleys in Chiang Mai: Bully Bowl (05322 4444, Kad Suan Kaew); PS Bowling (05341 6217-8, Sri Phum), UFO Bowling, (05380 1446-9, Highway 106). All are open until late.

Cooking Courses ★
AGES 8 AND UP

If your children like Thai food, Chiang Mai is an excellent place to sign up for a cooking class. These generally start in the market, progress to the kitchen, and end up with a lavish multi-course meal. Most also provide a folder with the original recipes to make it easy to recreate the meals at home. Smart Cook (21 Moonmuang Road, Soi 5, Sriphum A Muang, 05341 8309, www.chiangmaismartcook.com)

operates out of a 100-year-old teak home, courses costing from 700B per person. They also teach fruit-carving. The Thai Cookery School (25 Moon Muang Road, Soi 9, 05321 9896) charges 700B for a full day. Tom Yam Cookery School (Lake View Park II, Maejo Road, 05384 4877) operates courses just outside Chiang Mai (free pickup) with the advantage of the use of a swimming pool at lunchtime. The original pioneer is the Chiang Mai Thai Cookery School (47/2 Thanon Moonmuang, 05320 6388, www.thaicookeryschool.com), which offers courses lasting from one (990B) to five days.

Cruises ALL AGES

Though Chiang Mai is far from rushed by Thai standards, river cruises are a good way to introduce the city without traffic or crowds. Mae Ping River Cruises (Wat Chai Mongkol Pier, 05327 4822) operates daytime longtail boat tours at 350B per person, including some food and drinks, and night-time dinner cruises (7pm–9pm) with a set menu at 450B per person. From Nawarat Bridge Pier (081 885 0663) cruises depart at 10am, midday, 2pm, 4pm and 5.30pm: 350B. Scorpion Tailed River Cruises (081 960 9398, www.scorpion tailed.com, 500B adults, 250B children under 1.5m) runs tours that also explain fishing techniques and the area's history and lays on a mid-tour feast of Thai dessert snacks. Their cruises leave every two hours

(9am–5pm) from Wat Srikong boat landing, just north of the Nakhorn Ping Bridge.

Glide through the Sky ALL AGES

Chiang Mai Sky Adventure, 143 M.6 T.Cherngdoi, Doisaket, Chiang Mai 50220, ☎ *05386 8460, www.sky adventures.info.*

Earth Wind and Fire Company Limited, 158/60 Moo 6 Cheungdoi, Doi Saket, Chiang Mai, 50220, ☎ *05329 2224, http://balloon.wind-and-fire.com.*

For much of the year the air above Chiang Mai hangs limpid and still, making it perfect for balloon flights. Starting in the darkness before dawn it's an unforgettable family adventure. First the burners heat the air to raise the balloon. Once it hovers overhead you take off and drift above a magical landscape. There are Buddhist stupas often wreathed in morning mist, monks processing from their temples to collect alms as the streets begin to flow, while a patchwork of rice paddies stretches away to majestic Doi Suthep. When the burners die down it's infinitely quiet and without any breeze – a balloon travels with the air, its path and speed in the lap of the gods.

Times 6am–9.30am, including 1–1½ hours in the air. Balloons fly most mornings Nov–Mar, depending on weather. Cost 9850B per person with Chiang Mai Sky Adventures, or an eye-watering 20,000B per person with rival Earth Wind and Fire.

Museums AGES 8 AND OVER

As the capital of the north, Chiang Mai has a selection of excellent museums. The largest is the National Museum (Wednesday to Sunday 9am–4pm, 30B, *www.thailand museum.com*) although it's hard to imagine many children finding much of interest in the selection of Buddha heads, ceramics and sculptures. Mine were only briefly stirred by the occasional skeleton dug up from archaeological digs around the country.

If there's a trek planned, the Tribal Museum ★ (Monday to Friday 8.30am–4pm, free, ☎ 05322 1933) is a better bet, as it introduces the costumes and customs of the six major ethnic groups, and a video shown at 10am and 2pm is interesting, despite a somewhat cheesy voiceover. There are also reconstructed hill-tribe houses on the south side of the lake's park, and the army cool down their horses in the waters. A visit to this museum might also become your family's first experience of a hot-weather walk, as its stunning setting in the extensive grounds of Ratchamangka Park means it takes about 15 minutes to walk back to the road. To avoid this persuade (or pay) your taxi to wait.

For children who love creepy-crawlies, take a taxi to the Museum of World Insects and Natural Wonders ★ FIND (daily 9am–4.30pm, 100B adults, 50B children, 72 Nimmanhaemin Soi 13, Srimankalajarn Road, ☎ 05321 1891), a private collection of insects and bugs including all 422 of Thailand's mosquito species but also plenty of big creatures – tarantulas and giant scorpions. Not many taxi-drivers

Walking Street Markets ★★

Better – and increasingly more popular – than Chiang Mai's famous Night Market is the Sunday Walking Street Market. This sees Ratchadamnoen Street in the city centre closed off to traffic from about 3pm onwards, leaving the roads for walking and the pavements free to host a stunning selection of stalls. Everything you could possibly imagine is on sale, including edible insects, dried and filed by species, but the temples get involved too. Most Wats have performances of classical music at their gates, while inside volunteers set up stalls selling spicy traditional snacks that, like the temples themselves, reflect influences from Laos, Burma and beyond. This is a very good time to introduce the family to a wat or two. On Saturdays many of the same stalls appear on another Walking Street Market on Wua Lai, south of Chiang Mai Gate.

know where it is. Tell them it's midway between Suithep and Huay Kaew roads near Suan Dok Hospital.

Finally there is the Chiang Mai Doll-Making Centre and Museum, ☏ 05383 7229, 187/2 Moo 9, Dong Khee Lek, Sanpatong.

Shopping

Shopping is a major part of the Chiang Mai experience and generally much cheaper than further south. The city is most famous for its Night Market which takes over the streets west of the Ping River from about 5pm until late, but edging along broken pavements and hemmed in by stalls and other tourists is far from relaxing with children, and anyway serious shoppers are better off making the most of daylight at Wararot Market, slightly to the north, operating every day.

The village of Sankampaeng is known for its silk and textiles and these days the road out there has turned into a sort of craft alley, known locally as the 'Handicraft Highway', especially around the village of Bo Sang, 9km out of Chiang Mai, also called 'Umbrella Village'. However, you need your own vehicle to get there.

If you prefer your shopping air-conditioned, head out along Wua Lai to the Central Airport Plaza. This major mall has everything grown-ups might want to buy but also a Fantasy Zone and Robinson's Small World Playland. If you reach the Tesco Lotus Superstore you've gone too far and are in serious danger of reaching a strip of woodcarving, décor and antique shops where you could easily shop away a day or more.

Wats ALL AGES

Chiang Mai has hundreds of wats – estimates vary between 300 and more than 700 – and even if your children aren't especially spiritual they often find the atmosphere of devotion

Play in the Park

Unusually for Thailand, Chiang Mai has a city-centre park with a public playground. Called the Buak Pat Public Park it is set in the south-west corner of the old city. Toddlers can play on a sandy-floored playground, and grown-ups can rent mats for 10B to sit by the lake. There are ducks to feed, pigeons to chase, other children to meet and snacks on sale.

surprisingly moving. It's not just the countless candles, offerings and golden Buddha sculptures: wats invariably have monasteries attached and many of the novices may be the same age as your children. Naturally friendly, they are keen to practise their English and will soon make the young feel at home.

Wat Phra Singh, at the northern end of the central Rachtadamnoen Street, is the largest. Other impressive temples include the nearby Wat Chedi Luang and Wat Pan Tao which are next door to each other on Phra Pokklao. Outside the Old Town Wat Saen and Wat Bupparam are also well worth a visit. The monks are very open and at least one wat, Wat Srisuphan, offers 'Monk Chats' (5.30pm–7pm, Tuesday, Thursday and Saturday), followed by meditation classes.

Make an adventure out of a wat tour by hiring a *tuk-tuk* or even pedalled *samloor* (rickshaw), or do it yourself on rented bikes: most hotels have some for hire. The single best temple to visit with young children is without doubt Wat Doi Suthep, just out of town: see p 214 for further details.

Wat Doi Suthep, Chiang Mai

Around Chiang Mai

Active Families AGES 8 AND UP

There are countless adventurous options on offer in the Chiang Mai area.

Explore the forest on all-terrain vehicles, better known as quad bikes, with ATV Chiang Mai Tours (☎ 05329 0153, *www.atv-chiangmai-tours.com*). They will pick you up from your hotel and head out on half-day or full-day adventures on 150cc or 250cc quads: prices from 1950B per person, including insurance.

Take to the air in a microlight with Chiang Mai Sky Adventures (☎ 05386 8460, *www.skyadventures.info*): 15 minutes from 1700B, maximum weight 110kg, hotel pickup times 8am or 3pm. Mountain biking tours, mainly downhill, are offered by several companies, one of the best being Chiang Mai Mountain Biking (☎ 081 0247 046, *www.mountainbiking chiangmai.com*, 1 Samlan Road, just south of Wat Phra Sing), which offers a selection of guided tours at various levels, from 1250B per person.

Rock climbing, for beginners or professionals, is offered by Chiang Mai Rock Climbing Adventures Co. Ltd (☎ 05320 7102, ☎ 086 911 1470, *www.thailandclimbing.com*, 55/3 Ratchapakhinai Road, 50200), with introductory climbing and caving courses from 1800B per person and more adventurous expeditions to suit your level.

Bungee jumping is on offer at Mae Rim (☎ 05329 7700) and Mae Sa (☎ 05329 8442).

Rivers can be explored by bamboo raft or whitewater adventure. Try Chiang Mai Adventure Tours (☎ 05327 7810, 131–133 Rachadamnern Road, T. Prasing, A. Muang), Chiang Mai, *www.chiangmai-adventure-tour.com*; Marvel Travel (143 M.1 T.Nhong-Hoi, Mahidol Road, A.Muang Chiang Mai 50000, ☎ 05327 7230, *www.cmmarvel.com*); or The Peak Adventure Tours (☎ 05380 0567-8, Thanon Chang Klang, *www.the peakadventure.com*) where the office is enlivened by a 15m climbing wall. That should keep your children quiet while you plan their next adventure.

Elephant Camps ★ ★ ★
ALL AGES

Riding elephants all a bit tame? The elephant camps around Chiang Mai go several steps further. Before you head off in a howdah across the hills for an action-packed hour the elephants play instruments, burst balloons with darts and – perhaps most impressive of all – paint strikingly competent pictures that, for a few baht, you can buy to take home. Supplied with a large, elephant-sized football, star elephants take part in penalty shootouts and, when they score celebrate with a telling parody of the drama-queening boastfulness of real football players.

The leading camp among several north of Chiang Mai is Maesa Elephant Camp (☎ 05320 6247-8, *www.maesaelephant camp.com*, 100B adults, 50B

Maesa Elephant Camp

children, shows 8am, 9.40am, 1.30pm, elephant rides 80B to 800B extra, depending on length) which puts on perhaps the best show.

All the camps now take good care of elephants that otherwise would struggle to find a role in Thai society, but the most conservation-minded is the Thai Elephant Conservation Centre (76km south of Chiang Mai, 60km west of Lampang on highway 11), the elephants demonstrating logging, painting and orchestral skills (50B, 10am, 11am and (weekends) 1.30pm, ☎ 05422 9042, *www.thailand elephant.org*). It also runs a hospital for sick and ageing elephants, and offers homestays

and *mahout* (elephant training) courses. Charges for rides (100B 10 minutes, 400B 1 hour) are about the lowest in the north.

Show times at all elephant camps change depending on season so phone ahead, check with a local travel agent, or take the easy way out and book through a local travel agent.

Fly Like a Gibbon ★★★
AGES 7 AND UP

Zip wires come to northern Thailand in this new enterprise that explores the jungle at tree-top level, on a series of wires that gradually descend a thickly forested valley. Though it's a blatant copy of an eco-tourist venture across the border in a remote part of Laos, while in Laos children aren't allowed to take part, here they are. The operation is based around the village of Mai Kampong, 45 minutes out of Chiang Mai (transport provided from your hotel). A usual day will include two hours in the canopy, securely attached with lifelines, zip-wiring across canyons and between 15 treetop stations, in a 2km adventure of tree houses, platforms, sky bridges and cables, occasionally rappelling

Go Karting

Find out where the Thai's hone their driving skills at Chiang Mai Speed Go Karts   **AGES 8 AND UP** (☎ 05343 0059, Hang Dong-San Patong, daily 9am–6.30pm), prices from 200B for beginners, to 400B for faster machines. There are tracks to suit all experience levels but international contests are also held here: call ahead to make sure the track is clear.

down huge trees from one level to another. This is followed by an hour's jungle hike and lunch in the village. It fills an unforgettable day for those not scared of heights. A proportion of the takings, they claim, goes to help endangered gibbons, though they are long extinct in the area and a more convincing excuse would be that it brought revenue to the village, where you can, if you wish, stay overnight. Flight of the Gibbon (☎ 089 970 5511, *www.treetopasia.com*) costs 2200B per person, including transport and lunch. There is no reduction for children. Safety standards are good, though it remains to be seen how the course will be maintained. Unforgettable.

Jungle Treks ★★ ALL AGES

In many destinations trekking is all about natural beauty. In Thailand you get to walk through beautiful, forested mountain regions but you also get more: the chance to see and interact with the many mountain people, their traditional way of life still miraculously resisting change.

The most heavily trekked areas are in the Mae Tang Valley and the Kok Valley west of Chiang Rai, and here – and on any day-trek or coach-party visit – you may find the experience somewhat spoiled. There's nothing too exciting about walking through a dusty, flyblown village where every house is racked out with identikit handicrafts for sale. Unspoiled villages take

longer to find and you'll need to trek for several days, staying in local houses along the way, to discover authentic villages and really get a feel for mountain life. Though by now even the most remote village will be thoroughly familiar with the wider world, the less trekked villages still live a very different way of life and observe a range of traditional taboos.

Although it is possible to trek independently it is much better to take a guide who can help you communicate with your village hosts, and trekking is most commonly in groups of between six and 12 people, who pay about 2500B per person for a three-day trek, including short periods riding an elephant and river rafting on a bamboo raft. There should be two guides, one to lead and another to make sure any stragglers don't get lost.

Longer treks will let you get further off the beaten trail and if you are travelling with your family you may well choose to hire a guide of your own. This can be easily arranged but you have to make it absolutely clear you don't want to be tagged on to another group. Good operators include Eagle House (☎ 05323 5387, *www.eaglehouse.com*, 16 Thanon Chang Moi Kao Soi 3), and the Trekking Collective (☎ 05320 8340, *www.trekking collective.com*, 3/5 Loy Kroh Road, Soi 1). Both have policies that feed benefits back into local communities.

If the family don't want to trek you can get a feel for the

hill-tribe culture, cuisine and countryside by staying in a hill lodge. Expensive ones tend to be a bit Disney, with all staff in hill-tribe garb, but there are plenty of elephant rides and bamboo-raft rides. Options (see Accommodation) include Lisu Lodge, or on a tighter budget, Chiang Dao Nest for a family-friendly rural experience.

Monkey Theatre ★ ALL AGES

📞 05329 9414, www.monkey centre.com. Take the 107 Mae Rim Road out of Chiang Mai, after 12km turn left towards Samoeng, the Monkey Centre is 4km on the left.

Classic Thai Monkey Theatre: see p 171 for a full description of what to expect.

Shows 11am, 12.15pm, 1.15pm, 2.15pm, 3.15pm, 4.15pm. Costs 200B adults, 100B children.

Wat Doi Suthep ★★★ ALL AGES

Taxi from town about 200B, or catch a songtaew from the zoo for 20B per person. By car Doi Suthep is clearly signposted from the centre: head west.

If your children are only going to see one Thai temple, when the weather is fine this should be it. Set at the top of Doi Suthep Mountain, just to the west of Chiang Mai, this is Buddhism at its most lavish and lurid, a spectacular symphony of gold-leaf statues gleaming in the sun, small candles and incense wreathing dark shady shrines and gaudy murals, while on every side a constant stream of supplicants pay homage. Getting there is half the adventure. From the city the road

hairpins up the mountain and, should your children balk at the 300 steps up the final *naga* staircase, there is a new cable car (20B per person) to make their – and therefore your – life easy. To enter the upper level you'll have to remove your shoes, and there is a counter where you will be persuaded to rent discreet shirts or sarongs should you be showing any leg or shoulder.

Once you're into the upper level it's impossible not to be moved by the sheer quantity of gold leaf, the bells to be rung, the offerings being made and candles lit, infused with the sincere devotion of the Thai visitors who far outnumber the occasional camera-toting westerner. The views over Chiang Mai, weather permitting, are superb.

Open until 4.30pm. Admission 30B for foreigners only.

Loops from Chiang Mai

Most Chiang Mai travel agents link the major attractions in looping drives that can last a day or more. If you find an agent you like it is well worth talking through the options. With a family you could easily fill a taxi and let them tailor-make your day. They are likely to book a cheaper vehicle than you can arrange yourself and will get commission on your entry tickets. It is easy, for example, to see an elephant show and the monkey theatre in the morning, have lunch at an orchid and butterfly farm, visit Doi Suthep in the

Trekkiquette

It's not the fault of the mountain people that they are flooded with western visitors, and it's important that you minimise your own impact on a fragile society. Without a guide it is easy to infringe complex taboos that outsiders will never understand. Dress modestly, as the locals do, in long trousers and a shirt. Don't shout or raise your voice. Avoid public displays of affection. Take photographs with care: most villagers don't like to be photographed, especially when pregnant, as many believe a camera takes part of their soul. Don't photograph shrines without permission. Instead of handing out money, cigarettes or sweets, which encourages begging, channel more useful items such as pens, small tools, lighters or torches, through the headman.

afternoon, and take a twilight tour of the zoo on the way home.

Longer loops, easily completed in a rental car, curve up through the mountains to spend nights in the small hippy village of Pai, continue southwest to Mae Hong Son on the Burmese border, then either returning directly to Chiang Mai or continuing south to explore sleepy Mae Sarieng. The roads are beautiful (if you like hairpins and hills) and there is plenty to see along the way: With countless caves, hill-tribe villages worth a detour, viewpoints and parks you could allow several days.

A detailed large-scale map, produced by motorcyclists but also useful for car drivers, is available from car rental outlets in Chiang Mai: ask for the KT Riders Map or go to *www.gt-rider.com* and get a copy posted to your home.

OTHER NORTHERN TOWNS

Mae Hong Son

Deep within a mountain valley, mist-shrouded Mae Hong Son was only linked by tarmac road to the rest of Thailand in 1968. Even now, despite the floods of tour buses and minivans that descend on the town from November to February, it retains a quiet, provincial feel. The population is made up of Shan, Karen, Hmong, Lahu and Lisu hill-tribe minorities, as well as a substantial population of refugees from Burma.

Mae Hong Son's principle commercial street, Thanon Khunlumprapas, runs north–south, and is where you'll find the Tourist Office (daily 8.30am–4.30pm, ☎ 05361 2982-3, *www.travelmaehongson.org*), banks and ATMs, post office and the bus station.

The most beautiful part of town is just to the west, around

the postcard-pretty Jong Kham Lake, with parkland on one side and two nineteenth-century, Burmese-style *wats* on the other, their gleaming white-and-gold colours reflecting in the waters.

Mae Hong Son is Thailand's third-largest trekking centre. Good operators include TN Tours (℘ 05362 0059-60, 107 Khunlumprapas Rd), Central Tour (℘ 05361 1309, 112/2 Khunlumprapas Rd) and Rose Garden Tours (℘ 5361 1681, 86/4 Khunlumprapas Rd). Apart from visiting relatively unspoiled villages, it is also possible to do whitewater rafting, river cruises and bamboo-raft drifts. For Mae Hong Son accommodation see p 224.

Chiang Rai

A few decades ago Chiang Rai was a small, remote town in thrall to the drug trade and far from central government control. Today the opium scene has gone, replaced with a host of new hotels and attractions marketing themselves as trekking bases for the 'Golden Triangle' region, where Burma, Laos and Thailand meet.

There are also elephant rides, *mahout* courses, and rafting expeditions.

The Triangle marketing is being amended to a 'Golden Rectangle' to include southern China, and at the frontiers you will see plenty of cross-border activity.

Getting There

By Air The airport (℘ 05379 3048) is 8km north of town and has a currency exchange desk (9am–5pm) and ATM: a taxi should charge about 200B to reach the centre.

By Bus The bus station (℘ 05371 1369) on Prasopsuk Road is a long walk to the south of the centre – take a taxi or *tuk-tuk* – but has good links to cities in Thailand and beyond, Bangkok being 11 hours away.

Visitor Information

Tourist information (TAT) (℘ 05371 7433, 448/16 Thanon Singhaklai) is open daily 8.30am–4.40pm.

ATMs, exchange bureaux, travel agents and Internet cafés are easily found along the town's main road, the north–south Phaholyothin Road that ends at the Mae Kok River. Getting about is by *tuk-tuk*, *samlor* or taxi.

Attractions

Trekking & Hill-Tribe Tours
ALL AGES

Most of the villages within day-trip range of Chiang Rai have been thoroughly commercialised and you need to put a few days aside for anything approaching an authentic trekking experience. Chiang Rai operators include Golden Triangle Tours (℘ 05371 3918, *www.golden chiangrai.com*, 590 Phaholyothin Road), which offers a wide

Long-Necked Women

The Padaung people are most famous for their long-necked women. From childhood girls begin to wear metal rings around their neck, adding two each year until the age of 16. It is thought that these don't so much stretch the vertebrae as compress the collar-bones and ribs, but the effect is to produce a neck that seems 30cm in length. Although the custom does persist amongst the young, most of the long-necked women are now quite old and cut rather pathetic figures. Though originally from Burma, political and financial problems have caused several to cross to Thailand as refugees, and as tourists like to take photographs they are 'employed' by local Thai businessmen to pose for visitors in makeshift 'villages', now on offer everywhere you find tourists, including Mae Sa near Chiang Mai and around Chiang Rai where, confusingly, they're referred to as Karen long-necked women. The villagers often don't have papers or any legal right to residence in Thailand and so don't need to be paid much or at all. However, posing and charging for tourist photographs does offer them an income of sorts and the alternative can be to return to Burma to face torture, discrimination and poverty.

selection of tours. Prices are fixed by the tourist authority at a rather steep 2300B per person per day, and private tours will cost even more. Options include trekking amongst Akha, Hmong, Yao, Karen and Lahu tribes, riding elephants, and driving 4×4 vehicles along paths built by the authorities to help villagers diversify out of opium production.

Two non-profit foundations offer more intensive community-based treks and tours: Natural Focus (✆ 05371 5696, *www.naturalfocusecotour.com*, 129/1 Moo 4, Thanon Pa-Ngiw) and PDA (✆ 05374 0088, *www. pda.org.th*, 620/25 Thanon Tanalai, part of the Hill Tribe Museum and Handicraft Shop).

Excursions from Chiang Rai
Follow the Opium Trail ★
ALL AGES

Sop Ruak, Hall of Opium, Chiang Saen, ✆ 05365 2151, www.golden trianglepark.com. Head north to explore the 'GoldenTriangle'.

The Opium Museum at Sop Ruak offers views over Laos and Burma and the best way to get there is by speedboat along the Mekhong River from the newly built Hall of Opium.

Other family-friendly excursions include visits to interesting towns such as Mae Salong and Mae Sai Mekong cruises along Thailand's northern border, and excursions into Burma and Laos.

Give your children a taste of the wild by travelling to Tha Ton, 50km west of Chiang Rai, returning by river on a floating raft made of bundled bamboo poles, stopping for a night on the riverbank (only with mosquito nets) or staying in a village along the way. It makes an unforgettable adventure at any age.

The same journey can be completed in one day on a motorised raft or four hours in a noisy, fast longtailed boat, but it's hardly the same and too long to be comfortable for children.

Raft excursions *any of Chiang Mai's travel agents or guest houses or try Chiang Mai Marvel Travel, 143 M.1 T.Nhong-Hoi, Mahidol Road, A. Muang Chiang Mai 50000, ☎ 05327 7230, www.cmmarvel.com. Three-day, two-night adventures from 12,500B per person.*

Opium Museum *daily 7am–6pm, entry 50B.* **Hall of Opium** *Tues–Sun 8.30am–5pm, 300B adults, 200B children. Speedboat ticket between the two 400B per person.*

FAMILY-FRIENDLY ACCOMMODATION

Chiang Mai

There is nowhere in Thailand to match Chiang Mai for the variety, quality and price of accommodation, staid package-tourist options being thoroughly shaken up by the new boutique properties that spring regularly from behind construction hoardings, gleaming with polished woods. Sometimes the relentless focus on *Lanna*-themed minimal chic can make them a little daunting – to both children and parents – but usually the friendliness of the staff soon belies the property's formal façade. And all this

competition keeps prices keen and standards high.

Prices are notoriously variable and change according to season, occupancy and sometimes – seemingly – on a whim. In the hottest months, when Chiang Mai is flooded with Thais escaping the summer heat, and during the festivals of Songkran (April) and Loy Krathong (November), the town is packed and rooms at their most expensive. Reservations are essential for expensive hotels, and advisable for all. Prices given can be reduced by booking through an Internet discount broker – dramatically so in low season.

Hotels in the moderate and expensive categories are more than happy to arrange for airport pickups, though even if this is complimentary somehow it usually ends up costing more than taking a normal taxi.

The normal 7% government tax has a supplement here: Chiang Mai adds a further 0.8% of its own, which applies to expensive and moderate hotels but not the cheapies.

This selection of family-friendly hotels includes city-centre properties and rural resorts, and should suit most budgets and tastes.

VERY EXPENSIVE

The Chedi ★

123 Charoen Prathet Road, Chang Klan Road, 50100, ☎ 05325 3333, www.ghmhotels.com.

Built around the old British Consulate on the banks of the

Ping River the Chedi set new standards for sophisticated, five-star accommodation. It's not an obvious family choice but those with older children will find plenty to appreciate, and those with younger ones will like some of the touches, like the complimentary laundry service and minibar when staying in a Club Suite. And even the smallest toddler will appreciate the elegant décor, with plenty of polished wood to slide on. There are excellent views of the Ping River from the pool, and the hotel is in easy walking distance of the night market, though the Old Town is a bit far for young families: better flag down a *tuk-tuk*.

Rooms *52 deluxe rooms and 32 Chedi club suites.* **Rates** *deluxe room 16,235B, club suite 24,411B, extra bed in suite room 3500B including benefits. Under 12s not in extra bed, breakfast charge 325B, under fours free room and breakfast, baby cot free. All prices subject to 10% service charge and 7.8% tax.*

Credit *AE, DC, MC, V.* **Amenities** *pool, restaurant, parking, babysitting and child care.* **In room** *cable/satellite TV, minibar, espresso machine.*

Dhara Dhevi ★★★

51/4 Thanon Chiang Mai-Sankamphaeng, Moo 1 Ti Tasala, ☎ 05388 8888, ***www.mandarinoriental.com.*** *Take the main road to San Kamphaeng weaving village and after 5km look out for signs on your right.*

Constructed in the style of a traditional Lanna village in 60 acres of rice paddies just to the north of Chiang Mai, this five-star property is one hotel your family will never want to leave. Effectively run by the Mandarin Oriental group, it takes childcare seriously. Let them know the ages and names of your children in advance and they will lay on everything from baby bottles to nappies to colouring books and toys. There is a child's library stocked with books and films, children's yoga

Dhara Dhevi

courses, and the Lanna Kids' Club that teaches how to plant rice, ride a buffalo, or train for a day to be a *mahout* (elephant handler), while kickboxing (*Muay Thai*) courses can melt the resistance of the most surly adolescent.

While their children are off being turned into little Thais, parents can enjoy the luxurious spa and golf nearby, but there are also tennis courts and two large swimming pools in which to relax together. Accommodation is in private residences – the villas are better than suites – some with two bedrooms and some with private pools, with stunning views of the rice paddies and spires of the other buildings rising through the palms. Even if you notice that the buffalo in your view has had a shampoo and blow-dry and the herdsman – often playing traditional flutes – is straight from central casting, your children won't mind – ancient Thailand with all mod cons.

Rooms *54 suites and 69 two-story villas.* **Rates** *from 11,899B for a room low season, villas 13,999B–16,800B. All prices + 10% service and 7.8% tax, cots and roll-out beds for under 12s complimentary but should be reserved.* **Credit** *AE, DC, MC, V.* **Amenities** *pools, shops, restaurants, sauna, fitness room, bicycles, golf carts.* **In room** *A/C, wifi, TV, DVD, remote control air/curtains/lights, balcony, fridge, minibar, jetted tub, tea- and coffee-making facilities.*

EXPENSIVE

Dusit D2

100 Chang Klan Road, Tambol Chang Klan, Amphur Muang, 50100, 📞 *05399 9999, www.dusit.com.*

Centrally located near Chiang Mai's Night Market and the epitome of new Thai chic (though here expressed in a somewhat oppressive orange) this is a good place to stay for those who like their comforts slick, cool and smooth. It is family friendly – though there's not a huge amount of space around the pool – with babysitting arranged quickly and easily for when parents want some down-time or a trip to the spa. Moxey's Restaurant is reliably good.

Rooms *131.* **Rates** *4000B–6200B.* **Credit** *MC, V.* **Amenities** *spa, pool, babysitting, laundry, restaurant, fitness room,* **In room** *flat-screen TV, full cable access, DVD, tea- and coffee-making facilities, high-speed Internet access.*

The Tamarind Village ★

50/1 Rajdamnoen Road, Sri Phoom, Muang, 50200, 📞 *0418 896-9, www.tamarindvillage.com.*

This boutique hotel has a fantastic location, set back off the main drag through the heart of Chiang Mai, in the shade of a 200-year-old tamarind tree. Head out along the entrance drive lined with rustling bamboo and you're slap bang in the middle of the Old Town, with monasteries and temples to left and right. Though central, this isn't a particularly busy road, and on Sundays it is completely pedestrianised for the Walking Market. The garden setting is quiet and tranquil and, a hot-weather blessing, there is a decent-sized swimming pool.

Loungers at the tranquil Tamarind Village

Though many Thai hotels only allow one child to share a room with two parents, the Tamarind Village allows two under 10s to share free. A standard room might be fine for a couple but if you're introducing roller-beds and cots, go for a deluxe room or suite.

Rooms *42 guest rooms and three suites.* **Rates** *Lanna room 4200B–6000B, suite 9800B–14,000B, extra bed 1000B, cot free, + 7% government tax and 10%VAT.* **Credit** *MC, V.* **Amenities** *spa, pool, restaurant (northern Thai specialities), babysitting, laundry, dry cleaning.* **In room** *A/C, satellite TV, fridge.*

MODERATE

Rimping Village ★★ FIND

Chiang Mai. 13/1 Soi 2, Chiangmai-Lamphun Rd, T.Wat Gate, A. Muang Chiang Mai 50000, ☎ 5324 3915, **www.rimpingvillage.com**.

Unusually in this price bracket, this beautiful little hotel in the heart of Chiang Mai clearly understands family requirements. There are huge family suites, and you could easily sleep four in their – less expensive – deluxe suites. They will collect guests from the airport, and staff are famously helpful. They might be working harder on enhancing guests' experiences because they're a bit away from the action, east of the Ping River. The Night Market is across the bridge and within walking distance, but most families will flag down a *tuk-tuk* rather than face the traffic-fretted 2km walk into the Old Town. The swimming pool doesn't have an especially shallow end so isn't suitable for toddlers, but the peace and quiet makes this a restful family base.

Rooms *24 guest bedrooms including two family suites.* **Rates** *double 4000B, family suite 7500B, room only, extra bed 700B + taxes and 10% service.* **Credit** *MC, V.* **Amenities** *pool, garden, restaurant, laundry, bike hire, wifi.* **In room** *A/C, fridge, tea- and coffee-making facilities, satellite TV.*

Yaang Come Village ★

90/3 Sridonchai Road, T.Changklan, A. Muang, 50100, ☎ 05323 7222, **www.yaangcome.com**.

Despite being right by Chiang Mai's Night Market and an easy walk to Tha Pae Gate into the old city, the Yaang Come Village is a shady garden hotel that feels far removed from the rush of urban life. It is especially good

Yaang Come Village

for families, with the larger rooms able to fit several extra beds and a lovely and well-maintained pool – a winner in the heat. The two-storey buildings are well spaced, and the international restaurant good value. It won't suit those who like super-modern facilities, and occasionally you might come across a mosquito, but it's a friendly place with traditional Lanna architecture and art everywhere.

Rooms 42 rooms. *Rates* double 4000B–4600B, four people (two under 16) in a superior room 6000B–7200B including tax, VAT and breakfast. *Credit* MC, V. *Amenities* pool and Jacuzzi, traditional massage, wifi, DVD players to borrow from reception. *In room* TV, A/C, mosquito spray.

INEXPENSIVE

These are small, character properties which, by their nature, may sometimes be full. If so there are 540 guest rooms – and a rooftop pool – at the nearby Centara Duangtawan 132 Loykroh Road, Chang-Klan, Muang, 50100, ☎ 05390 5000.

Tadkham Village ★ ★ ★ FIND

8 Nantaram Road Soi 1, off Suriyawong Road, ☎ 05320 3799. *www.tadkhamvillage.com.*

New is often good in this fast-changing society, and the Tadkham Village – which should be well up into the price range above – is proof of this. It is just outside Chiang Mai Gate to the south of the city walls – therefore close to the Old Town rather than the Night Market – but offers excellent accommodation in character Lanna-style rooms. Breakfast is provided, and though there's no restaurant as such, they will provide simple meals – fried rice, perhaps, or noodles – if required.

Rooms 24. **Rates** *suite 1500B, extra person 500B, extra bed 300B, including breakfast.* **Credit** *MC, V.* **Amenities** *cable TV.*

There are little nests of inexpensive hotels in Chiang Mai's old town and two of the best budget selections have grown up on two quiet *sois* close to Tha Pae Gate. Walk into the Old City through Tha Pae Gate and take the first *soi* on the right, passing around the back of the Montri Hotel. This leads to several stalwarts, including the **Water Well Guest House**, Soi 1 14 Rachtadamnoen Rd, ☎ *05321 5809*, which is one of the cheapest with double rooms for 350B: add 500B for A/C. They have a downstairs café where you can park the family while you scout out alternatives.

Immediately opposite are **Nice Apartments** (☎ *05321 8290*, a double with fan 500B, A/C 1000B), and the rather smart new **Mini Cost** ★ (☎ *05341 8787-8*, doubles 750B, triples 1050B).

In the very unlikely event they are all full head out through the Tha Pae Gate, cross the ring road to the east and your first minor right is Soi 6. This leads to, among others, the **Thapae Garden Guest House**, Thapae Road Soi 3, ☎ *05327 2499*, with a small and shady pool, family A/C rooms (two beds, one large) for 800B; also the somewhat basic **Home Place Hotel**, 9 Soi 6, Tha Pae Road, ☎ *05327 6468*,

where small double en-suite rooms go for 400B.

Nearby are several alternatives, including two new properties that might still be discounting their prices to get established: the **BanThai Village** ★★ (19 Soi 3, Tha Pae Road, ☎ *05325 2789*, *www.banthaivillage.com*, (double rooms, set around a pool, interconnect but cost 2500B each) and **Studios 99** (48 Soi 3, Tha Pae Road, ☎ *05320 6960*, *www.chiangmaiserviced apartments.com*), a brand new development of one- and two-bedroom flats where 4000B will get you a fully specced two-bedroom, serviced apartment with kitchen, flat-screen TV and balconies front and back.

Rural Chiang Mai

EXPENSIVE

Lisu Lodge ★

North of Mae Malai, Dton Loong Village, Chiang Mai 50100. Head office in Bangkok: Asian Oasis, 7th floor, Nai Lert Tower, 2/4 Wireless Road, Bangkok 10330, ☎ 02655 6246-48, www.asian-oasis.com.

Active options for children over 10 are in store at this leading 'Hill-Tribe Experience' lodge. Accommodation is simple and fan-cooled, but your stay includes adventures like mountain biking, river rafting, light trekking and cultural shows. It's a fair way from Chiang Mai but one night won't really leave enough time to do all that is on offer.

Rooms 24. **Rates** *two-day/one-night soft adventure 3650B–3,920B, three-day/two-night 10770B–11,580B,*

White water rafting at Lisu Lodge

under 12s 50% discount. Transfer from Chiang Mai in A/C van for up to six 2100B (one hour's drive, taxi cheaper). **Amenities** *pool, restaurant.* **In room** *fan-cooled (no A/C), no phone.*

INEXPENSIVE

Chiang Dao Nest ★ ★ ★ FIND

80km north of Chiang Mai, Chiang Dao Nest, 144/4 m.5 Chiang Dao, Chiang Mai, 50170, ☏ 05345 6242 or ☏ 05345 5795, www.chiangdao.com.

This tremendously pleasant retreat is run by a young Anglo–Thai couple and consists of two hilltop settlements 700m apart, each with own restaurant. The owners have young children of their own so there are toys all over the place, including table tennis, sand pit, fenced play area and child bikes for rent. From here you can head out on half-day treks or longer trips, or simply relax and enjoy the outstanding

food. Accommodation is rustic but acceptable.

Rooms *16.* **Rates** *595B–1095B, extra bed 250B.* **Amenities** *restaurant, pool.* **In room** *fan, no phone, wifi in some chalets.*

Mae Hong Son

There are a few brand-new large hotels in Mae Hong Son, none of them expensive, while character options range from a cluster of inexpensive town-centre guest houses to a few out-of-town resorts.

MODERATE

Fern Resort Mae Hong Son ★ ★ FIND

Near Mae Hong Son, 64 Ban Hua Num Maesakhut 58000, ☏ 05368 6110-1, www.fernresort.info.

Six kilometres south of Mae Hong Son's centre, this is

perhaps the best option. Deluxe rooms and suites are large enough to fit extra beds or put mattresses on the floor and the staff, mainly Karen girls being trained for the hospitality industry, are very good with children. The swimming pool is heaven in the warmer months but at any time of year children can chase dragonflies and butterflies around the rice paddies on one side of the resort and explore the National Park on the other. Shuttle buses link the resort with the Fern Restaurant in Mae Hong Son but once in the resort there are no TVs or telephones, just the sounds of nature. Most families are happy to spend several days here.

Rooms 31. **Rates** *deluxe room 2500B, suite 3500B, under 12s sharing 150B, inc. breakfast, extra bed 500B.* **Amenities** *pool.* **In room** *A/C.*

Imperial Mae Hong Son

Mae Hong Son. 149 Moo 8, Pang Moo, Muang Mae Hong Son 58000, 📞 *05368 4444-5,* ***www.imperial hotels.com.***

Good, clean resort close to the lake and the centre of town. Many rooms interconnect and there is a swimming pool. This is a useful standby for mid-market accommodation close to town.

Rooms 104. **Rates** *deluxe room 2200B–4500B, extra bed 850B.* **Credit** *AE, MC, V.* **Amenities** *restaurant, swimming pool, laundry, tour desk, gym.* **In room** *A/C, satellite TV, fridge.*

Chiang Rai

VERY EXPENSIVE

Anantara

229 Moo 1, Chiang Saen, Chiang Rai 57150, 📞 *05378 4084,* ***www.anantara.com.***

Right up on the Burmese border in the heart of the Golden Triangle, the Anantara is some distance from Chiang Rai but is a superb place for all the family to experience river journeys, elephant rides and gentle hill-tribe treks. The property also has its own elephant camp for rescued elephants, and a *mahout* training school. Courses, open to adults and children, can be just for a few hours or last three days, but as there are only a few elephants working with visitors, it's important to book ahead. The view over the Mekong at breakfast, as the mist lifts, is expansive and unforgettable.

Chiang Dao Nest

Elephant camp at Anantara

Rooms 77. Seven rooms interconnect via a balcony. **Rates** deluxe room 17,000B–20,000B, Antantara suite 27,000B–32,000B, extra bed 1900B. **Credit** AE, MC, V. **Amenities** elephant camp, swimming pool, spa. **In room** A/C, satellite TV, minibar, fridge.

EXPENSIVE

Dusit Island Resort Hotel

1129 Kraisorasit Road, Chiang Rai 57000, ☎ 05371 5777, **www.dusit. com** (over bridge at northwest corner of town).

Set on an island in the Mae Kok River, this is one of Chiang Rai's leading resort hotels. Rooms are luxuriously appointed and can interconnect for families, there is a large swimming pool, a family pool, and babysitting if required. The 10th-floor Peak Restaurant has great views but is rather formal for most families.

Rooms 271. **Rates** superior/deluxe double 3873B–4202B, suite 6427B. **Credit** AE, DC, MC, V. **Amenities** three restaurants, pub, floodlit tennis, games rooms, laundry. **In room** A/C, satellite TV, minibar, fridge.

The Legend Chiang Rai ★★ FIND

124/15 Kohloy Road, Chiang Rai 57000. ☎ 05391 0400, **www.the legend-chiangrai.com**.

This boutique Chiang Rai property is ideal for families with rooms in various configurations, with two-bedroom pool villas as well as family suites. All have large outdoor showers and grand canopy beds. It's a lot of hotel for the price.

Rooms 76. **Rates** single/twin studio 3300B–3900B, triple 4300B–4900B, inc. breakfast, pool villas 7500B–8100B. First under 12 sharing bed with parents 400B inc. breakfast; second under 12 on sofa bed inc.

breakfast 600B; extra bed 1000B inc. breakfast. **Credit** MC, V. **Amenities** Thai and Italian restaurants, pool, spa, babysitting, laundry. **In room** A/C, satellite TV, minibar, fridge, coffeemaker, safe.

INEXPENSIVE

The Golden Triangle Inn ★

590 Phaholyothin Road, Chiang Rai 57000, ☏ 05371 3918, **www. goldenchiangrai.com** (two blocks north of bus station).

Larger-than-average rooms make this garden hotel in the centre of Chiang Rai a good family choice. The attractions of town are just outside your door but in this oasis of terracotta tile floors, traditional furniture, Lanna artefacts and paintings all the family will be able to relax. The restaurant is good too, and the family also runs a useful tour operation and can help with travel plans.

Rooms 30. **Rates** double 900B, extra bed 350B. **Credit** MC, V. **Amenities** restaurant, laundry. **In room** A/C, fan, no TV or phone.

FAMILY-FRIENDLY DINING

Chiang Mai

When travelling with a young family, your hotel can become an important dining venue and the hotels listed can usually satisfy most requirements. One local speciality children are likely to enjoy is the sticky rice, *khao miaow*, which northern farmers take into the fields in small bamboo baskets and eat with their fingers, something children quite enjoy too. Though eating with the hands is still traditional in rural areas, it's rather gone out of fashion in modern Thailand. Where hands are used, parents and grandparents quickly train the young to use only fingers, keeping food off the palms.

International cuisine tends to be more expensive than Thai food, but is often an easier sell to children. Chiang Mai has a huge selection of good options, with Italian cuisine especially prevalent.

Brasserie ★ THAI/INTERNATIONAL

37 Charoaenraj Road, ☏ 05324 1665. East bank of the Ping River opposite the Night Market.

Most guidebooks rate the Chiang Mai's Riverside Restaurant but the Brasserie, just along the river, is better – and much safer, with a fence to keep children out of the river. You'll have the place to yourself for a sunset meal of either Thai or international food before it gradually fills up, music starting around 8pm with a live band pumping out generally bluesy sounds.

Open daily 4.30pm–2am. **Main courses** 170B–300B. **Credit** MC, V.

Girasole Ristorante Italiano
NORTHERN ITALIAN

Kad Klang Vieng, Wat Pan-On Intersection, 17 Ratchadamnoen Road, ☏ 05327 6388, **www.lagondola thailand.com**.

In the heart of Chiang Mai's Old Town, Girasole is part of a low-rise block of shops enclosing a relaxing garden with benches and

The Legend Chiang Rai

seats, cooled in the warmer months by a gentle mist of sprayed water. This is an especially welcome refuge during the Sunday Walking Market: the food is excellent and while the children play on the grass you can browse the low-pressure, high-quality shops in the block. The chef is from Como and his risotto with saffron and mushrooms goes down well with children pining for a simple meal that is herbed rather than spiced. It makes an ideal prelude to the Girasole's captivating Italian ice-creams.

Open *daily, midday–3pm, 6pm–midnight.* **Main courses** *200B–300B.* **Credit** *MC, V.* **Amenities** *highchairs.*

Le Grand Lanna ★ ★ THAI

51/4 Chiang Mai-Sankampaeng Road (part of the Dhara Dhevi, 5km east of town on Charoen Muang). ☎ *0538 8888, www.mandarinoriental.com.*

Even if you can't afford to stay at this hotel just outside Chiang Mai, a leisurely lunch in the idyllic setting makes an ideal interlude during a shopping visit to the silk-weaving workshops of Sankampaeng. Built of old teak, raised on stilts and set among beautiful rice paddies, it offers luxurious dining – at a price – with icy air-conditioning inside plus an outside terrace, cooled in hot weather by mist-spraying fans. While you relax children can chase birds and butterflies around the grounds during the day, or gaze entranced at the candles in the evening. An ideal starter is the spicy *pomelo* salad, and the *gaeng hang lan mop* is a dry, fiery red curry that makes the home-made ice-cream dessert something of a medicinal necessity.

Open *daily, 11.30am–2.30pm; 6.30pm–10.30pm.* **Main courses**

400B– 1200B. **Credit** AE, MC, V.
Amenities children's menu, highchairs.

Old Chiang Mai Cultural Centre ★ ★ THAI

185/3 Thanon Wualai, 📞 05320
2993-5, *www.oldchiangmai.com*.

As important for the experience
as for the food, the Old Chiang
Mai Cultural Centre lays on a
good show of traditional dancing
by lavishly-costumed women,
men doing tricks with swords
and knives, and performances of
Lanna music. Meanwhile settle
down to a *khan toke* dinner, a
selection of traditional dishes
served on low lacquer tables and
eaten with chopsticks and
Chinese spoons. Highlights
include *sai ua* (Chiang Mai
sausage) and *khao sawy*, a yellow,
Burmese-style curry with fried
and boiled noodles, as well as
sweet meat and fish curries.

You'll be there with multiple
coach tours but service is good
and children with the stamina to
last through a three-hour show
usually love it. Even if you've been
to a dinner show in Bangkok, the
northern 'Lanna' experience is
altogether more relaxing.

Several companies offer versions of the same, but this is
widely thought to be the best.
Call ahead and they'll take care
of transport from your hotel.

Open nightly 7pm–9.30pm. **Prices**
320B including performance and set
meal. **Credit** MC, V. **Amenities** no
highchairs: they would leave toddlers
towering over the adults on the floor.
Reservations advised.

Palaad Tawanron ★ ★ ★ FIND
THAI/INTERNATIONAL

*100 Huay Kaew Road, Tambon
Suthep, Amphoe Muang, 50200,*
📞 *05387 4126 or* 📞 *05321 0620,*
*www.palaadtawanron.com. Above
Chiang Mai Zoo on the flanks of Doi
Suthep, entry through a zoo rear gate.*

Overlooking Chiang Mai Zoo
and the city beyond, this is a
delightful and popular restaurant
that goes out of its way to cater
for children. There is a separate
children's menu, highchairs are
provided, and most evenings a
clown comes around making balloon animals. A telescope (by the
loo, strangely enough) opens up
views of the city, particularly captivating as night falls, and there is
live music every night.

As an extra bonus a meal here
can be combined with a twilight
safari, with Zoo buses leaving
from the restaurant at 7pm,
7.30pm and 8pm (200B adults,
100B children, toddlers free)
which includes a visit to the
pandas.

Dining is in seven zones scattered around the forest and the
Palaad Waterfall, and the food is
delicious. Specialities include
crab and freshwater prawn.

Live music every night tempts
you to stay until your children
flag. Call ahead to reserve your
table – outside to enjoy the view –
and check taxi rates from town.

Open daily 11.30am–11pm. Main
courses 230B–300B. **Credit** AE, MC,
V. **Amenities** playground, potty, training toilet seats, feature loo with view,
breastfeeding area, nappy-changing
facilities.

The Insider

THAI TO GET BY

Thai is the official language, and accents vary widely across the country. However, English is increasingly spoken in the major cities at hotels, some restaurants and a few smart shops, and is the second language of the professional class.

Given all of this and faced with the difficulties of mastering Thai, most visitors give up. This is a shame. Polite greetings in Thai will make all the difference to the reception you'll be accorded and children will enjoy trying out new words.

Thai is a tonal language, with low, mid, high, rising or falling tones: these can dramatically affect the meaning of each word. There are five tonal markings:

low tone: `

falling tone: ^

middle tone (no marking)

rising tone: ˇ

high tone: ´

Thai also differentiates between the language used by a male or a female. Thus, males use **Pôm** for I, and females use **Deè-chân**. The suffix **khrap** is an affirmation used by men only, and **kha** is used similarly for women. It can be used as a lazy reply, like 'Uh-huh', but whether you say Khrap or Kha to do this will depend on if you're male or female.

It's not easy to master the tonal distinctions from the written page but at **www.travlang.com** you can click on Thai words to hear what they should sound like. The following table gives a basic selection.

English	Thai Pronunciation	Phonetic Pronunciation
Hello (male)	Sa-wat-dii-khrap	sah-wah-dee-kup
Hello (female)	Sa-wat-dii-kha	sah-wah-dee-kah
How are you?	Sabai-dii mai?	sah-bye-dee-my
I am fine	Sabai-dii	sah-bye-dee
Do you speak English?	Phuut phaa-saa angrit dai mai?	poot pa-sah ang-krit dye-my
I do not understand	mâi khâo jai	my-cow-jy
Excuse me/Sorry	Khaw thoht	cor-tort(-khrap, -kha) (-kup, -kah)
Thank you	Khòp khun	cop-koon (-khrap, -kha) (-kup, -kah)
No, I do not want	Mai âo	my ow

English	Thai Pronunciation	Phonetic Pronunciation
Yes, I want	Chai, ao	chai, ow
Stop here!	Yut tii nii!	jortinnee
Where is the (public) toilet?	Hawng nam yùu thii nâi?	hong-nam yutin-nye
I need to see a doctor	Pôm/Deè-chán tawngkaan mâw	pom/dee-charn tong-garn mor
Call the police!	Riâk tam-rùat nawy!	Reeyuk tamru-at noy!
Never mind/no problem	Mâi pen rai	my pen rye
Do you have . . .	Mii . . . mai?	mee . . . my?

Getting Around

English	Thai Pronunciation	Phonetic Pronunciation
I want to go to...	yak ja pai...	yark jar by...
Where is the...	yuu thii nai...	yutin-nye...
taxi	thaek-sii	dek-see
bus station	sa thaânee khon song	sartarnee kornsong
train station	sa thaânee rót fai	sartarnee rot fye
airport	sa nâam bin	sanam-bin
boat	jetty thâ reua	taa-ru-er
hotel	rohng ra-em	rorngrem or lornglem
hospital	rohng pha yaa baan	rorn-pye-aban
How much?	Thâo rai?	Tao-rye?
What time?	(jà àwk) kii mohng?	Jar-ork-kee-mung? (does it depart)?

Shopping

English	Thai Pronunciation	Phonetic Pronunciation
It's too expensive	Phaeng koen pai	peng kurn-pye
I don't like this one	Mai chawp anii	my chorp a-nee
Do you have a (smaller/larger) size?	Mii sai (lék /yài) nii mâi?	mee sai (lek/yai) nee my
Do you have a black one?	Mii sii tham mai?	mee see dam my

THAI FOOD

Staples of Thai cooking are fried rice – *khao phat* (pronounced cow pat) – and noodles *kway tiaw* (pr kway-tee-ow). Plain rice is *khâo* (pr cow). Noodles come in soups, sauces and stir fried, generally with a tiny bit of vegetable, egg or meat, treated as a snack food, available throughout the day. *Kway tiaw phat thai* for example combines noodles, beansprouts, egg and tofu with ground peanuts and juice of half a lime plus sometimes dried shrimps.

For main meals there are multiple variants on vegetables, fish *plaa* (pr blar), seafood (shrimp is *kung* pr goong), beef *neúa* (pr nuhr), chicken *kài* (pr guy) and pork *muu* (pr moo), often in sauce based on coconut milk. Soup is also standard at every proper meal, and salad is popular, made with noodles, meat, seafood or vegetables plus fresh lime juice. Other flavourings include mint, lemon grass coriander and ginger. Salty sauces from fish and seafood, plus soy sauce add further flavour, one of the pleasures of the food being the many combinations, which vary regionally.

Most dishes also feature a liberal sprinkling of chilli so you might prefer to stick to stir fries which are cooked on the spot, so you can request that chillies be omitted. To avoid too much spice ask for *mai phet* which means mild.

Watch out in particular for the tiny birds eye green chilli that look like innocuous greenery but set your mouth on fire. If the dish includes them pick the chillies out before starting, but if children do eat something that burns their mouth give them plain steamed rice, not water which just exacerbates the problem.

Puddings are rare, though you might find mango with sticky rice *khao niaw mamuang* (pr cow-neeow mar-mwang). Fruit is outstanding and includes not just pineapple, mango and papaya, but also exotics like the lemon sorbet-like mangosteen, custard apple (considered to taste of strawberry plus pear), guava – the apple of the tropics – rambutan and lychee with their white, opaque flesh, sapodilla with its almost honeyed yellow pulp, and the custardy jackfruit. Children may well enjoy fruit shakes and fresh coconut water, drunk straight from the green shell. Fruit juices, however, might come with salt and sugar already added. If they have a really, really sweet tooth the children can try sugar cane juice.

Useful words include coffee *kaa-fae* (pr gar-fay); tea (hot) *châa-rawn* (pr char-rawn); bottled water *nam khuât* (pr nam kwat); water *nam* (pr nam); ice *nam khaeng* (pr nam-keng); and beer *bia* (pr bee-ya).

Useful phrases include: I am a vegetarian *kin ahaan mang-sawirat* (pr gin aharn mang-saweerat); delicious! *Ah-ròy!* (pr Ah-roy); and bill please *Khaw chek-bin* (pr gor chek-bin).

HEALTHY TRAVEL

Children are more likely than adults to get ill. Explain the importance of avoiding insect bites, eating with clean hands and only drinking clean water. Common illnesses include ear and eye infections, especially from badly maintained swimming pools. Be alert to these and treat them quickly.

Illnesses

Bites

Train your children, if you can, not to scratch bites, or if they must take action, to scratch around them. After a mosquito or sandfly has bitten there's a moment when it itches: leave it alone and the feeling passes. Scratch and it itches more, until almost unbearable, and it is the itching, not the bite, that causes inflammation. In time that can develop into a tropical ulcer, all because a bite has been scratched. Particularly in the evenings it is a good idea to have plasters with you so if you see your child scratching a bite you can cover it immediately, preferably before there's anything to see. By the next morning it should be gone. If they are happy to tolerate the light zip it gives, Zanza-Click and similar devices are also extremely helpful for the over fours in reducing itching once it starts.

Cuts & Scratches

In the tropics cuts and scratches heal slower and are more likely to become infected, especially when from coral. Clean any cuts as much as possible and let them dry out while in a clean environment, covering them with a plaster when out and about.

Dengue Fever

This unpleasant but rarely fatal illness is borne by day-biting mosquitoes. Symptoms include joint pains, fever and intensely itchy skin for a week or so and if severe may affect the liver. I know several people who have contracted dengue fever from Koh Chang in the Gulf of Thailand but it can be contracted throughout the country.

Diarrhoea

Prevention is important, including making sure you all wash your hands carefully before eating. Be careful not to drink tap water and ensure iced water is made with purified water – in Thailand it usually is as, generally, is ice. Be wary of salads which may not have been washed with purified water, and of food left on display. Generally roadside food stalls are safe because the food is usually freshly cooked in front of you. The same cannot be said of major resort hotels where you have no idea how often the food has been reheated or how it has been handled. Beware too of pre-cut fruit: you are best sticking to items you peel yourself.

Diarrhoea can quickly lead children to become dehydrated so it is a good idea to carry rehydration salts, though Coca-Cola is surprisingly effective as is a teaspoon of sugar in a glass of water as salty as tears. If a child has diarrhoea and is also vomiting, see a doctor. Most travel diarrhoea is bacterial and can be stopped in its tracks with antibiotics. Some is viral and more difficult to treat.

Heat Exhaustion/Stroke

Symptoms of heat exhaustion include faintness, dizziness, nausea, headache and weakness. It is caused by getting too hot and not drinking enough. The treatment is to drink (not alcoholic) fluids beyond the point where you're thirsty, take a cool shower and rest in an air-conditioned room. Infants and the elderly are especially vulnerable to heat exhaustion, and untreated it can quickly develop into heat stroke. This is a true clinical emergency that can be fatal. Symptoms of heat stroke are the same as exhaustion plus a rapid pulse, strange behaviour, hallucinations, seizures and coma.

Jellyfish

Thailand isn't particularly infested by jellyfish but there are about 2000 species found in its waters. Most stings are painful but not dangerous. Wash the jelly off with seawater rather than your hands and immerse the sting in vinegar. The pain may last a few hours and the rash for a week or so. Some beach cafés swear by a local ground ivy that they whisk in the liquidiser and apply as a poultice and this seems to work even better, not even leaving a rash.

The most dangerous jellyfish in the world, the box jellyfish, is found in Thai waters and kills one or two people a year though, to protect the tourist industry, is under-reported. This should be kept in perspective against several thousand traffic fatalities each year, but it's worth being aware of the danger. Vinegar neutralises box jellyfish stings as well but be ready to administer mouth-to-mouth resuscitation.

Malaria

Most visitors to Thailand don't take malaria prophylaxis, and if you're staying in the major cities and resorts there is no need to. But while Malaria is rare in the cities and central areas it is a real risk in some areas, especially Koh Chang in the eastern Gulf of Thailand, and the forested areas near Thailand's land borders in the west, east and north. The disease is even more dangerous for children than it is for adults. You could avoid the pills altogether by avoiding these parts of the country, but if you are sure you want to visit them, you should seriously consider a course of prophylaxis. The new drug of choice is Malarone, which is highly effective though expensive, and like all malaria treatments has side effects. It is, however, available in a paediatric dose for children weighing more than 15kg: ask your doctor for details. Child pills are even coated in sugar to make them easier to swallow, but the long-term drawback is that it can give very young children the idea that swallowing pills is a good thing. Malarial mosquitoes bite at dawn and dusk, so cover up at these times, light mosquito coils and apply repellent (though not DEET on infants). It's best to buy Malarone in the UK (on private prescription only) as it's not an easy drug to obtain in Thailand and, with a low prevalent risk and the high value per dose, it's a tempting pill to counterfeit.

Prickly Heat

Thailand's humid heat makes prickly heat a constant travellers' companion and it affects children even more. Wash the area in cool water, pat dry and powder with a talc or calamine lotion. Fortunately a locally manufactured anti-fungal dusting powder is highly effective and sold in all tourist areas. Make sure clothes are loose and 100% cotton as synthetic fabrics make prickly heat much worse.

Rabies

This is a real risk for children. Thailand has any number of stray dogs and children often play with them. Don't let them! Licks and scratches should be thoroughly disinfected and if bitten by a dog, cat, monkey, rat or bat, wash the wound thoroughly. If possible contain the animal that did the biting so it can be monitored for a few days to see if it develops symptoms (frothing at the mouth, staggers) but meanwhile go straight to a doctor and begin a course of rabies vaccinations. By the time rabies symptoms appear it is too late for treatment and death is inevitable.

Sea Urchins

These are not common in Thailand but can be a problem. Pull out as much of each spine as you can, apply antiseptic and see a doctor. Usually there are no long-term complications but it can take a month for the last few spine tips to be absorbed by the body or work their way out.

Sun

Children's skin burns quickly in tropical sunlight, especially when cooled by waves or in swimming pools. Wear hats which cover the nape of the neck, light but long-sleeved tops and trousers, find indoor things to do in the middle of the day, and apply high-factor sunscreen on exposed skin. Think carefully before setting off on all-day sailing cruises or treks and if you or your children do get sunburnt bathe the affected area with cool water or cold compresses and apply calamine lotion or even better a product such as Forever Living Aloe Vera gel *www.forever living.com/*. If necessary give an analgesic such as Paracetamol. Extensive sunburn in children can allow them to lose body heat and become hypothermic, but before that point you should have seen a doctor.

Water

Don't drink Thai tap water. It can be purified by boiling for five minutes, or add puritabs (chlorine) or Pota Aqua (iodine). Bottled water is safe – check the seal is unbroken – cheap and widely available. Many hotels provide a certain amount of complimentary drinking water but sometimes in minibars one type may be free and another charged expensively. Check you're drinking the right one. Drink carefully but drink plenty.

If You Fall Ill

Many minor ailments can be dealt with by pharmacists, who openly provide prescription drugs. Thai doctors are generally good and much of their training is in English so communication is normally straightforward. The major regional hospitals are listed in the relevant chapters.

If your child has an existing condition such as diabetes, epilepsy or asthma that might require quick, specialist treatment, consider buying a Medicalert bracelet. This is engraved with details of your child's condition and comes with an emergency number through which the child's medical conditions can be instantly accessed, 24 hours a day in more than 100 languages. (*www.medicalert.org.uk*).

Further health information online: Foreign Office *www.fco.gov.uk*, National Travel Health Network and Centre *www.nathnac.org*, World Health Organization *www.who.int*, Fit for Travel *www.fitfortravel.scot.nhs.uk*.

THAILAND AT A GLANCE

Most of Thailand's population of 64 million still live in rural areas, subsisting on farming, though there's a fast and continual drift to the cities. Over 90% of the population is Buddhist, and the southern coasts and islands have a significant Muslim population that approaches a local majority in some areas.

Urban Thailand has a wealthy elite, often ethnically Chinese, a growing middle class and a vast pool of unskilled labour. There is a strict and discriminating class system in operation. As a foreigner you're rated relatively high status unless you flout basic rules of etiquette (see p 34).

Thailand is tremendously proud that it's never been colonised but has a colonial history of its own. Much of the Isaan region in the northeast was ethnically Lao, but is now a part of Thailand, the poorest, driest and least developed region, but one with a population of 40 million. This goes to explain the country's recent instability, as the democratic mandate does not reflect the views of the economically active society of Thailand's affluent western cities and towns. Gain the Isaan vote and a politician can gain power, but not necessarily keep it. Mainstream western Thailand's interests are protected by the hugely respected King of Thailand and the army.

A Glimpse of the Past

Archaeologists are constantly uncovering secrets from Thailand's past, with stone tools dating back 700,000 years and cave paintings, found throughout the country, up to 4000 years old. Thailand's Bronze Age happened alongside that of China, at about 2500BC.

Modern Thailand dates back about 1000 years and probably started with a drift of Tai tribal communities from central and southern China. From the 6th century AD the scattered Tai societies became known as the Mon, with settlements across the region. Merchants and missionaries from India brought Hinduism and Buddhism, while the south was influenced more by traders from the great empires of Java.

For hundreds of years the Tai people came under the influences of the Khmer civilisation from Cambodia, and it wasn't until 1000 AD that it started to develop distinct civilisations of its own. The Lanna Kingdom was established around Chiang Mai, while Sukothai became central to a society powerful enough to fight off Khmers to the east and the Burmese to the

east. For the first time Thailand had a distinctively Siamese culture of its own, reflected in art, sculpture and religion.

In the 14th century Sukothai's spark faded, and power shifted south to Ayutthaya, near modern-day Bangkok. This was the kingdom that the first European explorers encountered, when Portuguese seamen arrived in 1511. Despite falling briefly to an invading army, the Kingdom of Ayutthaya enjoyed many years of prosperity, adroitly handling western traders to emerge as the only country in Southeast Asia that was never colonised.

Another Burmese invasion in the 1760s bought Ayutthaya's rule to an end, and the Chakri Dynasty decided to move upstream along the Chao Phraya for a more defensible site, choosing a swampy marshland riven with canals: the site of present-day Bangkok. Here Tai, Mon and Khmer bloodlines mixed with Arab, Indian, European and Chinese clans in a truly global city and a powerhouse of trade.

Siam entered the 20th century as a dynamic, forward-looking kingdom, but the Great Depression of the 1920s weakened royal rule, and in 1935 it became a constitutional monarchy, adopting the name of 'Thailand' in 1939.

Modern Thailand

In the Second World War Thailand avoided invasion by Japan by choosing to collaborate, and through the Vietnamese War allowed America to operate military bases on its land. They were richly rewarded by the American government but at a price: consumerism grew, the indigenous sex industry exploded to handle a new overseas market, and a rich elite emerged. To the average Thai, communism started to seem a viable alternative, and protests were violently put down through the 1970s.

Since the 1980s Thailand has enjoyed steady growth with blips and now is one of the most prosperous countries and powerful forces in the region – though the majority of the population still lives in poverty.

Index

Poy Sang Long, 203
Prams, 21
Prebooked itineraries, 25–26
Prickly heat, 237
Princess Mother Memorial Park
  (Bangkok), 62
Pro Dive, 134
PS Bowl (Pattaya), 99
PS Bowling (Chiang Mai), 207

Q

Quad bikes, 103, 169, 172, 211
Queen's Birthday, 20

R

Rabies, 237
Rafting, 5, 37, 211, 216–218
Railay Beach (Krabi), 6, 140–143
Ratchamangka Park, 208
Rattanakosin (Bangkok), 49, 62
Rawai Beach (Phuket), 122
Real Divers (Pattaya), 100
Rentals
  car, 27, 123, 125, 164, 168, 182
  quad bike, 103, 169, 172, 211
  sailboat, 100, 103
  scooter, 27–28, 102–103, 168
  sea canoe, 103, 126, 131–134, 140,
    169–170
Ripley's Believe It or Not (Pattaya), 96–97
River Rovers (Phuket), 132
River taxis, 5, 50, 62–63
Rock climbing, 37
  best, 6
  Chiang Mai, 211
  Koh Phi Phi, 144, 145
  Krabi, 127, 140, 142–143
Rose Garden Tours (Mae Hong Sun), 216
Royal Barge Museum (Bangkok), 63
Royal Palace (Bangkok), 72

S

Safari World (Bangkok), 64, 65
Safety, 39–40, 56, 92, 103, 105, 205
Sailboat rentals, 100, 103
Sai ua, 229
Sala Rim Nam (Bangkok), 83–84
Samlor, 68, 182, 210
Samui Aquarium and Tiger Zoo (Koh
  Samui), 172–173
Samui Butterfly Farm (Koh Samui),
  169, 173
Samui Crocodile Farm (Koh Samui), 173
Samui Go Karts (Koh Samui), 172
Samui International Diving School (Koh
  Samui), 174
Samui Quad Motor (Koh Samui), 172

Samui Snake Farm (Koh Samui),
  169, 173, 174
Samut Prakan Crocodile Farm
  (Bangkok), 63
Sanam Luang Royal Parade Ground
  (Bangkok), 60
Sanctuary of Truth (Pattaya), 99
Sankampaeng, 209
Sankampaeng Handicrafts Festival, 203
Saphan Hin Stadium (Phuket), 135
Scooters, 27–28, 102–103, 168
Scorpion Tail River Cruises (Chiang Mai),
  207–208
Sea canoes, 3, 103, 126, 131–134, 140,
  169–170
Sea Cave Canoe, 134
Seafari Diving Centre (Pattaya), 100
Sea urchins, 237
Seelor, 202
Self-catering, accommodations with, 7–8
Service charges, 40
Shipping, 40
Shopping, 35, 209
Siam Niramit (Bangkok), 10, 66, 83
Siam Ocean World (Bangkok), 5, 63, 64
Siam Paragon Shopping Mall
  (Bangkok), 63
Siam Safari Nature Tours (Chalong), 135
Siam Water Park (Bangkok), 64, 65
Simba Trips, 134
Sirinart National Park (Phuket), 123
Siriraj Hospital (Bangkok), 62–63
Sky Fox Super Ride, 175, 176
Slings and carriers, for babies, 21
Smart Cook (Chiang Mai), 207
Smart Cookery School (Ao Nang), 143
Smoking, 40
Snake farms, 175
  Bangkok, 65–66
  Samui Snake Farm (Koh Samui),
    169, 173, 174
  Thonburi Snake Farm (Bangkok), 61
Snorkelling, 36
  best, 3–4
  Koh Chang, 106
  Koh Phi Phi, 144, 145
  Koh Samet, 103
  Koh Samui, 169, 174
  Krabi, 139
  Phuket, 4, 122, 134
  power snorkelling, 126, 132
Sois, 90
Songkran, 3, 19, 53, 91, 203–204
Songserm Express Boat (Koh
  Phangan), 178
Songthaew, 29
Speedboats, chartered, 134, 142, 170, 179
Spirit Houses, 57
Squid Piers (Hua Hin), 182, 183
Sri Racha Tiger Zoo (Pattaya), 5, 93, 97–98
Street markets, 209
Suan Siam (Bangkok), 64
Subways, 51
Sub Zero Ice Skate Club (Bangkok), 59
Sunburns, 237–238
Sunscreen, 21